THE REED
DICTIONARY OF
NEW ZEALAND
SLANG

David McGill

REED

To Harry Orsman

Published by Reed Books, a division of Reed Publishing (NZ) Ltd,
39, Rawene Rd, Birkenhead, Auckland.
Associated companies, branches and representatives throughout the world.

ISBN 0 7900 0912 9
© David McGill 2003
The author asserts his moral rights in the work.

Edited by Gillian Kootstra
Cover design by Craig Violich
Printed in New Zealand

Please send examples of New Zealand slang to the author at info@reed.co.nz

Introduction

This fifth collection of Kiwi slang and catchphrases has been revised and updated to include slang generated in the five years since the last edition. The slang comes mostly from young people, spread faster than a speeding bullet through text messaging and the Internet, which have joined conversation as communicators of the quicksilver informal language of New Zealanders.

I began collecting Kiwi slang in London in 1968, when I found irresistible the phrases of a New Zealand flatmate, Brett, who startled me with language as exuberant as any Barry Humphries was using in his Bazza McKenzie strip cartoon of the time. In my diary I recorded Brett assuring me that if something was not so then 'my arse is a red cabbage', or vouching for something to the extent of 'ten bob to a knob of goatshit'. I have been collecting Kiwiana ever since.

This book is based on my 1988, 1989, 1995 and 1998 collections of Kiwi slang. The first was tutored by my English lecturer of the early 1960s, Kiwi lexicographer extraordinaire Harry Orsman, who compiled the *Heinemann New Zealand Dictionary* (1979); with Jan Moore the *Heinemann Dictionary of New Zealand Quotations* (1988); the *New Zealand Slang Dictionary* and *The Beaut Little Book of New Zealand Slang* (Reed, 1992); with Elizabeth Orsman *The New Zealand Dictionary* (New House Publishers, 1994); his magnum opus, *The Oxford Dictionary of New Zealand English* (1997); and *A Dictionary of Modern New Zealand Slang* (OUP, 1999). The New Zealand Dictionary Centre at Victoria University of Wellington impressively expanded the work that began for him as a PhD thesis in 1951 and took until his 1997 publication to earn him a doctorate, which may be worthy of a *Guinness Book of Records* entry. The Centre, established in his honour, threatens a slew of doctorates, and a lot more rapidly than Harry managed in the pre-electronic era.

It was Harry's thoroughness that allowed my 1988 Kiwi slang collection to be the first since my solitary predecessor, Sidney Baker's *New Zealand Slang, A Dictionary of Colloquialisms* (Whitcombe & Tombs, 1941). Harry's generosity extended to critiquing and assisting me with my subsequent collections, right up to several weeks before his death. Good on ya, Harry, you live on in your tomes as the mother and father of all Kiwi commentators.

I have attempted to sift out Kiwi slang from the flood of comparative Australian, American, English and Canadian collections of slang, and also from the hybrid *A Personal Kiwi–Yankee Dictionary* by Louis S. Leland Jnr (1980). It is as easy as counting the spring hairs shed by your housecat. The slang that is irrefutably Kiwi is the mix and muddle of Maori and English, the likes of 'electric puha' and 'up the boohai'.

My arbiters in the many grey areas have often been Harry Orsman and two other internationally renowned lexicographers who also happen to be New Zealanders — Eric Partridge with the bible of slang books, *A Dictionary of Slang and Unconventional English*, which I also first encountered in London in 1968, and Robert Burchfield, editor of the *Oxford English Dictionary Supplement*. Other valuable publications are George Turner, *The English Language in Australia and New Zealand* (Longmans, 1966); J.A.W. Bennett, 'English as it is spoken in New Zealand' in *English Transported* (Australian University Press, Canberra, 1970); and my former professor of English at Victoria University of Wellington, Scotsman Ian Gordon, editor of *The New Collins Concise English Dictionary New Zealand Edition* (1982).

New Zealand writers and social commentators have yielded much slang, including Jim Henderson, Gordon Slatter, Keri Hulme, Noel Hilliard, Stevan Eldred-Grigg, Frank S. Anthony, Barry Crump, Edward Jerningham Wakefield, John A. Lee, Charles Money, Tom Scott, C.R. Thatcher, Lady Barker, Roger Hall, Alison Gray, Alex Veysey, Judith Fyfe and Hugo Manson, Burton Silver, Ruth Mason, Peter Cape, L.G.D.

Acland, David Burton, A.S. Thomson, Arnold Wall, Jim and Mary Barr, Gordon McLauchlan, Peter Mahon, Frank Haden, Bill Pearson, J. Magurk, John McDermott, Austin Mitchell, A.W. Reed, Herbert W. Williams. I am grateful to television, radio, the press and magazines, most particularly the *New Zealand Listener* where I worked for many years and whose editor kindly publicised my search for slang updates. Sports commentators such as Keith Quinn, Stu Wilson and Graham Lowe, and the indefatigable Paul Holmes and enthusiastic Jim Hickey, are all significant users of Kiwi slang.

I am grateful to those who have written or rung or confronted me with contributions, including Geoff Churchman, Roger Steele, Joy and Lloyd Shepard, Ian Forsyth, M. Fletcher, Jacob de Ruiter, Charles Johnstone, Bob Hancock, Nigel Watson, Tony Burton, Jo Mildenhall, Grant Tilly, Tom Ward, Brian Sergent, Anna Rogers, Tracey Williams, N.A. Rigden, J. Waddell, N. Butt, L.J. Nielson, M. Malmanche, Erena Josling, Greg Peacocke, L. Hyslop, G. Hurdle, M. Hiddlestone, N. Frew, A. Dick, J. White, M. Geddes, R. Newton, K.J. Davis, C. Hampson, C. Corbett, David V. Coy, R.M. Cairns, Mrs Spinner, C. Johnstone, F.C. Smith, M. Rodwell, M. Burnside, G., P., R. and K. McDonald, Kay Barraclough, R.L. Jackman, G. Clark, G. Hall, M.B. Taylor, Paul Robinson, Hugh Young, T. Williams, Neville Mack, Stan Butcher, Glenn Johnston, Frank Nerney, P.R. Stephens, Tony Yelash, S. Cleland, Rick and Tina De Bes, Sydney Seddon, Kate, Alison and John McGill, Robyn and Duncan White, Ross Alexander, Lester Goodfellow, J.H. Bentley, Roger Boshier, Murray Gray, Gillian Kootstra, Mana College students and the dozens of talkback respondents to radio programmes in which I participated in most parts of the country.

This collection adds my harvesting over the last five years, including some of the new computer slang. New additions may soon be as dated as the verb 'to be lomu-ed' from Jonah Lomu's comet-like trail across the international rugby scene, which I have cut from this collection. There is a question mark over the staying powers of such new entries as 'scody' to indicate approval or disapproval, while 'tukus' is already fading. I have reservations about the influx of Los Angeles and New York slang via music, television and the Internet; however, often a Kiwi slant is added to the Americana. I have generally avoided subculture slang that has not crossed into general use, such as that used by birdwatchers, the armed forces, gardeners or those in jail, of which there is enough for a book apiece. I have dropped from this collection much of the rarely heard historical slang, usually of a farm, military or nautical nature, in the interests of reflecting the organic, active nature of our informal language.

Our more formal educators share with the French the dread of the classical language and grammar being polluted by mongrel imports. The opposite problem applies at the other end of the spectrum where slang, the cutting edge of language developing at the street and school and social level, is disappearing before it ever makes the formal records. This book attempts to catch it on the wing.

Nowhere is slang moving faster than in the teenage and subteen worlds, and I am grateful to and admiring of the work of Phil Coogan and his Unitec colleagues for not only spreading slang into the school system but tapping schoolchildren's knowledge of their own language. This is comprehensively presented in the Kiwi English Project, available on the Internet, with its research from schools all over the country.

When Harry Orsman was finally finishing his doctorate, it was still unthinkable among many teachers that children should be exposed to slang, let alone appreciate that they are at the forefront of developing new slang and ensuring New Zealand has its own distinctive language culture. I know this to my cost, because my first collection of Kiwi slang drew on young people as well as anybody else I could find. There was no doubting that there was a keen response, for the book went on to sell heaps and it was difficult to get off talkback programmes for people wanting me to include all the Kiwi slang I had missed. Back then, only fifteen years ago, few sales were achieved in schools or libraries. Slang was scarcely acceptable to formal educators until Harry Orsman made it so.

They didn't know how much fun they were missing. Over the period of collecting slang I have never passed up an opportunity to ask a young person what slang they are using. The response is invariably amusing and, for me, rewarding. Unitec has structured this informal process.

With the aim of keeping the book accessible and obvious, I have reduced abbreviations to a minimum. The common ones are 'C' for century, as in 'C19' for nineteenth century; 'c' for circa, which means about or approximately the date, as in 'c1920'; and 'WW' for World War. I have put examples in quotes when they are either from somebody or could be confusing in the context.

Dating slang is problematic. Undated entries are probably C20. Entries marked ANZ do not intend Australian paramountcy, but are rather too close to call as to which country used the word first. This collection makes a good case for us joining up with Australia, such is the commingling of our informal language, but it makes just as good a case for retaining our differences. It perhaps reflects our greater interest in them than theirs in us that we have adopted more Aboriginal bastardisations than Australians have Maori.

However, slang is rarely the exclusive property of a single nation state; even less so in these mobile times. I heard on an Australian television show on 6 January 2003 the phrase 'as big as a Maori bull', which I have not come across in New Zealand. Hence I have reservations about place as well as date sourcing. Slang does not respect national borders. Nor time, for that matter, as witness the number of references to British, English or Scottish dialect origins which, in many cases, have lapsed in the place of origin as surely as Elizabethan speech died out in England but has lingered on in some remote parts of the United States. Sometimes the word changes; sometimes, as with 'barracking', it reverses its common meaning when it moves 'Down Under' and retains the British meaning too, which must be confusing for new Pom chums here.

Some of the slang entries can be used offensively. However, slang is mostly (and almost by definition) used for fun, and sometimes to defuse tensions with mock abuse. Maori entries often came from Maori themselves. The offence is in the mind of the beholder who is not considering the casual context in which slang flourishes. A feminist reviewed an earlier Kiwi slang collection of mine and found much fault, even accusing the collector of representing one of the entries, namely 'root-faced'. Other collections of slang from around the world, including Partridge, offer more comprehensive offence to decontextualised sensibilities.

Slang is the yeast that good communicators use to leaven the dough of officialese. Politicians like to use slang to show the voters they are one of them, and to lighten the stifling prose that bureaucratic and judicial minds employ to solemnise and mystify their proceedings. If politicians do not communicate, they are not good at what they do. Slang is a sure bet for getting their message across. Slang is at the opposite pole from obfuscation — it is the language we use when we are relaxed. It is our wordplay. This is where we can all be poets, for slang is metaphor. Slang tells us what we are like with our guard down.

Kiwi slang defines us as Kiwis, warts and all. Some entries have been challenged as Australian, English and, in recent examples, American slang. This is often true, and many such examples have been omitted. Yet it can also be an example of colonial cringe (see entry), for New Zealanders might have used the example first, or at about the same time; or we perhaps use it with slightly different emphasis and make it our own. We are inveterate travellers, we export as well as import words and phrases. In this informal area, nobody can claim absolute authority. The main thing is to enjoy our distinctive language, slang, which defines us as surely as our accent. If you want an example, try 'togs' on any visitor to these shores.

Be a happy Kiwi camper!

a into g Arse into gear, usually intended to advise a hurry up.

a over k Arse over kite, a wild tumble.

AB A woman's monthly period, an abbreviation of 'Annie Brown'.

ab-fab Total approval, an abbreviation of 'absolutely fabulous', teen jargon 1950s.

ABs, The The All Blacks.

ace Alone, like the single spot in the playing card of this name, used in the phrase on one's ace. ANZ early C20.

acid Pressure; usually in the phrase to put the acid on, meaning to apply pressure. Probably derives from the acid test in chemistry to determine components. ANZ C20.

acre Buttocks. ANZ from late 1930s.

act the angora Silly behaviour of a high-spirited nature, a variation on 'acting the goat'. ANZ C20.

afghan A popular biscuit made with cocoa powder.

afterdinner mint Woman who provides sexual favours in exchange for dinner. ANZ.

aftermatch/aftermatch function A boozy celebration after the game, mostly of the sporty kind, usually restricted to males. From 1970s.

afto/arvo Afternoon, in its diminutive forms. ANZ.

aggies Panties (underpants), as in 'agapanthus' plant.

Airstrip, The The principal corridor through Paremoremo Prison, north of Auckland.

alchie Alcoholic, often the outdoor variety.

all around the houses All over the place.

all around the pig's arse there is pork Reinforcement of the obvious, often resigned in delivery, sometimes tinged with sarcasm, akin to 'Is the Pope a Catholic?'

All Blacks The New Zealand national rugby union team, from the colour of the strip and said to be from a printer's error: *Daily Mail* reporter Buttery wrote of the 11 October 1905 match against Hartlepool clubs, won 63–0 by New Zealand, that the whole team played with precision and speed as if they were 'all backs', printed as 'all blacks'.

all cock and ribs like a drover's dog Very thin animal or human.

all done up like a sore toe Disparaging reference to someone overdressed and overimpressed with it. ANZ.

all hair oil and no socks Flashy but unimpressive; often used of a superficially impressive performer, who ultimately disappoints.

all hands to dance and skylark Encouragement to have a rousing good time.

all hunched up like a dog on a bag of staples Looking extremely uncomfortable.

all over the place like a madwoman's shit An unacceptable situation, often used scornfully of a sportsperson who falls below expectations.

All Whites Now unofficial name for the national men's soccer team, administrators not wishing to promote a team with such a politically incorrect name.

alpha geek The most knowledgeable person in the office. Mid 1990s.

aluminium rain Debris from a midair collision. Mid 1990s.

amber fluid/liquid Beer. ANZ early C20.

amber gambler Driver who runs through the amber or orange light. Latter C20.

am-dram Amateur dramatic, usually dismissive of a production or performer judged to be below professional standard. Latter C20.

American Invasion Semi-jocular concern at American language and customs swamping our own, recorded as early as 1920, possibly fuelled by the huge American Pacific Fleet visiting Wellington in 1925.

anaconda The penis, among teenage appreciators of a recent movie of that name.

angel gear Coasting your car downhill with the ignition switched off. 'Engine off, no brakes, just a straight, silent run', *Dominion* review 30 September 1989 of *Angel Gear*, Colin Hogg writing on Sam Hunt as travelling poet/performer.

angry man, the New Zealand soldiers used this term to describe the enemy in North Africa in WWII.

angus Angry, as in Angus bull.

animated straw The stick insect, called that by the early settlers.

anklebiter An infant crawling around at about the height of a small dog and humorously supposed to display the same tendency to nip at ankles. ANZ 1980s.

Antipodes, The The name attributed to both New Zealand and Australia, though New Zealand is much closer to the true antipode or exact geographical opposite of London, which is east of us.

any sodium glutamate of yours is a sodium glutamate of mine Another way of saying 'any friend of yours is a friend of mine'; used among young people not unacquainted with the favoured seasoning in some Chinese takeaways.

Anzac Acronym for the Australian and New Zealand Army Corps from WWI. The Anzac entries following date from WWI or soon after.

Anzac biscuit Firm, teeth-challenging biscuit made with oats.

Anzac button A safety pin or nail.

Anzac Day dinner Anzac Day lunch of the liquid variety.

Anzac hare Meat loaf.

Anzac shandy Champagne and beer.

Anzac tile/wafer A hard army biscuit; later, any hard biscuit.

Aotea biscuit Biscuits made with brown sugar, cornflour and cornflakes.

apple 1. $100 bill, arrived at in a roundabout way from the rhyming slang 'apples and spice' for 'nice'.

2. Guts or intestinal fortitude, usually directed at a contact sportsperson falling below the aggressive par expected. From rhyming 'apple tart' and 'heart'.

apples Desirable state, usually in the phrase offering reassurance, **she'll be apples**, same derivation as **apple** above. ANZ mid C20.

Aratanic Nickname for a Cook Strait ferry which kept breaking down in recent years, mercifully not to the extent of the *Titanic*.

are your arms and legs painted on? A sarcastic way of suggesting you do something yourself.

aristotle of alison A bottle of bourbon, rhyming slang for 'bottle' and the Kiwi singer Alison Durbin.

army golf Hitting the ball inaccurately both sides of the fairway. Michael Campbell said he had no excuse for his army golf after his relative failure in the last round of the 2003 New Zealand Open, the *Dominion Post* of 20 January 2003 noting he 'drove the ball army style — left right, left right'.

aroha job Work done for love, not money. From 1980s.

arse into gear, get your Advice to somebody proving sluggish. ANZ.

arse like a working bullock Big buttocks; the phrase can be approving or disapproving.

arse over kite Head over heels. Raconteur Brian Bell described a haymaker punch from poet James K. Baxter, concluding 'arse over kite I went into the gutter'. They were fighting over a woman after a twenty-first birthday party in Wellington in 1954.

arsehole Incompetent and/or objectionable person, eg, 'I don't know why you've got that arsehole building your extension.' ANZ.

arsepaper Despicable or useless person or thing, eg, 'That builder is arsepaper.' ANZ.

arsey-boo A mess.

arsy Lucky, a contraction of **tin arse**. ANZ 1930s.

arsy-tarsy A tangle.

artesian Freisian Watered-down milk.

Arthur or Martha A confused person, usually described as **not knowing if he's/she's Arthur or Martha**, from earlier C20. ANZ.

articulated/articulator Short for articulated truck, with the detachable truck bed. From mid C20.

Arty Farty Ngati Karate Club A pretentious group.

as Stand-in word for anticipated phrase, used to maximise or increase the impact of a statement, eg, 'I'm hungry as.' 1990s.

Asian moll A prostitute who services Asian fishermen.

ask the question/ask the big question Whether a challenge can be responded to; the answer is implied. For example: 'And now the big question is being asked of Waikato,' John McBeth commentating on TVOne on the game between Waikato and New Zealand Maoris, 8 July 1995, at the stage when the Maoris were drawing away and Waikato needed a huge effort.

Association of Consultants and Tax-dodgers A jokey nickname for the Act political party.

ate the cow and worried the tail Leftovers.

Auks, The The Auckland rugby team.

auntie Male homosexual mid C20.

Aussie Diminutive of Australian.

Australian haka, the A transparent attempt to avoid paying your way, developed in a television ad in which a group of drinkers inform one it is his turn to shout. He pats pockets vigorously and then whines, 'Where's me flamin' wallet?' 1990s.

away laughing Some task that is or is likely to be readily achieved, as in, 'The America's Cup guys are away laughing.' Mid C20.

away with the birds/fairies/pixies Not paying attention, sometimes because a person is mentally deficient, usually because they are not focused, maybe daydreaming of something unrealistic, such as a favourable response from Petra Bagust or Lucy Lawless to a request for a date. ANZ latter C20.

away/up in the teatree Resident in a remote area literally or figuratively.

babbler/babbling brook   1. Cook.

2. Unwell, as in 'crook'. Both rhyming ANZ slang from early C20.

babe   Attractive person to a contemporary teenager, male or female. ANZ.

Baby Blacks   The young All Blacks team which replaced the rebel Cavaliers team of established All Blacks, who defied the New Zealand Rugby Football Union in 1986 and toured South Africa.

bach   From early 1900s a weekend or holiday hut or cottage by sea or lake or in the wilderness, cobbled together from secondhand or free odds and ends, sporting raddled furniture, cold showers and outback toilet. In the C19 a bach was stand-alone spartan rental accommodation only big enough for one of the many bachelors who developed this country. A **bacher** is an occupant of a bach or a type who prefers to live alone; **baching**, looking after oneself, often a male living alone in a hut or crude accommodation. To **bachelorise** is a male making do when his female partner is away, or males flatting together; the latter **bach with** each other. From US *bach*, a bachelor, mid C19.

bachelors and benedicts   A contest between married and single men, the 'benedict' being an old term for a newly married man.

bachelor's button   1. A native button-shaped yellow wildflower found in bogs, or any round little flower. From c1920.

2. A button in the Christmas pudding from 1920s. If a man got the button, he was condemned to be a bachelor who had to sew on his own buttons.

back of beyond   Really remote place. ANZ late C19.

back teeth are floating, my   Urgent need to urinate. Latter C20.

backblocks   Remote place. Hence **backblocker**, a dweller in remote rural area, perceived as crudely civilised. ANZ from latter C19.

backbone of the country   Farmers, whose primary produce is the country's main earner. From early C20.

backdoor bandit   Male homosexual. ANZ.

backdoor pensioner   Retired sheepdog. Latter C20.

backwash   Drinking from a bottle being passed around. From c2000.

bad   Good, to a teenager influenced by American rap music. From late 1990s.

baffle with bullshit   Deceive. ANZ latter C20.

bag   1.To disparage or 'knock' someone, such that they have received a **bagging**. From late C19 ANZ reaction to a cricketer missing an easy catch.

2. The breathalyser plastic bag police require suspected drinkers to blow into, or **put the bag on**, and they fail because they are **in the bag**, ie, drunk. Mid 1980s.

bagful of busted arseholes   Ugly person or unpleasant condition, such as a hangover, usually preceded by a comparative phrase such as 'He looks like a . . .' or 'I feel like a . . .'

bail up   To confront or constrain; from C19 bushranger's command. ANZ.

ball of fire/muscle   Energetic person, and maybe overly so, from 1930s.

banana   Disparaging term for New Zealand-born Chinese, suggesting yellow on the outside, white within, used by Chinese immigrants about local Chinese from 1980s.

bandicooting   Artfully and craftily removing root vegetables not your own. A term imported here from Australia in the 1930s Depression, named after the marsupial that occasionally disturbs Aussie gardens. Being **bald as a bandicoot** is popular this side of the Tasman too.

bang   1. To have sex, ANZ C20, often in phrases such as **bangs like a leaky pipe when the tap's turned on/like a shithouse rat/like a dunny door in a high wind** in regard to an enthusiastic fornicator.

2. An all-encompassing intensive, ANZ late C19, often used in the phrase **the whole bang lot**; positioned first in **bang slap**, used of any rugged encounter, when elsewhere people prefer 'slap bang'. Anything said to **go with a bang** is a successful activity, often said of a party.

bang on To hassle, eg, a pupil might complain that teachers 'bang on you'. ANZ latter C20.

banged up Pregnant. ANZ C20.

banjo 1. Head-high tackle, probably imported from Australia. 'The old banjo,' said rugby commentator Keith Quinn on TVOne, 25 August 1990.

2. Leg of mutton; the shape is reminiscent of the musical instrument. From early C20.

bank, the Popular exposed seating area of many sportsgrounds, especially, footy grounds, attracting the more unruly element. Short for an earth 'embankment'. Covered stands and all-stadium seating are making the bank a thing of the past. If a player is sent off the field by the referee he or she is **sent to the bank/given an order for the bank**. From early C20.

banker A flooding river almost risen to the bank. ANZ latter C19.

bantie Bantam fowl. Here from 1890, possibly via US.

Barber, the A keen wind, especially that scything out of the gorge into Greymouth.

barbie The barbecue, an ANZ necessity from at least the second half of the C20.

bare-bottom haka Presenting the bottom to disconcert, ritualised in pre-Pakeha days in the *whakapohane*.

bark To vomit.

barker's egg Dog dropping.

barker's nest A pile of dog droppings.

barmaid's blush Rum and raspberry or port and lemonade. Early C20 ANZ.

Barn Dance, the The diagonally-striped pedestrian crossing, named after its inventor, New York City Traffic Commissioner Barnes. From c1950, ANZ.

barney   An argument in Australasia, a celebration elsewhere, though the difference could be slight.

barrack   Cheering or jeering, often a sporting occasion. Origins have several contenders, Orsman offering the Aboriginal *burag* meaning 'no' and *borak*, which Partridge enters as meaning 'fun', the Cockney *barrakin* or gibberish, the Northern Irish *barrack* for bragging. At least when you **barrack for** somebody or some team you know you are supporting them.

barracouta   Long, narrow, crusty loaf reminiscent of the fish of that name.

barrelarse   Short and stubby person.

bash   1. A party. ANZ from 1930s. To **go on the bash** is to have a spree, usually the alcoholic variety.

2. Tramping term for difficult terrain.

bash up   To casually create, the very nature of much do-it-yourself activity; you bash up a deck/evening meal/job application in no time flat.

bash artist   Somebody too ready to use fists to solve frustrations.

Basin, the   The Basin Reserve oval sports ground in central Wellington. Result of the 1855 earthquake lifting the land and draining a large pond.

basket case   Somebody adjudged mentally deficient. ANZ.

bastards on a raft   Poached eggs on toast.

bathers/bathing togs   Swimming apparel.

battle   Make pregnant or make love. Vince Boyle of Winton, researching the history of Mossburn, recorded a former wagoner in northern Southland in 1914 as having 'battled a woman'. He had intended to marry her until, a few days before the wedding, she had her teeth removed and sent him the bill.

battler   Dogged worker or performer, often in sport, generally admired for honest endeavour, even if skill factor is modest. In the past has meant a swagman and also a prostitute working on her own without a pimp or brothel. Now also used of a child enduring a severe illness such as cancer. ANZ early C20.

Bay, the   The provinces of either the Bay of Plenty or Hawkes Bay.

beach, the   The name for the entire holiday area by the sea in New Zealand.

beachball   A multi-coloured marble.

beachcomber   Shoreline scavenger, noted here by Edward Jerningham Wakefield in the early 1840s, before the *Oxford Dictionary* recorded the word.

beacher   Retired whaler or sailor in the earliest Otago days.

beastie   Excellent, to a teenager today.

beat about the bush   Prevaricate. ANZ.

beat the feet   Walk or run. Latter C20.

beat to death with a stocking full of hot crap   A jocular threat perhaps first heard in Bendigo, Central Otago.

beaudy/beaut/beauty/beautee/bewdy   Appreciative exclamation, also used as adjective or noun: 'That goal. Beaudy!', 'That was a beaudy goal'. Often accompanied by a reinforcing word, as in 'wee beaut', 'little beaudy', 'you beauty' and 'you blimmin beaut'. In the phrase **put across a beaudy**, you have been praised for a successful trick. ANZ late C19.

Beaver Station   Blenheim from its flooding days, attributed to Sir Joseph Ward or an unknown squatter.

beebee gun   A slug gun or toy rifle which fires soft metal pellets. Latter C20.

beef bayonet/bugle   Penis. ANZ later C20.

Beehive, The   Cone-shaped concrete maze designed for the New Zealand Cabinet and staff by Sir Basil Spence, named after its shape without any implication that drones or a queen bee are resident within.

been there, done that   A dismissive remark indicating speaker knows all about something. ANZ.

beer fleas Tummy tingling from too much of it. Late C20.

beer goitre Large, generally collapsed stomach from excessive beer drinking. Mid C20.

beer sandwich A liquid lunch. Latter C20.

bee's dick Insignificant or tiniest measure, eg 'The maiden speech of the Member for Wewe was a bee's dick.' ANZ.

beeswax! Rubbish! Rhyming slang with 'cracks', which are what cheeky people make. Usually used in the phrase **mind your beeswax**, meaning to watch your manners, or mind your own business. C20.

beggars-on-coals Damper or the unleavened bread made from flour and water and cooked on an open fire. ANZ mid C20.

belly-buster/flop A disastrous dive in which belly hits the water, or any financial disaster; eg 'The 1987 stockmarket crash was the mother of all bellyflops.' ANZ late C19.

belt A stiff drink. **To belt down** is to drink alcohol quickly; **to belt one on** is to get very drunk. ANZ later C20.

Ben Doon and Phil McCavity Two mythical Celts inviting an easy laugh that glosses over uneasy feelings about homosexual activity. Mid C20.

bench, the The seat on which the rugby reserves sit hoping for the call on to the field.

bend one's back Work hard. ANZ C20.

bend the bank Pressure your bank to apply creative accounting to your account.

bender A Catholic, from the bending of the knee to genuflect upon entering and leaving church. In Australia means a homosexual.

Benghazi boiler A thermette or chip heater for boiling a 'cuppa', made by John Ashley Hart as a young plumber with A & T Burt, patented 1930. Hart waived his rights to it in WWII, where it acquired the nickname with Kiwi troops in Benghazi, North Africa. Hart also invented the Lawnboy and Lawn Lass for cutting grass against walls, the tent coathanger, the Terra Grip umbrella stand and the Adjustaflow for controlling milk flow from a baby's bottle.

benny A state beneficiary. On **benny day** the day the state pays beneficiaries. Puzzling to other English-speaking nations, who understand it to mean a Benzedrine pill.

berkers/berko Somebody considered excessively silly or angry, crazy or out of control, as in berserk, usually in the phrase 'to go berko'. ANZ mid C20.

bet on two flies walking up the wall/across the ceiling Betting enthusiasm that knows no bounds, usually used of a compulsive gambler. ANZ.

bet your balls Guarantee to and probably from a functioning male, eg 'Bet your balls that's the last time he shows his face around here.' ANZ.

better to bust your arse than die a cripple Encouragement to do some task to your utmost, rather than be left wondering and wimpish. ·

Bible-basher A clergyman or layman given to excessive biblical proselytising, and fundamentalist Christians who shove their beliefs down others' throats. ANZ mid C20.

bickies/bikkies Money, often in the phrases **big bickies**, for lots of money or some operation that is on the grand scale and will usually involve big amounts of money, and **small bickies**, a paltry sum of money, often used dismissively. A jokey extension of the nursery name for biscuits, which can also be used to indicate bad luck in **stiff/tough bikkies**. ANZ latter C20.

biddy-bid The Maori plant *piripiri*.

biffed Bothered, eg, 'I couldn't be biffed doing that'.

big as the Waimak Big-hearted; from the large Christchurch river the Waimakariri.

big ask, a Difficult achievement. Sports commentators refer this way to a player or team trying to overtake an opponent who is well ahead. In the second cricket test between New Zealand and Pakistan in 1994 New Zealand's task was described as 'a big ask'.

big bird Aeroplane.

Big Frisbee, The Australia. From 1990s television weather maps of the Other Side.

big girl's blouse   Weak, timid wimp, often addressed disparagingly to an effeminate or irresolute male.

Big One, The   The anticipated catastrophic earthquake in many parts of New Zealand, particularly Wellington.

big picture, the   A complete appreciation of all the elements that concentration on detail may miss, eg, 'Conservation Department bureaucrats in their single-issue drive to save the pied stilt, fail to see the big picture that without a bridge through its habitat, State Highway One traffic will grind to a halt.'

Big Red   A Wellington bus when they were all red, before advertising transformed them into a rainbow fleet.

Big Smoke, the   A large town, in the surrounding rural perception. From Aboriginal application to Australian towns from mid C19, NZ 1904.

big spit, the   To vomit. ANZ mid C20.

Big Wet, the   Continuous downpour for days, so-called by Aucklanders rightly fearful it will spoil sporting fixtures. One amply justified example was before the Bledisloe Cup test on 22 July 1995.

big wraps on, have   Be highly impressed. The *Sunday Star-Times*, 23 June 1996, said Little 'has big wraps on Andrew Mehrtens'; the All Black first five-eighth Little played outside.

big yellow ball, the   The sun.

bigger than the back of an ARA bus   Very big, often in reference to the size of someone's bum; the letters stand for Auckland Regional Authority.

biggie   1. Large turd.

2. Big businessman.

big-note   Unacceptable level of boasting. ANZ c1935.

bikie   Member of a motorbike gang. ANZ from 1960s.

billy   Tin can with a wire handle for boiling water over an open fire, ANZ c1850. Also a can with a lid for carrying milk. Both uses combine in making tea. Hence, **billy-tea**, which is made by tossing tea leaves into the boiling billy. The word has extended into the phrase **to boil the billy** meaning to make tea, and to stop for a tea or refreshment break, the latter meaning also in the phrase **to sling the billy,** which also has the general meaning of preparing a drink of tea. A **billy boy** is the tea-maker, a **billy fire** is the outdoor fire for the purpose of boiling the billy, a **billy-can** is a billy, a **billy-hook** is the hook to hang the billy on, while **billybread/cake/loaf/sponge** are all cooked in a billy, probably one with a lid. You can get sets of billies fitting one inside the other like Russian dolls, known as a **nest**. Probably from Scottish word *billy*, a pot.

billycart   Trolleys boys of all ages cobble together from bits of wood and spare wheels, probably less finished than the original carts pulled by billygoats. ANZ from 1930s.

binder   A solid meal, from cWWI, often in the phrase **to go a binder**, meaning to eat a meal. British dialect word for a large quantity, particularly of food. ANZ.

binocs   Binoculars from c1945.

biodegradable Poms   Kiwis, as described by Australians.

bird   Success, used in the phrase **make a bird of**, to make a success of some project. If you **make a dead bird of** then you have made very sure of whatever you are doing, from late C19 Australia in reference to pigeon shoots, where the released bird is going to be dead, for sure.

birdcage   1. Fenced area where horses parade before and after a race, in show-jumping where ponies and riders wait to compete, adapted C20 from the so-called saddling area at Newmarket racecourse in England.

2. Used-car dealer's lot, from 1950s, when chickenwire fencing was prominent around caryards. The dealer was known as a **birdcage boy**.

biscuit class   Non-business class air travel on internal flights where only a biscuit pack snack served, from 1980s.

bish   To throw, a variation on 'biff'. ANZ c1920.

bite on, to put the   To seek a loan. From c1918 ANZ, from British dialect word for money.

bitser/bitzer/bitsa   A mongrel dog or any object that is constructed from disparate bits, such as a billycart, from mid C20 ANZ.

bitumen blonde   A dark-skinned woman. From Australia mid C20.

bitumen man   Any male town or city dweller, where the streets are paved with bitumen. From 1960s.

biv/bivvy   A campsite or shelter such as a rock bivvy, short for the military word 'bivouac'. From mid C20.

bizzo   Any business or activity. ANZ surfie slang from 1950s.

BJ   A blow job or oral excitation of the penis. 1990s.

black as   An intensive in a myriad of phrases, including **black as the back end of a bull/a leper's armpit/midnight in Naseby/Sunday morning in a West Coast coalmine.**

Black Budget, the   The name was given to a deflationary 1930 budget taxing popular items, but now linked with the 1958 budget of non-drinking, non-smoking, non-conformist Minister of Religion and Finance Arnold Nordmeyer, who taxed items such as beer and cigarettes, provoking irate voters to vote his party out of office.

Black Caps   National men's cricket team. 'Slack Caps' was the *Evening Post* headline after a March 2000 batting collapse.

Black Ferns   National women's rugby team.

Black Fins   National swimming team this millennium.

Black Magic   Successful Kiwi yacht in the contest for the 1995 America's Cup.

Black Sox   National softball team, with a nod to the Chicago White Sox baseball team.

Black Sticks   National women's hockey team, maybe. 'Stick Chicks' was firmly rejected.

black velvet   Vulgar name for sex with a coloured woman, linked perhaps to the sketches of voluptuous coloured women on black velvet found increasingly in secondhand shops. ANZ.

blackbait   Gutty bait or whitebait which have been in fresh water long enough to develop intestines. Scarcely edible, tasting a bit like sardines.

BlackHeart Organisation campaigning late 2002 against the allegedly unpatriotic behaviour of New Zealand sailors such as America's Cup winners Russell Coutts and Brad Butterworth, who left Team New Zealand and signed on with the Swiss syndicate sailing the successful challenger *Alinghi*.

blacksmith A poor station cook who burns the food.

blade To clear an area, from the use of the bulldozer's blade. From 1960s.

blades Manually operated sheep shears.

blades of meat Feet; rhyming slang.

blatherskite A boaster talking voluble nonsense. ANZ variant since late C19 of Scottish dialect *bletherskate*.

blender Copycat. Teenage usage late 1990s.

Blenheimers Loss of memory from too much wine. A play on Alzheimer's disease and Blenheimer wine.

Blerta Acronym for Bruno Lawrence's band Electric Revelation and Travelling Apparition. A group of musicians and entertainers travelling the country in the 1970s, including singer Beaver, artist Fane Flaws, actors Ian Watkin and Tony Barry, film director Geoff Murphy. Bruno became the country's favourite actor, starring in successful Kiwi films such as *Goodbye Pork Pie* and *Smash Palace*. David Charles 'Bruno' Lawrence died of cancer on 10 June 1995 aged 53.

bless your garters Folksy phrase of gratitude.

blimey, Charlie! Expression of mild-mannered relief; watered down from its Cockney origin in 'Gorblimey', meaning 'God blind me'. ANZ C20.

blimmin The mild version of 'bloody', sometimes in the phrase **blimmin eck**, where 'eck' is 'heck', a euphemism for 'hell'.

blinded with science Brains defeating brawn, in its derivation from the rise of the scientific boxers such as Gentleman Jim Corbett, at the expense of bruisers like John L. Sullivan. The phrase was extended during WWII to mean bewildering or overwhelming somebody with a mass of detail. ANZ.

blister   1. Sister, rhyming ANZ slang from c1920.

2. Official reprimand in writing. Originally a court summons. From 1920s. ANZ.

block   A pack rape, or a female subjected by a group of men to serial sexual activities, often associated with bikie gangs in the phrase **to put/go on the block**. From 1970s.

block, use your   Advice to show common sense, where 'block' means head. ANZ mid C20.

blocked   Satisfied, usually in regard to food.

blockie   Small-time, casual hobby farmer of a lifestyle block. ANZ 1980s.

blokery   Mates who are men, particularly bachelors. ANZ early C20.

blokess   A female bloke or acceptable mixer among ordinary working folk. Mid C20.

blood's worth bottling   Hearty appreciation of a splendid fellow, ANZ mid C20.

bloody oath!   Affirmative intensive, as in response to the question whether you want your glass topped up. 'Bloody' has been a historically popular ANZ swearword, its impact declining from excessive use, latterly inserted into words such as 'fan-bloody-tastic'.

blow a tank   Dynamite a safe open. From c1920.

blow, have a   1. Sniff of glue, among streetkids. From 1980s.

2. A stroke of the sheep shears. ANZ c1920.

blow me down with a fencepost!   I am surprised. Kiwi landed version of nautical 'blow me down'.

blow off/blow out/blow through   Sudden or casual departure, while 'blow through' can also mean to pass through a place on a journey. ANZ c1920.

blow that for a joke!   A phrase of rejection, an extension of euphemism 'blow'.

blow trout   Use gelignite; a blow-back usage from catching fish by dynamiting their environs.

blow up   1. Referee use of whistle to stop play.

2. To confront or chastise verbally.

blowfly cake   Lurid yellow fruit cake with raisins prominent.

blowhard   Boaster. ANZ from late C19.

blowie   A blowfly. ANZ early C20.

blow-in   Unexpected arrival. ANZ C20.

blowing/blowing off   Boasting. From 1860s.

bludge   To cadge whilst loafing, consuming without working like those around you. A **bludger** lives off others, a **dole-bludger** lives off state benefits. Derives from the prostitute's bully and his inclination to bludgeon problem clients. ANZ.

blue   1. A brawl, perhaps anticipating the piece of blue paper that would summon brawlers to court.

2. A mistake. Again possibly linked to use of blue paper by authorities calling you to account.

3. Red-haired person.

4. Drunk, perhaps from its association with blue devils that appear in extreme cases involving the drinking of methylated spirits.

5. Extravagant spending. The phrase **to blue a cheque** could be wordplay for 'blew' or could indicate the blue inking of the cheque.

All meanings distinctively ANZ C20.

blue-arsed fly, running around like a   A dithery condition akin to a blowfly after being hit by flyspray. ANZ.

Bluebird chip   A ten dollar note, a pun on the blue-packaged potato chip brand.

blue duck   A failure or a lost cause, as in 'This super tax is a blue duck.' Could be a combination of the American phrase 'dead duck' and the local blue duck, which in the shooting season is potential dead duck. Late C19 ANZ.

blue fit/blue vinegar fit   Extreme anger or shock or drunken behaviour, as can follow the imbibing of blue vinegar or turpentine. Mid C20.

blue flu   Leave the blue-uniformed police take because legally they may not strike, popular late C20 during periods of industrial unrest.

blue lady   Methylated spirits, which has a blue tinge.

Blue Orchid   Member of the Royal New Zealand Air Force, whose blue uniform and conditions of service were considered namby-pamby by the khaki army lads.

blue rinse brigade/set   Middle-aged ladies comfortably off, distinguished by the blue rinse through their perms, often wearing twinsets and pearls, to be found in National Party blue-ribbon enclaves such as Remuera, Kelburn and Fendalton. ANZ.

blue veiner/blue vein flute   The penis. ANZ.

blunt as a bull's ear   Very blunt; used by Otago high country farmers about poorly sharpened sheath knives.

blurter   The anus, which blurts or emits noxious noise. ANZ.

boar's nest   A mess. Rhyming slang, eg, 'It was supposed to be selective logging, but it's a boar's nest.'

boatie   Operator of small, often motorised, boat. ANZ.

bob each way, to have a   Hedging your bet, probably from putting a bob or the imperial shilling on a win and a place in horseracing. Decimalisation in 1967 made shillings and pence obsolete, but words like 'bob' and 'penny' linger on in popular phrases.

bobbycalf   Milk-fed calf slaughtered very young for its tender flesh. Also known as a vealer. Defined by the Bobby Calf Marketing Regulations as a calf intended for human consumption as boneless veal. From the British dialect *bob*, a young calf.

bobsled   Two-footed soccer tackle.

bobsy-die   A fuss, maybe a fun one. Often used in the phrase **kicking up bobsy-die**. From the British nautical rhyming slang *bob's a dying* for 'idling', sometimes appearing in that form, as Ngaio Marsh in *Surfeit of Lampreys*: 'It plays Bob's-a-dying with the whole blooming case.' ANZ.

bodgie   1. ANZ male youth of the 1950s acting tough in copycat versions of rebel British and American gear such as greased-back hair, long, thin sideburns, black leather jackets, stovepipe trousers, white socks and winklepicker shoes. Originally American slang for a male jitterbug with long hair and oversized sports jacket.

2. Now something of dodgy quality or origin, such as very cheap stereo equipment in sidestreet stores.

body snatcher   A stock buyer.

bogacka/bojack   Pukeko. Pakeha corruptions of the Maori word for the swamp bird.

bogan   Idiot or misfit, acting stupid or clumsy; a long-haired, heavy metal listener; those favouring the black leather jacket and black jeans and a taste for bourbon. Possibly from the Bogan River in outback New South Wales, though the phrase was applied to the less couth western suburbs of Melbourne in the 1980s, promoted by the Australian TV comic character Kylie Mole.

bog in   Work hard at something, often the eating of a meal. ANZ mid C20.

boiled dog   Affectation, eg, 'Don't come the boiled dog with me, mate. I know you grew up in a railway house in Papakura.' From about 1910. Probably from a combination of 'boiled shirt' and 'putting on the dog'.

boil up   To become angry. In use1874. ANZ.

boil-up   Brew of tea, often outdoors, as in **to have a boil-up**. ANZ.

boiler   A tough old chicken or other just acceptable animal fodder judged fit only for boiling. Mid C20.

boilover   A surprise sporting result. Partridge sources to Australian horseracing c1870.

bolter   An outsider or racehorse on long odds that wins; sometimes applied to humans, usually in the footrace context. ANZ mid C20.

bomb   1. Ancient vehicle or other dilapidated piece of machinery, likely to blow up at any minute. Mid C20 ANZ.

2. A rugby ball punted high towards the opposition, who have to catch it before the advancing players.

3. Jumping into the water with arms around knees.

bomb-up   Wild party with much boozing. From c2000.

bomb out   To lose. Sporting teams often bomb out of contention. Specific use of 1970s British word for failed expectations. ANZ.

Bombay bloomers   Baggy sports shorts; originally WWII servicemen's shorts, made in Bombay. ANZ.

Bombay Hills/Bombays   Dividing line between civilisation and the peasants, or between Auckland and the rest of the country; actual hills just beyond Pukekohe. Used in the phrase **south/north of the Bombays/Bombay Hills.**

bomb-squasher/bombie/bum-squasher   Big marble, a menace to small marbles, especially when dropped from head height.

bone people   Pakeha wearing Maori pendants or other carved ornaments as gesture of solidarity with Maoritanga, in perhaps an oblique play on Keri Hulme's book *The Bone People*. Used contemptuously of such people. From 1980s.

boner   Penis, usually erect. ANZ.

bong   1.To hit somebody, usually on the head. Perhaps a combination of the British public school 'bonk' and the Aboriginal word *bung* for 'dead'.

2. A plastic contraption involving a funnel and hose for competitive ingestion of alcohol, popular among students. Adaptation of word for a waterpipe used to smoke marijuana.

bonker   Large marble used to shoot other marbles.

bonny new nothing with a thistle/throstle/whistle on the end, a   Answer to a silly question, usually from a child, eg, 'Please, Miss, what's that s'posed to be?'

bonza/bonzer   1. Pleasing or well regarded. Less commonly a **bosker** or **boshta**. Possibly came with goldrushes from California, contraction of Spanish word 'bonanza'. ANZ.

2. A large marble which was highly prized. ANZ early C20.

booai/booay/booeye/boohai   A remote place. Refers to Puhoi, 50 kilometres north of Auckland, which was so isolated in the early days, its pioneering Bohemians almost died of starvation. This Pakeha corruption of *puhoi*, Maori for dull, slow or phlegmatic, is used in the phrase **up the boohai**, meaning to be lost or in trouble.

boob tat A tattoo acquired in prison, from *boob*, a prison, originally military detention cell in WWI.

booboo A mistake. Usually you **make a booboo**. Extended from the American *boob* with maybe a cry-baby notion thrown in. ANZ.

boogie board Small surfboard for juveniles. ANZ later C20.

boomer First-rate, large, successful. Surfies talk of a boomer wave. A boomer is a large male kangaroo, from British dialect word for 'a whopper'. Contrarily the phrase **a little boomer** can mean the opposite, ie, a big and desirable wave.

boonga/bunga Pacific Islander; an offensive adaptation of *boong*, name of unknown origin for an Australian Aboriginal. ANZ early C20.

boot, in your Contemptuous expression akin to 'in your face'.

boot, put in the/put the boot in Rugby union forward habit of kicking and stomping at any part of an opponent's body that comes between the booter and the ball. Also means any rough or unfair treatment of a vulnerable opponent. ANZ.

boot home Strain to finish, from the racing term for urging the horse to cross the line first.

boots and all/boots'n'all Total commitment. ANZ early C20. Used as the title of All Black lock Andy Haden's autobiography. The All Black fullback Don Clarke was known as 'The Boot' because of his prowess at kicking goals and kicking for touch. Used generally for any enthusiastic engagement.

boots leak, someone's That person is daft, eg, 'Notice the way the new student stares into space? I'd say his boots leak.'

booze artist Drunkard. Early C20 extension of old English word 'booze' for liquor and the early C20 word 'artist' for a person, which came to mean a specialist and in that context much favoured in Australasia for drinking experts.

booze balloon The heavy beer drinker's pot belly.

booze barn Large tavern with ready access for consumption of alcohol, popular in 1970s. The **booze-barn mentality** was binge drinking before the pub closed, or generalised liquor swilling, particularly among groups.

booze rooster Drunkard. The word 'rooster' is employed on its own for a man, often in amiable or dismissive fashion.

boozeroo/boozelum Drinking spree or place where you do it. Early C20.

bo-peep A look. From nursery rhyme 'Little Bo-Peep'. ANZ c1920.

borax Banter. Originally 'borak', almost invariably in the phrase **poke the borax at**, to tease somebody. From an Aboriginal development of *burag*, no. ANZ C19. By the middle of C20 **the borax** had come to mean blame or a scolding, eg, 'Jacko copped the borax from the coach for being late to footy practice.'

bot 1. A bug or germ such as a cold or the flu, perhaps from the botfly whose larvae afflict farm animals. In the 1920s the bot signified a tubercular patient. **To have the bot** is to be in the grip of a cold or flu, or perhaps just feeling out of sorts and/or irritable. **How are the bots biting?** is a cheery greeting.

2. The posterior, probably in mind with the ANZ meaning of borrowing money, in the phrase **bot on** when bludging or looking for a handout, where the Americans would be bumming off you. **The bot** is a juvenile reference to junior's bum, or a jovial semi-euphemism, such as enquiring of somebody with piles, **How's the old bot?** ANZ.

botoss A boy, maybe contracted from 'boy' and 'tosser' or masturbator. Recent teenage slang.

bottle drive A bottle collection to raise funds.

bottle store The room in the pub selling bottles of beer, wine and spirituous liquors. Australians have a bottle shop.

bottler A person or object of splendid account, often used in the phrase, 'you bloody bottler, mate'. ANZ from WWII.

boulder-bashing/hopping/jumping/scrambling Trampers' term for crossing rocky terrain. From 1930s.

bounce of the ball Luck, often expressed in resigned fashion as 'that was the bounce of the ball, there is nothing you can do'. Sometimes just **the bounce**. From the erratic bounce of a rugby ball. ANZ.

bounce the ball   Testing public opinion, usually by politicians. From about 1920, from the habit of rugby union players, especially the first five-eighth, bouncing the ball to test the bounce before dropkicking off. The phrase evolved in recent times into **bouncing it off**, something favoured by advertisers in particular.

bowl   To fell a tree or a deer or a pig, or to seduce a woman, eg, for all four, 'Reckon I bowled her, eh?'

bowldacks   Bullshit. Teenage Kiwi slang.

bowser   1. Petrol pump from early C20, when manufactured by S.F. Bowser & Co. of Indiana. The petrol station was also known by this name. ANZ.

2. The measure stuck in the bottles above the liquor bar, reminiscent of the glass bobble on bowsers which filled with the other amber fluid.

3. A dog, contraction of 'a bow-wow-ser'. ANZ.

box   1. Female genitals, the 'box of tricks'. ANZ C20.

2. Mixing accidentally or deliberately two herds or flocks. ANZ c1870.

3. Muddling or making a mistake. ANZ from c1920.

4. That dodgy area in rugby union games behind the scrum and in front of the last lines of defence, the winger and fullback: a clever opponent will **kick into the box**.

box and dice, the whole   Everything, eg, 'How about a spring clean of your room, dear. Pick up everything, dust, clean the windows, the whole box and dice.' From British dialect *box and dice* for 'the sum total'. ANZ from late C19.

box seat   The most favourable place to be. Originally the position atop the coach taken by the driver, most famously Ned 'Cabbage Tree' Devine, the Central Otago goldrush driver who could turn his horses on a coin. Everybody wanted to ride in his box seat. He once refused the request from the Minister of Mines, saying it was taken. The minister informed Ned who he was. Ned replied that was a fine post and he should see he hung on to it. ANZ.

box of birds/boxa birds   Fit and/or well and/or deliriously happy. Often a cheery response to a greeting, like 'Corker, mate. Boxa birds, eh.' From WWII. Sometimes with the additions **and all singing** or **all feathers and shit**. ANZ.

box of fluffies/box of fluffy ducks   Fit, well and happy, thank you.

box of fruit   A suit. Rhyming slang from 1960s.

box on/box on regardless/box on with   Persevere, originally in fighting. Mid C20 ANZ.

box outside the ring   Unconventional or illicit activity, such as having an extramarital affair.

boxed/boxed up   Lost or confused, from the tramping term for getting lost; **to be in a box**, to be in a confused state. ANZ from 1930s.

boxhead   A numbskull, one possessing a head like an empty box. Mid C20.

boy   1. Polynesian man, used until recent times in sport. C19 for a servant and/or missionary convert.

2. A greeting, particularly among Maori, as in 'G'day, boy, how's it goin.'

boya   A man on the West Coast.

Boys on the Hill, the   Members of Parliament, a hangover from when they were all male.

brain like a cow's udder   Dim-witted. Brains or the lack of feature in a variety of scornful phrases, such as **if he had another brain it would be lonely** and **he hasn't enough brains to give himself a headache**.

brass razoo   A minute, virtually worthless, imaginary coin, once approximating the status of a farthing, usually used in the phrase **doesn't have a brass razoo**. Said to have been a gambling chip and/or to be a corruption of the Maori word *raho*, a testicle. Thus **razoos** testicles; **not worth a brass razoo/a razoo**, to be useless, and **not give a razoo**, not to care one iota, not the smallest bit. Eg, 'Some foreign exchange dealers after the crash were not worth a razoo/Some foreign exchange dealers never gave a razoo about the implications of gambling with a person's lifesavings.' In use from the 1930s. ANZ.

bread and scrape/bread and spit   Very little to eat.

breakfast, have for   Boast that somebody or something will be easily conquered or acquired. You might say you **could do it before breakfast**, meaning it is so easy. ANZ.

break down/break it down   Modify or mute, take it easy, stop that, desist from speech. A command that is often a reprimand. Eg, 'Break it down, fellas, I can't sleep with all that noise going on.' ANZ from 1920s.

break in   Clear and cultivate new ground.

break out   1. A new goldrush, C19.

2. A C20 boozing spree, sometimes to the extent of vandalism. ANZ.

3. The first cuts in shearing.

4. Hauling logs out of the bush.

breast/breast up to   Approach, face, sometimes confront, but popular in the up-close, anticipated pleasure when you **breast up to the bar** for a drink. ANZ from c1930.

brekkie   Breakfast. ANZ.

brewer's asthma   Beer hangover. ANZ c1925.

brewer's goitre   A beer gut. ANZ c1925.

bridge   A glance, c1920s. If a woman happens to **chuck a bridge** she has flashed her underwear. ANZ.

Britland   Jokey name for Britain.

Briton   Brave person, invoked as a role model for children, often in the phrase **be a brave little Briton**.

bro   Greeting, particularly popular among Maori, short for 'brother', imported from the Black Brothers in America. Maori gangs are identified generally as **The Bros** and hospitals in some areas are known as **Bro-repairs**, a play on the Beaurepaires tyre retailing chain.

broiler/broiler fowl   A scrawny and usually older woman.

broken-arse   A prisoner who has caved in to the system and goes to the bottom of the pecking order among his fellow prisoners. 1980s.

broomie   Shearing floor sweeper.

bronzed Anzac   Suntanned Antipodean.

brown   Sulkiness and/or shame, in the phrase **do a brown**. Teenage slang.

brown ankles   Toadying behaviour, suggestive of being up to your bent ankles in your attempt to get up the bum of the person you are trying to impress. From 1970s.

brown derby   South Island chocolate dip ice-cream.

brown-eye, to   An unattractively active verb meaning to expose the anus. ANZ.

brownie   Cocoa or currant damper; treacle gingerbread among tramps; a **brownie gorger** is a shearer.

Brown's cows   In the phrase **all over the road like Brown's cows**, a disorderly state. Sometimes used in regard to a person with wobbling buttocks. ANZ 1920s.

Browntable   Establishment Maori. A play on the Business Roundtable group of business leaders. *The Dominion*, 5 August 1996, refers to 'Mr Henare . . . contemptuous of the "Browntable" as well as the Pakeha establishment.'

brumbie/brumby   Kaimanawa wild horse, probably from the Aboriginal word for wild, *booramby*.

brush   A woman, often as object of male sexual desire, the whole perceived from the pubic hair part. ANZ 1930s.

brush the teatree out of your hair   Admonition not to be a dolt or to somebody who has made a doltish remark worthy of somebody residing amongst teatree or manuka in the backblocks. Mid C20.

buck/buck at   1. To object to something. From c1890. In the phrases **have a buck at** and **to give it a buck** meaning to try something, maybe daunting. **Fair buck!** is an appeal to play fair, or an expression of astonishment.

2. A Kiwi dollar, adapted from American dollar.

buck in   Help the common cause, eg, 'We hope every local will buck in for the Thorndon Fair.'

buck rat, fit as a/wild as a Very fit or very wild. Mid C20.

bucket Harsh if not brutal criticism. Politicians give and take a **bucketing**.

bucket of pipis, goes off in the sun like a Promiscuous woman, in the perception of an insensitive male.

bucket-of-water wood Useless wood for burning. The *pukatea* is an example of this sappy sort of wood.

Buckley's/Buckley's chance No chance. From convict William Buckley, who escaped and lived for 32 years among Aborigines before giving himself up.

buffie Sultana, down south.

bugger A favourite exclamation, and consistently so from the goldrush era of the 1860s. It can refer to almost anything or anybody, often in an exasperated fashion made famous in a TV ad for a sports ute. ANZ.

bugger it!/bugger me!/bugger me Charlie/bugger me days!/ bugger me sideways!/bugger that for a joke Expressions of surprise or anything else in context, such as disbelief or distaste. ANZ.

bugger off! ANZ expression of denial or dismissal, as in 'Bugger off! I never laid a finger on him.'

buggerama! Expression of mild or jokey distress.

buggerise about Aimless behaviour. ANZ.

buggerlugs, sometimes spelled **bugalugs** Expression of exasperation usually of a mock variety and often directed at junior. Early C20. Likely northern British dialect originally. ANZ.

buggers afloat Doughnuts, dumplings or fried scones. Early C20.

buggers-on-the-coals Currant damper. ANZ mid C19.

build a feed To prepare food in the bush, originally South Island forestry workers and musterers.

buku Lots of anything. Army slang from Vietnam, mashing the French legacy of *beaucoup*, a lot.

bull artist/bullshit artist/bullshitter Boaster or conman or experienced liar. ANZ c1916.

Bull Ring, The   Rugby Park, New Plymouth, where the Taranaki rugby team disports its mascot Ferdinand the Bull and amiable All Black prop and Taranaki captain Mark 'Bull' Allen was wildly popular.

bull the tea   Put soda in your bush tea to boost its impact.

bull-bars   Thick metal pipes extended out from front and sometimes back of 4WDs and utes to protect from stock in rural areas and to make a statement in urban areas.

bulldogging   Catching wild deer by dropping on them from helicopters. In his thriller *The Idiot Played Rachmaninov*, Michael Brown says it was so common in Westland that it no longer raised eyebrows there.

bulldust   Nonsense, more genteely expressed than 'bullshit'. ANZ c1919.

bullocky   Bullock driver, ANZ from 1840. To **bullock** is to act belligerently, while **bullocking over** is a favourite description of how rugby union forwards crash in for tries.

bullers   Gumboots, from a brandname for a low-top, lace-up variety popular in bush country, usually cut down to lighten them, the laces replaced with wire and holes made in them to drain water.

bullet   A cannabis cigarette, from its shape, invariably crimped at both ends to stop the crumbled leaf falling out.

bull-a-bull/bulli-bull/bullybul   The flowering shrub *poroporo*, c1845.

bull's roar   Not even close, in regard to the desired distance or objective, eg, 'Norty's not within a bull's roar of qualifying for the sprints.' ANZ.

bullseye   Sheep's anus after shearing. Mid C20.

Bullshit Castle   Air Force headquarters, in the perception of our WWII airmen, applied frequently ever since to Parliament.

bullswool   Nonsense, in the nicer way of putting it. ANZ early C20.

bully   1. A tiny freshwater fish, also known as a cockabully.

2. A bulldozer.

3. A pig-dog that appears to have a bulldog among its antecedents.

4. Highly desired or approved, adapted here to apply to objects such as a bully loaf of bread from 1870, from the English word for a fine fellow.

bulsh Nonsense.

bum bandit Active male homosexual. ANZ.

bum barber Sheep shearer.

bum chum 1. Male homosexual.

2. Close friend.

bum man Male professing attraction for female buttocks, eg, 'Me, I'm a bum man when it comes to the sheilas.'

bum nuts Eggs, usually hen's eggs. ANZ.

bung 1. Ruined or bankrupted, often said to have 'gone bung' or to have something not right like 'a bung ear'. From the Aboriginal word *bung*, dead. ANZ late C19.

2. Move something, as in 'Bung the plate over to me, will you.' ANZ.

bung it on To boast or exaggerate. ANZ.

bunger A cave or shelter where you can bung yourself. WWII.

bungy The elastic cord that once simply held items on your bike or car roof has been stretched around the ankles to allow **bungy-jumping** off disused bridges and other high places, often down to a ducking in the river below, before springing back up again. A bungy was a typist's rubber. However, when you **bungy your swag** you are merely packing your bag or tramper's pack.

bunny hop A vehicle moving in fits and starts.

bunrunner Lunch and snack deliverer around offices. 1990s.

burger Vagina.

burk To dodge working. Maybe rhyming with 'shirk'. From c1880.

burl Give something a try, such as a relationship or a restaurant. From English word *birl*, a turn, via its use in the game of two-up to indicate spinning the coins. ANZ.

burn Fast and probably showy driving of a vehicle, usually in the phrase **to go for a burn**, the burn referring to the smell of burning rubber when subjected to a fast take-off. ANZ mid C20.

burn off Leave someone behind, usually by a rapid departure in a car. ANZ mid C20.

burn-off Clearing land by fire.

bush Forest or dense scrub from earliest days of European settlement. When you **go bush** you are leaving the city stress for the simple rural life, or you are hiding out. Disgraced touring All Black Keith Murdoch did not return to New Zealand but went bush in Australia. ANZ.

bush baptist Religious ranter from early C20, lacking the dog collar or authority of an organised religion. ANZ.

bush bash To tramp difficult terrain, or let your 4WD do the job. In Australia it refers to clearing virgin bush.

bush carpenter A rough and probably untrained carpenter, originally in 1870s an itinerant carpenter. ANZ.

bush champagne Meths and salt. ANZ.

bush fridge Damp sack or teatowel over the tin of food, the edges soaking in cold water. ANZ.

bush happy Somewhat deranged or eccentric person, from living alone too long in the bush.

bush justice The rough kind of justice decided without a properly constituted court.

bush lawyer 1. Laying down of the law by a layman, first spotted on the goldfields. ANZ

2. A thorny native plant of the blackberry family whose clutches are not easy to escape.

bush nightie The Swanndri shirt for outdoor slumber.

bush mechanic Amateur and untrained mechanic.

bush pig Ugly person.

bush telegraph The grapevine or gossipy means by which information and rumour is spread. ANZ C20.

bush whisky   Illegally distilled whisky, almost invariably done out in the bush, such as the celebrated McCrae efforts in the Hokonui Hills of Southland.

bushed   Very lost. ANZ C19.

bushfire blonde   1. A redheaded woman.

2. Cherry brandy and lemonade. Both ANZ.

bushie   Bushman, a person who lives in and off the bush, like a forester or hunter. ANZ C19.

bushman's breakfast   A yawn, a stretch, a piss and a look round. ANZ.

bushman's bunk   The *mangemange*, a springy shrub suitable for sleeping on.

bushman's friend   The *rangiora*, whose leaves are toilet-friendly to bushmen's bums.

bushman's mile   Much more than the mile you expected. From late C19.

bushman's singlet   Black, woollen, sleeveless singlet favoured for outdoor work.

bushwhacked   Totally tired. ANZ.

bushwhacker   1. Axeman who fells bush.

2. Any rugged, rural type or rough-and-ready effort. ANZ.

bust!   Exclamation, usually of disgust. Often **bust it!**, as my grandmother used to say when she dropped her crochet stitch and did not want to say anything stronger such as 'Bugger it!' From early C20.

bust your boiler   Collapse from over-exertion, eg, 'Don't bust your boiler digging that crib wall.'

buster   Short for a southerly buster or severe southerly storm. ANZ late C19.

busy as a bee with a bumful of honey   Very busy.

busy as a one-armed paperhanger with crabs/a one-eyed cat watching two rat holes   Decidedly busy. ANZ.

BUTA   Boot up the arse.

butcher's 1. To be angry, usually **to go butcher's at**, from rhyming 'butcher's hook' with 'crook', in the sense of 'going crook' meaning to be angry with somebody. ANZ late C19.

2. Indifferent, as in **not give a butcher's**, probably suggesting a butcher shares with a tinker not giving a very big curse or damn.

butcher's canary Blowfly, which butcher shops attract. ANZ c1925.

butcher's cat To attack, but not from rhyming slang so much as the reputation of butcher's cats for vigorous battle, such that the phrase for vicious fighting perhaps involving scratching and eye-gouging is to **be in like a butcher's cat**.

buttendski The buttocks.

buttinski To interrupt or butt in, from WWI soldiers. ANZ.

buttonhole Sheep crutching, with reference to the slang word for the genital area.

buzz around like a bee in a bottle Busy and/or confused.

by Christchurch — hooya? Euphemism for 'By Christ, who are you?'

by korry/py korry Allegedly Maori pidgin for 'By Gōd', elaborately presented in the nonsense rhyme:

'By korry said Hori to Hiki

We'd better sell our cows pretty slicky

For I've heard a mutter

That New Zealand butter

Comes from Bulls and Rangitikei.'

BYO Bring Your Own, wine usually, to an unlicensed restaurant; **BYOG** bring your own grog — to a party. ANZ.

by the limping cricket/thundering sardine Mock horror oaths.

cabbage Cannabis leaf, sometimes referred to dismissively when its quality is poor; **cabbaged** is made mellow if not sluggish by smoking cannabis; **cabbaged out** is to be affected by cannabis to the point of being almost comatose; **cabbaging** is smoking cannabis leaves.

cabbage-tree Hat made from cabbage tree leaves.

cabsav A cabernet sauvignon style of wine, a favourite ANZ.

cactus In difficulty, in the phrase **in the cactus,** sometimes in reference to being lost or in an out-of-the-way place. ANZ.

Cake Tin, The Nickname for the new millennium stadium on former railyards in downtown Wellington, replacing the revered but rugged Athletic Park.

call the game in Quit, eg, 'Time to call the game in, fellas, the fish ain't biting.' ANZ c1912.

can-a-piss Beer in a can, the favourite drug of those who want you to know they do not smoke cannabis.

Cannabis County Northland.

canary The yellow bus ticket that drivers used to dispense, with the discretion to **sell a canary,** give you a free ride. From 1950s.

cannon Rifle.

can't make honey out of dogshit You can't make something good out of something bad, like a silk purse out of a sow's ear.

Capital of Cow Country Hamilton.

captain cooker/cooker 1. Wild pig, supposed descendant of those released in New Zealand by Captain Cook.

2. **Cookers** were the British immigrants who came here aboard the

TSS *Captain Cook* in the 1950s, as part of a total of 27,000 British migrants.

carjacking   Raising a parked car on a jack before robbing and/or assaulting occupants. Late 1990s.

car surfing   Jumping for fun from car bonnet to car bonnet. Mid 1990s.

carbine   A fast or a slow horse, the latter jokey inversion, both referring to an internationally acclaimed Kiwi racehorse of that name early C20.

cardie   Cardigan. ANZ 1960s.

cardigan brigade   Public servants from post-WWII, when the wearing of usually grey cardigans was popular if not emblematic of grey government or local body employees.

career girl   A ewe who will not mother her lamb.

cark   To die, if a person, to collapse if machinery, such as a car. To **cark it** is to die, but to **cark out** is to fall into a drunken sleep. C20 ANZ of uncertain origin, possibly from the carking sound of crows feasting on corpses or, more likely, a contraction of the word 'carcass'.

Carlaw Coathanger   Stiff-arm tackle not unknown at Carlaw Park, the home of Auckland rugby league before the Auckland Warriors moved into Mt Smart Stadium in 1995.

carn!   Come on! Often invoked by sporting spectators desperate for their team to do better. ANZ.

carnie   Sexually available female under the lawful age for sexual intercourse; short for 'carnal' in the legal phrase 'carnal knowledge', an issue in the 1950s when youth rebellion surfaced.

Carrot County   Ohakune in recent years, since the adoption of the giant carrot icon in the town in celebration of its local crop.

carry matilda   To carry one's swag or 'matilda'. The Australians prefer to 'waltz matilda'.

cashed up, all   Money in hand, earned or saved. Mid C20 ANZ.

cashie   Cash sale that avoids paperwork, popular in used-car selling circles.

castor Approval of anything excellent, from castor sugar. Early C20 ANZ.

catch-up play A team having to come from behind to win a game, eg, 'The All Blacks have to play catch-up football in the second half if they are to win the Bledisloe Cup.'

Cathedral City Christchurch, because of its central Anglican cathedral.

cat's meat Anything of little significance. Mid C20.

cattledog Catholic schoolchild, in the jeering language of state schoolchildren with rhymes such as 'Cattledogs, cattledogs, stink like frogs and live under logs.'

caught short Unexpected need to use the toilet, or menstruate without tampons available, or lacking means to host surprise guests, or unable to meet a requirement for money. ANZ from 1930s.

cauli Cauliflower. ANZ.

cave in To defecate, with reference to subsidence experienced by trampers.

ceefa A cat, as in 'c' for cat.

Central Central Otago, radiating around Roxburgh.

chardonnay socialist A tepid socialist; used by Mike Moore 26 November 1993 of those Labour politicians planning his demise as leader of the party.

charge an arm and a leg/like a wounded bull Excessive pricing. ANZ.

Charles Ulysses Farley Jokey variation of the dismissive remark 'Fuck you, charlie.'

charlie A knee into the thigh, an unpleasant playground activity.

charlie/charlie over the water A children's game like chasey or tag.

chateau cardboard/chateau de cask Cheery 1980s terms for cheap bulk wine in cardboard box.

chateau collapsio Cheap bulk wine in a weak cardboard box.

Chateau Taranaki Beer.

cheer germ Somebody who makes negative remarks, eg, 'Mandy reckons nobody in the class will pass Bursary English, but ignore her, she's a cheer germ.' In the 1930s it was a get-well message, popularised by Aunt Molly of 2YA children's session.

cheeri Short for 'cheerio' or goodbye, from c1930. ANZ.

cheerio Small saveloy usually served at children's parties with a large bowl of tomato sauce.

chelsea Sugar, from the name of the Auckland sugar works.

cheque Worker's wages not in cheque form but cash in an envelope, except when it was a farmer receiving his **butter/wool cheque**, from mid C19 ANZ. If you are **cheque proud**, you are impatient about spending your cheque, from the restlessness of a collar-proud, harness-racing horse.

cher bro Excellent, to a contemporary teenager.

cherchez le sausage Sexual intercourse, a franglais play on the phrases 'cherchez la femme' and 'hide the sausage'.

Cherry Blacks Ex-All Blacks playing for Japan, land of cherry trees, used of Graeme Bachop on *The Tight Five*, TVOne, 22 October 1999.

cherrypicker A large nose. ANZ.

chew To talk. Often referring to a lengthy discussion of some issue, when people **chew it over**. From c1920, ANZ.

chew/suck the kumara Something going wrong, often mechanical. Originally a topdressing pilot crashing.

chews Lollies. Originally chewing gum dispensed by American servicemen in WWII.

chiack Vigorous teasing; also used as a verb. From the London street greeting, from late C19. ANZ.

chillybin Insulated plastic container for carrying food and drink. ANZ.

chinaman 1. Yellowish Central Otago stone that could have gold in it, the kind often found by Chinese miners following behind the more impatient European fossickers.

2. A chute for loading spoil onto trucks.

3. A length of wool on the sheep's rump the shearer left, looking like a pigtail.

Chinese ballast   Dismissive term for rice.

Chinese burn   Twisting wrist or leg skin between two hands, a children's playground pastime. From 1930s. ANZ.

Chinese lady   South Island toilet C19, indicative of low regard for Chinese miners.

Chinese smoke   Letting cigarette smoke trickle out of mouth upwards to be inhaled through nostrils. From 1960s.

Chink   A Chinese man, used contemptuously from goldmining days.

chip   1.To be impertinent, eg, 'That boy chips me one more time, he cops it.'

2. To chide. ANZ. British dialect *chip* meant a disagreement. From early C20.

3. Dried cow dung. ANZ.

chippie   Potato chip. From 1960s.

chippy   Wood-burning wetback stove or chip heater.

chocolate dip   An icecream in a cone, dipped in chocolate.

chocolate fish/frog   A popular candy bar, the former made of chocolate-coated marshmallow shaped like a fish, the latter solid chocolate or peppermint-filled chocolate shaped like a frog. **Have the brains of a chocolate fish/frog** is teenage slang for a dolt.

chocolate trout   A Taupo chocolate fish.

choke a darkie   To defecate. ANZ 1960s.

choke it   Stop something or turn it off, eg, 'Choke that radio, will ya.'

chook   1. Chicken, hen, even rooster, from British dialect variants of *chick*, a fowl. ANZ mid C19.

2. Woman, often an older woman, usually used dismissively. ANZ from mid 1930s.

3. Silly person. Often said to be **running around like a headless chook,** displaying **headless chookery**, spelled out by phrase **silly as a chook**, though it could be the drunken variety when you are **pissed as a chook**. ANZ.

chook raffle A quick and probably illegal raffle, often in a pub, prize a frozen chook.

chookie Girlfriend or young woman. ANZ from mid 1920s.

chook's bum The mouth. ANZ.

chop 1. Woodchopping contest, from late C19.

2. A fair share, often in the phrase **in for one's chop**. If something or someone is **not much chop**, it or he or she is of little value or not very good at something. ANZ.

chop short of a barbie, a Mentally deficient. ANZ.

chow Chinese person. Evolved from sailors calling food 'chow'; **chowchow** for yellow pickles, from Chinese perceived as yellow in skin pigment. A term of contempt that followed Chinese into market gardening, where a cabbage was known as a chow. ANZ.

Chowick Auckland suburb of Howick, drawing dismissive attention to where many Asian immigrants settled in 1990s.

Chrissie Christmas, often used in **Chrissie pressie**. ANZ.

Christchurch!/By Christchurch! Euphemistic modification of 'Christ!'

chrome dome Bald person. Late C20.

chuck/upchuck To vomit. ANZ mid C20.

chuck a mental/spaz/wobbly Lose temper or behave erratically. 'Spaz' is short for 'spastic'. ANZ.

chuck it in Surrender or give up. ANZ.

chuck off at To tease or abuse. Early C20 ANZ.

chuck-out Ejection or dismissal, usually the sack. Late C19 ANZ.

chuddy/chutty Chewing gum. ANZ c1925.

chuff Backside. Prime Minister Holyoake startled some people in 30 July 1967 when he talked about sitting on one's chuff, a phrase that usually means being lazy. ANZ.

chunder To vomit. Australia c1925, where Chunder Loo of Akin Foo was a well-known cartoon character in advertisements for Cobra bootpolish.

ciggie Cigarette. ANZ.

City of Sails Auckland, which has more yachts to the nautical mile than anywhere else.

claddy Flax stem, a corruption of *korari*.

clanger A smoke, teenage usage late 1990s.

clayie Clay marble.

Clayton's Anything phoney or imitation, from the 1980 Australian TV advertisement for the non-alcoholic 'Clayton's — the drink you have when you're not having a drink.' Hence **Clayton's choice**, ie, no choice at all.

clean up Defeat, often used to indicate comprehensive sporting victory, but first emerged in WWI. ANZ.

clever In good health or mood, usually in negative **not too clever**. ANZ mid C19.

clever gear Fashionable or smart clothes, sometimes used derisively. 'What's with the clever gear, new date?'

client-server action Sex, in late C20 corporate speak.

climb into Attack, phsyically or verbally.

clip around the ears with an iceblock, a Arrival of cold weather.

clobbering machine The way the system squashes individuality, known as **The Great Kiwi Clobbering Machine** in 1970s. An Education Department report on Maori achievement in 1989 observed **'the great brown clobbering machine'** of peer group pressure on Maori achievers in school and workplace.

clock To punch, usually in the head. Mid C20 extension of British word for the face.

clocking Illegal winding back of vehicle odometer. From British word 'clock', the speedometer.

clog clatterer Dutch person.

clonk To hit. ANZ.

clucky 1. Gushing, often over a baby, in the way hens cluck contentedly.

2. Pregnant.

3. Showing fussy, gushy signs of wanting to be pregnant. All ANZ.

Coaster   West Coaster, South Island.

Coastie   Maori from the East Coast of the North Island, mainly Ngati Porou and Whanau Apanui between Opotiki, the Cape and Gisborne.

coathanger   1. Close-pruned pine tree, the way it is supposed to be done.

2. Rigid arm across the neck, a very dangerous tackle in both rugby codes, whose practitioner should find himself in disciplinary trouble.

3. Auckland Harbour Bridge.

cobber   A mate or friend, or sometimes merely the fellow alongside in manual labour. Cheery diminutives are **cob** and **me old cob**. The phrase **to cobber up with** is to make friends. From Yiddish *chaber*, a comrade. ANZ late C19.

coca-colas/cokes/colas   Brown-coloured marbles.

cockabully   Grayling or small freshwater fish, a corruption of Maori *kokopu*.

cock-oi   Farmers' version of a hikoi or march on Parliament.

cocky   A small farmer, like the cocky or cockatoo scratching out a small patch of earth. Often extended to **cowcocky,** a dairy farmer. ANZ latter C19.

cocky's horror   Grease and oil, which are never used by a dinkum cocky or farmer.

cocky's implement shed   Any dumping corner for old farm machinery.

cocky's joy   Treacle or golden syrup, which came in half-gallon tins in the days before fridges and was thus a thing of joy for several months, being the only food that lasted that long. ANZ.

cocky's string   Number 8 fencing wire.

coconut   Pacific Islander, a dismissive term in 1960s, now positive.

coconut tackle   Head-high tackle. In March 1997 Northern Transvaal rugby coach Kitch Christie told the media: 'I never considered the term racist. It is like referring to it as a mango tackle.'

cold as a frog's tit Very cold, or sexually frigid.

cold as a stepmother's breath Very cold. The stepmother may have replaced the mother-in-law as the traditional family *bête noire*.

cold enough to freeze the nuts off a Massey Ferguson Very cold, to anyone familiar with that sturdy brand of tractor.

cold pigging Selling goods door-to-door.

colder than a mother-in-law's kiss Unfriendly.

collar Froth on a glass of beer. Sometimes objected to as 'big enough to take a Windsor knot' (a bulky way of tying your tie) — the implication that you are being deprived of beer by the large collar of froth. Mid C20.

colonial Uncouth, provincial, naive, wet behind the ears. Still used by the British to put down New Zealanders.

colonial cringe Kiwi putdown of ourselves as inferior in relation to Britain or any other country.

colonial goose Dressed mutton flaps. Originally a boned and stuffed leg or shoulder of mutton, popular when these cuts were less expensive.

colonial oven Cast iron box with a door, placed in an open fire.

colonial pudding Basic steamed pudding made from flour, butter and whatever dried fruit to hand.

coma'd Drunk to the point of being comatose.

come a thud A failure or figurative fall, eg, 'Keep up that bolshie attitude with your teachers, mate, you'll come a thud at assessment time.'

come at To attempt, often used negatively, as in 'Don't come at that with me, mate, or I'll drop ya.' Mid C20.

come good To succeed, something often said of sportspeople or racehorses after a period of disappointing performances. From British dialect phrase for injury and recovery.

come the uncooked crustacean Cause trouble, often by attempting to dupe. A variant on popular Australian phrase 'come the raw prawn'. Often negative use, **don't come the uncooked**

crustacean, meaning don't try to fool me. ANZ.

come to light with   To supply something, as in 'The coach finally came to light with the long-promised headgear.' ANZ early C20.

come up against   To encounter difficulties. ANZ.

come up for air   Take a rest. Even front-row forwards occasionally come up for air. ANZ from 1940s, probably from diving.

commercial traveller   A ram who doesn't stay in his own paddock.

complexion like an oxidised potato   An ugly face, perhaps pitted from boils or acne.

compo   Financial compensation for work injury, or alleged work injury, from mid C20 Workers' Compensation Act. Being **on compo** is to be receiving such compensation. ANZ.

compo king   Somebody perceived as illegally receiving compo after deliberately injuring him or herself, or pretending to be ill.

con-artist   A deceiver, somebody practised at cheating. ANZ.

convo   To talk, as in having a conversation.

cooee   Domestic hail, often calling the family to the dinner table, adapted from the Aboriginal *guwi*, a call. Something **within cooee** is available. If something is **not within cooee**, it is far from being attained. If you **come within cooee of** you have just missed out on. ANZ.

cooking with gas   A fast solution or ready to get going. 'Sign this and we're cooking with gas.' ANZ.

coot   A person of little or no account, still used with the jocular contempt popular in the 'Hori' stories published in post-WWII periodicals. ANZ early C20 spin on C18 US word for a simpleton.

cootie/kootie   A head louse, from the Maori *kutu*.

coozer   The penis, the active object aimed at the cooze, the vagina.

coral stomper   A Polynesian, dismissively.

corker   Anything appreciated, such as people saying they had a corker time at a party. It may go back to the meaning of 'caulker', a dram of liquor, but New Zealand was using it earliest in settler days. ANZ.

corned beef room Hospital ward where the terminally ill are placed apart from those likely to survive. Possibly adapted from the British 'corned beef island' for a housing estate early C20, whose residents favoured corned beef and/or lived in houses resembling tins thereof.

Coromandel green Marijuana grown in the Coromandel area.

corpus delicti An attractive woman. ANZ.

corrie iron Corrugated iron sheets, used for roofing, fencing, and sometimes to clad walls.

cossie A swimming costume. ANZ.

cot-case Somebody fit for the lunatic asylum, though it may only be a temporary craziness from too much alcohol. ANZ.

cough your cud To vomit.

could eat a baby's bum through a cane chair/a horse and chase the driver/the arse out of a dead horse/dead possum/the crotch out of a low-flying duck Extremely hungry. ANZ.

could eat an apple through a picket fence/eat peas through a tennis racquet Buck-toothed. ANZ.

could kick a bullock up the arse and walk away with the hide Big feet. ANZ.

could open a can of peaches with that nose A prominent nose. ANZ.

could play a piano while pouring concrete Can do anything, as Stu Wilson said of All Black centre Frank Bunce playing for North Harbour vs Auckland, TVOne, 19 September 1992.

could scull the cap off a can of beer Very thirsty.

could use her shit for toothpaste Indicative of extreme lust. ANZ.

could you stop a Presbyterian? Would you like a shot of whisky in your tea? A Deep South of the Mainland question, cannily concealed.

couldn't bat an eyelid Adjudged an appalling batsman, as did cricket commentator Glenn Turner of Indian spinner Bhagwat Chandrasekhar, 3 February 1991. Chandrasekhar averaged about four runs in approximately 80 matches.

couldn't care less if the cow calves or breaks a leg Indicative of extreme disinterest. From c1950.

couldn't catch a cold if he/she sat naked all night in an icy pond
Unlucky or incompetent.

couldn't fuck a frog trotting Inept.

couldn't hit a dead bull's bum with a tin can Without any
discernible skill in the motor coordination department. ANZ.

couldn't kick a hen off its nest Underachievement, a day to forget,
eg, 'Don Clarke had one of those days when he couldn't kick a hen
off its nest.' T.P. McLean, *Evening Post*, 30 June 1995.

couldn't knock the skin off a rice pudding Weak and incompetent.
ANZ.

couldn't lie straight in bed A liar. ANZ.

**couldn't piss out of a boot with the directions written on the
tongue** Clumsy.

couldn't poke a sharp stick up a dead dog's arsehole Astonishingly
incompetent.

couldn't see the road to the dunny if it had red flags on it Very
drunk or very stupid. ANZ.

couldn't sell a statue to a pigeon Ineffectual person.

country so poor a rabbit would have to take a cut lunch Rural
South Island saying about impoverished farmland.

cow Problem person or thing; **dirty/rotten/silly cow**, an
unacceptable person; **poor cow**, intended sympathy for the
pathetic; **fair cow,** any person, situation or object, either
unacceptably or as exclamation at viewing whatever; **a cow of a**,
anything troublesome. Early C20 ANZ.

cow-banger/cow-cocky/cow-spanker A dairy farmer or sharemilker.
ANZ.

cow-gravy Freshly poured cow manure.

cow-jockey The new kid in the cowshed who cops the chores around
the farm.

cowsh Term of dismissal for something regarded as nonsense or
rubbish, short for 'cowshit'.

cow's kipper/pie Cow pat.

cow-tree Karaka shrub.

crack a fat To achieve and/or express a sexual erection. ANZ.

cracker 1. Karaka tree, from 1860s.

  2. Smallest amount of money, usually employed in the negative, as in **not a cracker** or **not having a cracker**, ANZ mid C20. Refers to a plain, small, dry biscuit called a cracker.

  3. Rated highly, as in a cracker day. Probably shortened form of 'crackerjack'. ANZ.

  4. A cartridge. Usually plural. Early C20.

  5. The shredded end of the stockwhip or a flax whip, referred to in the phrase **Can he crack his whip?**, meaning 'Is he a good drinking man, and is he prepared to prove it by shouting the next round?' If somebody **cracks the whip**, they are urging or ordering greater effort or control, as a jockey cracks the whip over a horse's flank.

crack it To succeed in seducing a woman, or in anything else. ANZ from 1920s.

crack on Talk on and on past the listener's patience.

crappers' ditch, in In trouble, as one would be if one found oneself in the place where people have crapped or defecated.

crash hot! Exclamation of strong approval. Often used in the negative, as complaining about **not feeling too crash hot** to indicate you are feeling lousy. ANZ from c1950.

crate 1. Oblong wooden box specifically designed to carry 24 quart bottles of beer or six half-gallon flagons of beer. Almost obsolete, but still used as generic term for acquiring a quantity of beer. In 1991 Wellington's newspaper the *Evening Post* referred to 'fill a crate' for taking away beer.

  2. Car or bicycle or other machine either literally or jocularly suggesting rust or dilapidation. ANZ.

crawler/crawlie The *koura* or freshwater crayfish.

cray The $100 bill, red as a crayfish.

crayfish 1. A contemptible person, as in one who crawls to authority blabbing about his mates. From the army in WWI.

2. A coward, often used in phrase to **crayfish out**, meaning you back lost your nerve or backed away from something dangerous or risky. Late C19 ANZ.

cream   To defeat comprehensively, often in competitive sports. ANZ.

cream your jeans   To ejaculate sperm, or to become excessively excited. ANZ.

crib   Holiday cottage in the South Island.

crib/cribtime   Mealtime or smoko in the South Island.

cribtin   Lunchbox, mostly on the West Coast of the South Island.

crim   A criminal. ANZ c1925.

crimplene suit and Skoda brigade   A group of Social Crediters, the suits often crimson, 1970s.

crockery   Teeth, as called by commentator Keith Quinn in the Ireland vs New Zealand second rugby test, 6 June 1992.

crook   Ill or angry, deriving from *cronk*, obsolete word for 'ill', perhaps also from German *krank*, British dialect *crock* for an injured animal or person, and US *crook*, a swindler. Often used in the phrase **to go crook**, meaning to display annoyance or anger. If you **feel/look crook**, you are ill or unhealthy. If you are **in crook with** someone, you are in their bad books. If someone **puts you crook**, they have misled you. If they **go crook on** you, your status has declined in their eyes. A **crook deal/job** is something that goes wrong, perhaps through bad luck, bad judgement or simply the fates conspiring against you. A **crook do** is a poor party. A **crook run** or **trot** is a period of bad luck. A **crook steer** is being given misleading information. ANZ early C20.

crookie   Someone unreliable or plain bad and dishonest. ANZ.

cross-eyed spieler   A crafty character. The Yiddish *spiel* means patter.

Cross-roach   A Kiwi bludger sponging in King's Cross, Sydney, a rough area of lowlifes and deadbeats and hookers and strip joints; even there such activity would be regarded as at cockroach level.

crow   A farmhand forker of hay or shoveller of grain. Late C19 Australian.

crown jewels, the The treasured male genitalia. ANZ.

crumb-bum An oaf, by extension of the word crummy, meaning worthless. ANZ.

crust Livelihood, eg, 'It's no easier than it ever was to earn a decent crust.' ANZ early C20.

cu/cya Goodbye, possibly the first recorded text message slang.

Cuba Street Yank Flashy dresser and probably loud with it, the way WWII American servicemen were perceived walking up this central Wellington street.

cuff, a bit on the To be unfair or severe, usually in the form of a protest by the party who feels injured. Perhaps rhyming with 'rough' or 'tough'. ANZ c1930.

cunning as a Maori dog/hen Sly or cunning in a low fashion. Mid C20.

cunning as a shithouse rat/the proverbial outhouse rat Super sly or cunning. ANZ.

cunning stunt Jocular greeting, the meaning bearing no relation to its origination in the swapping of letters between the two words 'stunning' and 'cunt'.

cunt's hair/red cunt's hair The measure of some minute mechanical difference.

cupful of cold sick, a Indicative of low esteem. A poor game of rugby might be so described.

cuppa A cup of tea, tea break, often also in the figurative sense of the need for a rest, famously proposed by Prime Minister David Lange in 1988 when he called for a breather and a cuppa from the market reforms of his Finance Minister Roger Douglas. Habitual ANZ habit C20.

curly Difficult or attractive. Depending on the context or which team you back, a cricketer could bowl a curly ball that was tricky or superb, or both. Often the addition of 'extra' indicates strong approval, such as 'That was an **extra curly** ball he bowled.' Cricket is probably where the word originated, where the ball can curl in mysterious ways. ANZ mid C20.

curry   Aggressive encouragement, possibly abusive, not often physical anymore. Often used when you give the team you are supporting **a bit of curry**, screaming at them to do better. Borrowed from the English word for rubbing down a horse, and the idea of heat generated by the Indian curry dish. ANZ.

currymuncher   Term for an Indian or somebody intimate with an Indian woman.

custard, turning to   Popular phrase for anything going wrong, such as the recent America's Cup defence by Team NZ.

cut   1. A share, probably derived from sheep shearing, where to **get a cut** was to get a shearing job. When you are **in for your cut**, you anticipate a share. Furthermore, a cut could be the completion of a job. If you **take a cut**, you accept a reduction in your share or salary. ANZ late C19.

2. Finished, eg, a keg of beer. Mid C20.

3. Drunk. ANZ.

cut a track   Leave, usually in a hurry, eg, 'I've had this cannabis cultivation caper, I'll leave yous jokers to it and cut a track.'

cut cat, to go like a   To exit smartly, as you would expect from a cat that had been cut. ANZ.

cut lunch   Sandwiches. ANZ.

cut the rough/cut out the rough stuff   Desist from doing something aggressive or unpleasant to others, often used as an imperative against such rough stuff. ANZ 1930s.

cut the cheese   To fart.

cuz/cuzzy/cuzzy bro   Polynesian male greeting. Pakeha term for a Polynesian male. From late C20.

dab 1. A darting run on the rugby field, often the preserve of a nippy first five-eighth.

2. A baby flounder.

dag Entertaining, amusing or unusual person or thing. We say **what a dag** of somebody amusing, who can be called **a real dag,** immortalised in New Zealand and then Australia in John Clarke's comic rural character Fred Dagg. Probably combination of the British dialect word *dag*, a daring feat, crossed with 'wag'. ANZ.

daggish/daggy 1. Definitely amusing, maybe eccentric. ANZ.

2. Wilting or dated clothes and the person in them. ANZ.

dagpickers' ball Picking the wool from the dags.

dairy Small neighbourhood general store selling everything from toothpicks and soft drinks to sliced bread and sacks of coal from dawn to dusk seven days a week. Often run by new arrivals, nowadays especially Indians, who employ the whole family. Originally a shop for milk and still big on that and non-essential food items like sweeties and chippies, cigarettes, pet food, and piles of newspapers and magazines.

daks Trousers or underpants. Young male drinkers often enjoy 'dropping their daks' to expose themselves to each other and passersby. From 1930s brand of British trousers, Daks, contracting 'dad' and 'slacks'. ANZ.

Dallie/Dally A New Zealander whose ancestors came from Yugoslavia late C19, before it was called that, to dig gum up north. Mostly from Croatia, or the part of it then known as Dalmatia.

Dallie plonk Dismissive term mid C20 for the rough, sweet wine produced by Dalmatian vintners in Henderson area of Auckland for the sweet Kiwi palate, before Kiwis started drinking seriously the drier wine made by the same Dalmatians or their descendants.

Dallie Valley The area of West Auckland around Henderson where many Dalmatian gumdiggers moved to when the gum ran out.

dalmatian Black and white marble.

damper Basic bush bread made from flour and water cooked in the ashes of an open fire. ANZ early C19.

dance a haka An expression of pleasure, from the Maori dance chant, from late C19.

dancing dolly The small storm petrel seabird that appears to dance over the ocean, wings flapping, legs trailing in the water.

dancing the Pommy waltz Dodging dog turds on the pavements of London, a shock for newly arrived ANZs.

darl Darling. An affectionate diminutive ANZ mid C20, more recently a lesbian on the street and in prison, presently a term of endearment from girlfriends, gay hairdressers and café waiters to women.

Darth Vader's dunny The Bank of New Zealand headquarters in downtown Wellington, from its long black box appearance, supposedly suitable for the toilet purposes of the chief villain of *Star Wars* movies. **Darth Vader's pencil box** is a polite version. 1980s.

date The anus. ANZ mid C20.

date-driller/packer Active male homosexual.

daylight robbery Excessive and unrepentant overcharging for goods or services, such as the entire system of GST to some free market libertarians. ANZ.

dead as a moa Decidedly dead, as is the extinct, ostrich-like bird that once roamed New Zealand.

dead horse, to work off /bury a To pay a debt. Australian from mid C19.

dead house A hotel shed where drunks were dumped. ANZ.

dead right Absolutely correct; Steve Parr on *Sale of the Century*, 19 September 1989.

dead ring/ringer   Close likeness. Possibly from 'ringer' meaning originally a horse that has been disguised to look like another. ANZ C20.

dead tree edition/option   Paper version of an electronic publication, 1990s.

deadbeat   Unlucky or broke individual. ANZ from 1870s.

deadman's arm   A leg of lamb or a long, steamed currant roll pudding.

deadman's ears   Stewed dried apricots.

deadman's head   A round steamed pudding.

deal to   Physically account for somebody; eg 'Remember when they used to bring on Skinner to deal to those Springboks?' You can also **deal it out to**. ANZ early C20.

dee   Detective, in shortened form, or possibly from 'demon', by which name, among others, a colonial detective was known. Commonly **The Dees**. ANZ from mid C19.

deefa   A dog, as in 'd' for.

delec   Delectable, in teen shortspeak.

delish/delishimo!   Very tasty, teen slang for 'delicious'.ANZ.

demolition ball   The concentrated razing of the older buildings in the three main centres, mostly in the 1980s, an ironic play on the favoured object of mass destruction, the demolition steel ball swung from a crane into the walls to be tumbled.

demolition party   Tenants' last night in, destroying fixtures and fittings.

demon   A detective. ANZ late C19. Orsman suggests a pun on 'dee-man', though convicts in early records speak of harsh jailers as demons.

derision   Filthy weather among trampers, as in 'shit and derision', an Air Force phrase for bad weather.

dero   A derelict person, sleeping out, usually the worse for booze. ANZ.

des-res   Desirable residence, originally real estate parlance.

dew pond   Natural or manmade waterhole, usually reliant on rain. Mainly lower South Island usage.

DH   Down the hatch, or drink up, eg, 'DH, lads, it's almost closing time.'

dial-a-kaumatua   Compliant Maori elders ready to approve Maori policy in the view of critics, a play on 1990s commercial services such as 'dial-a-hangi'.

diarrhoea bags   Knickerbockers.

diarrhoea clips   Bicycle clips.

dick   To lose or be beaten, eg, 'We got dicked by St Bernards 50–0.'

dicken   Expression of disgust or disbelief, often **dicken on that!** as a way of telling somebody to take it easy. ANZ modification of 'the dickens', the devil.

dickhead   Idiot. The 'dick' is C19 military slang for penis. ANZ.

dickwhacker   Idiot, where a whacker is a male masturbator. ANZ.

dickydidoe   Penis.

diddlydieday   Reunion, on the West Coast.

diff   1.Difference. ANZ

2. Differential in a car engine, as in 'We hit a rock and cracked the diff.' ANZ.

differ   Difference. Early C20.

dig/digger/old dig   Friendly greeting, usually male to male. Specifically an Anzac soldier or returned Anzac serviceman, from WWI the Australians preferring 'digger', New Zealanders 'dig'. Originally a gold digger, who worked 'the diggings'.

dig deep   A supreme effort, as when the All Blacks had to 'dig deep' in the 1991 second test at Eden Park against the Wallabies for the Bledisloe Cup, having been walloped in the first test in Sydney.

digging for whoopcackers   The answer to the question, How come someone is so dirty?

digglers   Eggs.

dilberry/dill/dillbrain/dilly   Stupid person. From the British dialect combination of 'daft' and 'silly', without necessarily retaining any of the C19 British meaning of 'dilberry' as excrement. ANZ mid C20.

dindins Dinner. ANZ.

ding 1. A dent, usually in a car, or the accident that causes a dent, from the archaic verb 'to strike'. ANZ.

2. A boisterous party, short for the American 'whingding'.

dingbat Eccentric or crazy person. The plural **dingbats** means an extreme stage, as in delirium tremens from consuming excessive amounts of alcohol. A combination of 'bats' or 'batty', madness or eccentricity, and 'ding' in boisterous sense. ANZ.

dinger Anything regarded highly. Short for 'humdinger'. ANZ mid C20.

dingo Australian person, after the unappealing Australian wild dog of that name.

dinkies A couple with double income, no kids.

dinkum Fair, genuine or reliable, from English dialect *ding*, to work hard, and **fair dinkum**, an equitable share. The validity of something is often attested to as 'fair dinkum' or **square dinkum, real dinkum, the dinkum article, dinkumly** or **the dinkum truth**, while a New Zealander born and bred is a **dinkum Kiwi.** ANZ C19.

dinky Small and neat or cute. We might distinguish between our big milk trucks and the dinky electric vans of the British. The word is from Scottish dialect for neat or trim. ANZ.

dinkydi/dinkydidoe Absolutely okay, fair, true. ANZ mid C20 variation of 'dinkum'.

dip one's lid Honour somebody in the old gentlemanly days, by lowering your head and raising your hat. ANZ C20.

dip out Miss out on something, usually considered a failure. Many dip out on a Lotto strike every Saturday evening. ANZ 1960s.

dip south Search your pocket for money, particularly when there is not much there. ANZ C20.

dipshit Idiot. Variant on 'dippy', meaning silly. ANZ.

dirt-trackers Midweek non-test rugby players on tour. Late C20.

dirty/dirty on Angry or upset. Rugby players are frequently described as being dirty on each other after a dirty or thuggish tackle. ANZ.

dirty big Very bloody big. Early C20 ANZ.

dirty play Illegal or unfair sporting intervention, such as the use of fists or boots in a rugby ruck. ANZ.

Ditch, the The Tasman Sea; **across the Ditch** is Australia.

divvy A dividend, usually a payout from the TAB, but in use long before the TAB. Late C19 ANZ.

DIY Do it yourself, the home handyperson's hobby if not passion, known as **the DIY mentality** or **the DIY bug.** ANZ.

do/do your dough/chips To use up all your money, perhaps recklessly. Late C19 ANZ.

do a freeze To be ignored or overlooked, eg, 'Sinclair's done a freeze with the selectors this summer.' ANZ early C20.

do a get To retreat in a hurry. Early C20.

do your block/bun/melon/scone Lose your temper. The noun means 'head'. ANZ early C20.

dob/dob in To inform on someone, usually with the implication that this is not dinkum Kiwi behaviour. ANZ 1930s.

dob/dob over To drop-kick a ball over the rugby goalposts, which is literally closer than the previous entry to the English dialect word *dob*, to throw down heavily. ANZ.

doco Documentary film. From 1980s ANZ.

doctor 1. A West Coast publican. The original was Dr Schroder of the Central Hotel, Fitzherbert Street, Hokitika.

2. A sheepstation cook; originally a ship's cook in Britain 1821, here 1839. ANZ.

dog 1. Large iron nail for securing rails to sleepers or wire rope to timber.

2. Member of the Mongrel Mob gang.

dog cock Chub-style sausage.

dog tucker Defeated. Speaker of the House Doug Kidd suggested in May 1997 that the NZ First Party would be dog tucker at the next election. Mr Kidd would not have been unaware of the drought conditions that reduce his Marlborough electorate to **dog tucker country,** or unproductive land. If you live long enough you will experience **dog tucker years** when your body goes into decline. You might at any time of life be described as someone who **wouldn't go out to a dog-tucker's picnic**, an elaborate way of saying you are reclusive. The disparaging use of 'dog' comes from the gruff treatment of, and spartan living conditions imposed on, rural dogs. ANZ.

dog's breakfast   A mess. ANZ.

dog's dinner, done like a   You have been comprehensively defeated or outwitted.

dog-bludger/dog-walloper   Musterer.

dogbox, in the   In trouble or disgrace, from the word for railway carriages without corridors, and the confined cages for dogs on a train. ANZ.

doggy bag   Container restaurant provides on request to carry away your leftovers. ANZ.

dole bludger   Somebody who prefers, or is perceived as preferring, Social Welfare benefits to working for a living. ANZ.

Dolly Parton wine   An up-front red, after the American country singer with a large chest.

domestic   A family disagreement, so described by police called to the scene. ANZ.

dommie   A motorcyclist, after the diminutive for a Norton 'Dominator' motorbike.

dommyknocker   A stick to beat other children with.

Donald Duck, a   A fuck, a facetious rhyme employing Walt Disney's famous cartoon character. ANZ.

dong   To strike or punch. ANZ C20.

donger/dunga/dunger   1. The penis, variants of British *dong*.

2. An idiot.

3. A useless or dilapidated object, like a rusty old car which makes a 'dunger, dunger' sound.

4. If you are **in the dunga** you are in trouble.

dongyknocker A club, cousin of 'dommyknocker', invoking the concept of a dong or knock, such as a hunter might use to dispatch a possum.

D

donk A useless racehorse, one perceived as a donkey. Mid C20 ANZ.

donkey A deer, to those who stalk them.

donkey deep Enthusiastic participation, eg, 'MP Rodney Hide dives into any perks debate in Parliament donkey deep.' Early C20.

donkey-lick 1. Golden syrup or treacle.

2. Defeat, originally in a horse race. Both ANZ rural C20.

don't be ankyfooken A dismissive rejection. Reverse of 'don't be fucking anti'.

don't be an Uncle Willy Don't be silly (rhyming slang extension).

don't drink and drive home, smoke dope and fly home Flip advice from cannabis enthusiasts who assume dope is less harmful than booze.

don't get historical Goofy advice to calm down, spoonerising 'hysterical'.

don't get off your bike, we'll pick up the pump Advice to an angry person to calm down.

don't get off your horse Stay calm.

don't hand me that Dismissal of speaker's claim, eg, 'Don't hand me that load of malarkey.'

don't let the bastards grind you down Exhortation to stay cheerful or resolute, no matter how badly you are treated. The other version is cod Latin *nil caborundum bastardis*. ANZ.

doodackie A thingummybob or object of uncertain definition but probably useful. Early C20 version of American 'doohickey'.

dook To bob, used in the phrase **dooking for apples**, ducking face underwater to recover floating apples using only your mouth.

Recorded by Brian Sutton-Smith in his collection of children's games.

doolan An Irish Catholic, often a Micky Doolan, a popular Irish name. In Australia a doolan was a policeman because he was likely to be Irish and Catholic.

dork 1. Stupid person.

2. The penis. ANZ. Although popular in America, may have been used here first.

Dorkalofa Auckland.

dorkbrain Idiot.

Dorklander Aucklander.

DORKs Doddering Old Real Kiwis.

dosh Money, as in dollars and cash. In general use but Partridge credits Australian juvenile c1944. ANZ.

doss down Rough or makeshift bed or to sleep outdoors or in rough and temporary conditions. ANZ late C19.

doub/double-banking/dub/dubb Giving someone a lift on your bike, whereby the person sits on the handlebar or the carrier, as in doubling. As old as bikes.

double All Black A New Zealand representative at rugby and cricket.

double-banger Sexually superactive woman.

double-decker 1. A tram or bus with two levels as early as 1890. ANZ.

2. Ice-cream with two scoops, one on top of the other. ANZ.

3. Double-layered sandwich. ANZ.

4. A sheep sporting two seasons' worth of overcoat.

5. The stock truck with two levels.

double-dipping Two incomes from the state, illegal for all but politicians and judges. David Stevenson wrote in the *Evening Post* of 20 June 1991 of thirteen retired judges the previous year earning an average $54,000 for relieving work while drawing pensions.

doughboy Suet dumpling favoured by musterers; **golden doughboys** are dumplings cooked in golden syrup. ANZ.

doughnut   Round-patterned wheelies done in car or on motorbike.

doughroaster   The sheepstation cook.

down on, have a   To hold a grudge or poor opinion of another. Emerged in the suspicious confines of goldfield tents. ANZ.

down south   1. Somewhere in the South Island usually.

2. The trouser pocket bottom, where money may be unsuccessfully searched for. ANZ.

3. Below the hemline of a dress, where the petticoat or slip is visible.

down the coast diving for fish farts   A deadend job.

down the road   Dismissal from work. ANZ mid C20.

down the rocky road to the funny farm   Someone showing signs of mental instability, indicating the direction in which subject is heading.

down to the wire   Very close contest, only resolved at the finish.

down trou   The lowering of trousers to shock or amuse, usually by inebriated males at parties.

Down Under   New Zealand and/or Australia. Recorded in New Zealand in 1905, a decade before it appeared in Australia. In the 1920s NZ heavyweight boxing champion Tom Heeney was known as **The Hard Rock from Down Under**.

dozo   Fool, somebody who is dozy or sleepy in the brain department.

DPB   Domestic Purposes Benefit, state stipend to solo caregiver from 1968.

drack   Ugly or boring, often directed at a plain female, without intending the extreme condition of the probable origin, the fang-toothed, blood-imbibing Count Dracula. ANZ c1950.

drag the chain   Lagging behind in a group activity such as drinking beer in pubs. Originally slowest shearer. ANZ.

drama queen   Exaggerated performance to win attention, eg, 'That kid's a drama queen, screams the place down whenever another kid bumps into her.'

dressed pie   Pie in a brown paper bag with peas and potato and gravy on top.

drink the piss from a brewer's horse, would   Devotee of booze. ANZ.

drink up large   Exhortation to hit the booze.

drink with the flies   Drink alone. ANZ early C20.

drive the pigs home   To snore.

driver is safer when the road is dry, The/And the road is safer when the driver is dry   Don't drink and drive.

drongo   Stupid or clumsy fellow. From Australian bird, the *drongo*, popularised by a disappointing Australian racehorse of mid 1920s called Drongo.

drop   1. To get rid of somebody, eg, 'Drop that boyfriend before he drops you.' ANZ early C20.

2. To knock someone down, eg, 'One more word like that in front of the ladies and I'll drop ya.' ANZ mid C20.

3. To give birth. Originally referring to farm animals.

4. To deliver sly grog, the work by train or truck of a **dropper**, who could also be the hotel worker watching out for police while sly grog was sold out a side door mid C20.

5. Liquor, as in **not a bad drop**, meaning it is good. ANZ.

drop in it   Get someone in trouble, as in 'You dropped me in it, telling the cops it was my cannabis stash.'

drop like a hot scone   Abrupt cutting of contact.

drop off   1. To falter and fail. Racehorses and athletes 'drop off the pace' of a race, a rugby player 'drops off the tackle'. ANZ.

2. To give someone a lift in a car to a particular place. ANZ.

drop off the perch   Die, as parrots and chooks do.

drop shoulder   Idiot.

drop your bundle   1. To lose your temper or composure or control of a situation.

2. To give birth to a baby. ANZ.

3. To defecate.

drop your gear   Take off your clothes. ANZ.

drop your load   A male ejaculation. ANZ.

drophead   Idiot.

dropkick   Ineffectual, obnoxious or inept person. A loser. ANZ.

dropper   Fencepost.

droppie   A drop kick at goal in rugby union or Australian Rules. ANZ.

drum   1. A horseracing tip, or any information, from drum as a means of signalling. Also a tip-off or warning. ANZ C20.

2. A swag, rolled up in the shape of a drum for easier carrying; the swagman is a **drummer**. ANZ C19.

drummer   In shearing slang, the learner in the shed, or **drummer boy**, sarcastically applied also to the slowest shearer. Bush gangs use the term too. ANZ early C20.

dry as a cocky's selection/a dead dingo's dong/a nun's nasty/a Pommy jockstrap/a sack of gum-dust/a wooden cow/a wooden god   Very thirsty, usually for a quantity of beer. ANZ.

dry balls bastard   Parsimonious bowler in cricket, who gives away few runs.

dry horrors   Hangover, where dehydration is apparent. ANZ early C20.

dry root   Unlubricated sex.

dub in   To contribute to a collection. From a marble added to those in the ring awaiting shooting. ANZ.

duck away   To avoid something or somebody. Late C19.

duckfart   A stone plopping softly into water, maybe a failed skimmer. From c1940.

duck's breakfast/dinner   A drink of water. Early C20.

duck's disease   Short or vertically challenged person. ANZ.

duck's nuts, just the   Very desirable, a variant of 'the bee's knees'. ANZ.

ducks and drakes   1. The shakes, from excessive drinking. ANZ.

2. Somebody giving you a difficult or misleading time.

duckshove   To pass responsibility on to somebody else in an unfair if not cheating fashion. From Melbourne cabbies of 1870s jumping ranks.

ducks on the pond   Warning among shearers that a woman is present.

dudess   Girl, female version of the American 'dude', a person.

duds   Female breasts.

duff   To make pregnant, from British 'pudding club', to be pregnant, a duff being a suet pudding; **up the duff**, pregnant.

duffer   A failed goldmine. ANZ.

dumb-bum   Fool. ANZ.

dummy   1. Person who acquires land on behalf of another, usually not entitled to do so. ANZ mid C19. Nowadays, the plant an auctioneer uses to bid up a house auction.

2. Prison cell, usually a punishment one; **in dummy** is in solitary confinement. A dummy cell was originally a false one that served as a place of confinement.

dump   1. A place to conceal stolen goods; from army storage area for old materiel or ammunition.

2. A dilapidated residence. ANZ.

3. An inferior marble, eg, a clay one, that is dumped in the playing ring to be sacrificed.

dump one's load   Male ejaculation. ANZ.

dungpuncher   Active male homosexual. ANZ.

dunny   A toilet, from the British *dunneken*. ANZ from c1880. The carter who collected toilet refuse was called the **dunny man**. If an enterprise goes **down the dunny** it is a failure, yet a **dunny rat** was a byword for a cunning person. Not so the **dunny budgie**, the lurking blowfly. Climbing roses and rosemary were among the plants used to modify the dunny odour, but banana passionfruit was probably the top choice.

durry   A cigarette, specifically a roll-your-own. After the popular brand Bull Durham. ANZ.

dust Gunpowder, usage noted among whalers here by E.J. Wakefield before it was recorded elsewhere.

dustie Dustman or garbage collector.

Dutch oven A camp oven — a round iron pot with a lid, and a handle to suspend it over a fire.

Dutchie A Dutch person

dyke A toilet, often the outdoor variety whose bottom is not in sight. From the word for a ditch, whence it was a small leap to a water closet in 1920s. ANZ.

earbash   To talk aggressively and/or incessantly at someone. An **earbasher** is a person who talks too much. ANZ mid C20.

early doors   Early to bed or early to rise. ANZ.

early shower   Banished from the field of play by the referee for foul play. Extended to employees losing their jobs earlier than expected.

earthquake weather   Uncharacteristically settled weather, nary a breath of wind, so humid you can scarcely breathe; thought to presage an earthquake.

earwag   To gush gossip.

easies   Woman's elasticised corset, a relief after the earlier era of whalebone entrapment.

easy as carrying a kerosene tin full of cowshit uphill on your head   Not easy.

easy as hooking an eel with a blunt pin   Definitely not easy.

easy as pushing shit uphill with a pointed stick/a rubber fork   Pretty difficult. ANZ.

easy as shoving a pound of butter up a cow's bum with a size 5 knitting needle on a hot day   Extremely difficult.

easy come, easy go   Resigned attitude to a lost gain, usually money, eg, 'Doubled the value of me shares last year, this year they halved. Guess she's easy come, easy go.' ANZ.

eat toot   Period of adjustment to pioneering life, when the new immigrant learns to cope with a harsh new life. From Maori *tutu*, a poisonous plant.

educated boot   Elegant, effective kicking for touch in rugby, usually by the first five-eighth, and at its more elegant off the left foot.

eggbeater   Helicopter. ANZ.

egg-boiler   Any confining hat, originally a bowler hat — on a hot day your egghead boils in it. ANZ c1920.

eggs are cooked, one's   Visited by misfortune, if not disaster, as happens to farmers struck by floods or droughts. Early C20.

eggshell blonde   Bald person. ANZ c1935.

eh?   Interrogative or emphasising add-on at the end of sentences, possibly from the Maori *ne*, perhaps indicating a national uncertainty or need for reassurance or agreement, eg, 'We really put it to the Aussie cricketers, eh?' ANZ.

el cheapo   Inferior, often used of a restaurant. ANZ.

electric fireplace   Television.

electric puha   Marijuana, usually homegrown.

elevator doesn't go to the top storey   Somebody who is not too bright. ANZ.

empty house is better than a bad tenant   One way of apologising for farting.

empty sack can't stand, An/A full sack can't bend   Farming advice to labourers at harvest time to get on with the job.

emu parade   Detention involving cleaning up the grounds; originally military litter collection in WWII. ANZ.

endo   Cartwheeling over the handlebars of a bike, as in end-over-end. From 2000.

engine room, the   The front row and locks in a rugby forward pack, those who do the grunt and the 'hard yards'.

enough to choke a bull   A fat roll of money.

Enzed/Enzedder   New Zealand/New Zealander, from the pronounciation of the country's initials, from WWI. ANZ.

ethnic hay   Untended land.

euchred   Defeated or totally exhausted. From the card game, where you win by frustrating the other players' ability to win tricks. ANZ.

ever thought of renting your mouth out for a carpark? Loud mouth.

every man and his dog A wide cross-section of society, eg, 'Every man and his dog will love it.' ANZ.

everything but the cat's blanket A comprehensive effort, eg, 'The New Zealand Fifteen hit the Romanians with everything but the cat's blanket.' Keith Quinn commentating on Kiwi rugby on TVOne, 9 June 1991. A variant of 'everything but the kitchen sink'.

ewe Female.

ex Former wife/husband/partner, often **the ex**. ANZ.

extra Approving intensive, popular in phrases **extra early, extra curly** and **extra grouse** to mean something first rate or very attractive. ANZ C20.

eyedrop Shooting marble aimed from eye-height directly onto objective.

eyes like burn holes in a blanket Not looking well. ANZ.

eyes on him/her like a stinking eel Pop-eyes.

eyes out Maximum effort, such as 'going eyes out to win the race'. ANZ early C19.

eyes stick out like eggs in the wrong nest Very pop-eyed.

F word, the Fuck, eg, 'I won't have the F word used in this house, thank you.'

face, off your Drunk or drugged or acting crazy. ANZ.

face fart 1. A belch.

2. Ugly person.

face like a bull's/chook's bum Ugly, dreary, drenched in misery.

face like a twisted sandshoe Image of disgust, eg, 'One sip of port and the toddler had a face on her like a twisted sandshoe.' ANZ

face like an abandoned quarry Battered and ugly.

face like a festering pickle Bad case of acne or pimples. ANZ.

face like a yard of tripe Thoroughly miserable appearance. ANZ.

face like the north end of a southbound bus Fairly unattractive. ANZ.

faces The answer to the pestering question what is for tea?

facial Roughing up the face of a tackled opponent, a rugby league forward habit, eg, 'Kearney's been hammered, and he's copped a real facial.' Often observed by commentators but rarely by referees. ANZ.

fag hag Female friend of gay men.

fair intensifier in appeals for better treatment with **buck/burl/cow/dinkum/do/doos/go/spin**. Used ironically to challenge exaggeration. Part of the language in long-running TV consumer rights programme *Fair Go*. From British dialect word *fair*, reasonable. From c1900. ANZ.

fair crack of the whip/shake of the dice and **fair suck of the saucestick/saveloy** Appeals for fairness. ANZ.

fakawi?   Shortened form of 'Where the fuck are we?' The **fakawi bird** is signal at student parties for another rude repetitive chant, such as 'Long strong black pudding up my auntie's cat's pyjamas twice nightly.'

fang bosun/carpenter   Dentist. Originally in ANZ navy and army respectively, C20.

far canal   Euphemism for 'fucking hell', usually denoting exasperation.

farley fig noogan   Old person to a teenager today, possibly refers to fig newton biscuits.

farmgate intellectuals   Improvisational Kiwi achievers, such as beekeeper/climber Sir Edmund Hillary, jetboat inventor Bill Hamilton, aeroplane inventor Richard Pearse, filmmaker Peter Jackson.

farmyard confetti   Nonsense or rubbish, like the stuff free-range farm animals leave behind. ANZ.

fart sack   Where you sleep, etc. Popularised by trampers and army. ANZ.

farts like a motormower off its stroke/on the phut   Flatulence of a staccato, uncontrolled nature. ANZ.

Fast Ferns   National athletics team, its administrators hope.

fat   1. Male erection. To **crack a fat** is to release it. ANZ C20.

2. Fashionable. Early C21.

3. Cattle or sheep in prime condition, often **mud-fat/fat as mud.** ANZ C19.

fat show   No chance, eg, 'Doesn't matter who they rope in, the Chiefs have a fat show of winning the Super Twelve.' From 1930s.

fat lot of good   Extension of the British phrase 'fat lot', usually a caustic expression, eg, 'Fat lot of good it'll do you crying and sobbing, you're still not going to the party.'

Father Christmas hold, the old   The hand under the crotch of an opponent, inducing surrender. Commentator Keith Quinn called this in the All Blacks vs Swansea game on 22 October 1989.

feather to fly with, not having a   Broke, or lacking prospects or any excuse, from a 'feather' meaning a farthing. ANZ.

Featherston Street farmer Urban absentee farm owner, from a central Wellington business street.

feed a line Give somebody deliberately misleading information.

feeding the chooks Male masturbation, sometimes rammed home with the addition **on Master Bates' farm**. ANZ.

feel like a bagful of busted arseholes Not feeling well, usually because of a hangover.

feel like a haunted shithouse Very hungover.

feel like a pickpocket in a nudist colony Nervous. ANZ.

fellaress/fullaress Female fellow. C21.

fend off To take or steal. From early 1930s.

feral Bad or shocking, eg, 'Have you seen the way that new hooker gets stuck in? Man, he's feral.'

Fern A member of the Silver Ferns, the national netball team.

Fernleaf New Zealander, from the fernleaf badge worn by soldiers in WWI. ANZ.

fernrooter New Zealander, from association with pigs rooting ferns, in their case to eat. ANZ.

fevver clucker Reversal of 'clever fucker' or smart aleck.

few, a Too many beers; **have a few in**, drunk. ANZ from early C20.

fiddle 1. Hindquarter of mutton. From 1930s.

2. Car radio. Later C20.

fiddle-arse about Waste time. ANZ c1920.

fill the tins Housewifely act of baking cakes and biscuits; it was — and in some remote areas still is — a Kiwi housewife's prerogative to **keep the tins full**.

financial Carrying cash or enjoying credit in the bank. ANZ mid C20.

find another gear Competing person or animal that manages to make an extra effort.

fine art Expertise. Good front-row forwards in rugby have scrummaging down to a fine art. From mid C20.

finickerty Fussy. A blend of finicky and pernickety. ANZ mid 1930s.

firefly Tent fly.

firing a warmer into the bank The first beer of the session.

firing blanks Failing to fertilise the female.

fish-and-chip brigade Labour MPs who, over fish and chips in the first half of 1980s, plotted the replacement of Bill Rowling as party leader. The *Dominion Post* identified the four plotters as David Lange, Mike Moore, Roger Douglas and Michael Bassett on 16 January 2003, in an article marking the demolition of the fish and chip shop in Molesworth Street opposite Parliament which allegedly fuelled the plot.

fish hooks Difficulties. The first thing politicians look for in any commissioned report.

fit as a buck rat In good physical shape. Mid C20.

fitter and turner Army cook, from alleged habit of cramming food into big pots and doing little more than stirring or turning the food.

five to six The phrase that caused a stampede to the bar in the days when closing time was 6 pm.

five-million-dollar carrot, five-million-dollar banana and five-million-dollar hairdryer, the Nickname for the three concrete sculptures that replaced Broadcasting House beside Parliament in Wellington, demolished in the late 1990s to make way for proposed parliamentary premises that public objections ensured were never built.

five-acre Tory A small landholder with large opinions to the right of George W. Bush's.

fizzboat A small, flimsy, noisy boat with an outboard motor owned, not surprisingly, by a **fizzboater**. Latter C20.

fizzer Failed item of machinery or fireworks. ANZ c1920.

fizzies Sparkling wine as opposed to superior 'bubbly', champagne or champagne-style.

flag/flag away Give something up, lose patience or confidence, eg, 'C'mon, Col, let's flag this fishing lark, we haven't had a bite in hours.' From linesmen in rugby union flagging an unsuccessful kick at goal or a try not scored.

flagon party The partygoers bring half-gallon glass jars of draught beer known as **flagon beer**; the host might surprise them with a **flagon wagon**, a truck carrying crates of flagons, latterly a large keg or container of beer that can be siphoned direct to consumer. Latter C20.

flakers Collapsed from too much alcohol, or simply sleeping over at somebody's place. ANZ mid C20.

flapping like a dunny door in a high wind Panicky behaviour or compulsive talking.

flash a brown Expose the buttocks.

flash as a Chow on a red bike Ostentatious. A West Coast saying going back to the goldmining era, when a 'Chow' or Chinese man on a red bike was unlikely, for the Chinese kept a low profile.

flash your nasty A lewd request for a woman to expose her genitals, or a man flashing his genitals without being asked. ANZ.

flat as a strap A flat plain. ANZ.

flat stack/stick/strap/tack As fast as possible or maximum exertion. ANZ latter C20.

flat to the boards Maximum effort, as when the accelerator is pressed to the car floor. ANZ latter C20.

flathead A nail with a flat head as opposed to a raised head.

flatter than a shit carter's hat The dunny-man carrying the can on his shoulder gave rise to this phrase for being depressed.

flattie 1. Flat-dweller. Latter C20.

2. Puncture. ANZ.

3. A flat-bottomed rowboat, used in shallow water, possibly to fish for 4. From late C19.

4. A flatfish. ANZ.

5. A state of confusion or being flustered, a contraction of being 'in a flat spin'. From mid C20.

flax-bag terrorist Maori activist belittled. 1990s.

flaxie   A flax mill worker.

flaxroots level, at the   Activity among ordinary Maori, a variation of the grassroots level.

flea circus   A cheap cinema, variation of 'flea-pit'. ANZ from c1925.

flea taxi   A dog.

flea track   Parting in the hair.

flick your wick   Admonition to hurry up. Mid C20.

flimsy   A cheque. ANZ C20.

floater   1. A meat pie floating in gravy, popular at piecarts.

    2. A turd that refuses to flush.

    3. A penny that does not spin in game of two-up.

    4. A teacher without a classroom.

    5. A voter who has not made up his mind who to vote for.

    6. A fried scone floating on the fat. All ANZ C20.

float-up   A casual approach. Late 1930s.

flog   To masturbate. ANZ C20.

flog off   To depart quickly. Latter C20.

flog the log   To masturbate.

flog your chops   Talk incessantly.

flognosticate   Thrash, as in 'I'll flognosticate you', usually a jokey threat to a wayward child.

flower in a wet spot   Female on heat.

fluff   To fart. ANZ early C20.

fluff about   Dither instead of getting the job done.

fly cemetery   Square cake containing dried fruit between slices of pastry. ANZ mid C20.

flyblown   Broke, your money blown. ANZ mid C19.

flying fox   Rope declined across a gully or river with a pulley attached so that boy scouts, adventure campers, trampers and other outdoors folk can slide across. ANZ C20.

flying saucer   A fried slice of luncheon sausage.

Flymo toe Accident prone, from careless contact with the electric lawnmower of that name. Later C20.

FM/FY boots Fuck me or fuck you footwear, usually with exaggeratedly high heels and/or dangerously pointy toes, part of tarty apparel along with tacky blonde hair and very short skirt. Late C20.

fob Pacific Island immigrant, meaning 'fresh off the boat'. Second half of C20.

fong Booze. 'To be fonged' is to be drunk, **half-fonged** is on the way, but **to be fonged up** can also mean bewildered or bothered or in a mess. Mid C20.

footsteps on horseback Noisy kids.

footy Rugby union game. ANZ.

for goodness' sakes, it's chicken flakes Exclamation, particularly if you have done something wrong, like knocking over a glass of milk. Derives from the chook on the cornflakes packet.

forward pack The eight members of the rugby union team who lead the game to the opposition, operating as a unit at fixed positions such as scrum and lineout.

four by two The standard timber stud retaining its pre-metric sizing of four inches by two inches, used to describe the blunt approach, eg, 'Many have objected to Inland Revenue's four by two way of handling people filing late returns.' ANZ.

foxie A fox terrier. ANZ, early C20.

freckle The anus. ANZ.

freckle puncher Active male homosexual. ANZ.

freezer/freezing works Abattoir, because most carcasses are frozen for export. Employees are invariably **freezing workers.** From 1893 a 'freezer' was a sheep bred for export.

friend or enema? Jokey challenge to your loyalties.

Frogolia France. Even more derisive than its Pongolian inspiration.

frogs' eyes Boiled tapioca or sago in the view of the school boarders who have to eat it. ANZ.

frogs' eyes and onions   Jokey response to 'What's for tea, Mum?'

frogs' tits and watercress   Another answer to 'What's for tea?'

frogskin   Contraceptive sheath.

front bum   Vagina. ANZ, later C20.

front foot, go on the   Showing leadership or initiative, as batsmen are advised to do in cricket.

fruitfly   Female friend of gay men. Later C20.

fruits in suits   Gay or homosexual bar patrons in urban areas in new millennium.

fruit salad   Mixed fishbait, such as *pipi* and trevally.

fuck-knuckle   Idiot, but can be meant affectionately. From 1960s, ANZ.

fuck a town down and shake her arse at the ruins   A woman who likes sex. ANZ.

fuck me dead said Foreskin Fred as he waved his wooden leg!   Exuberant exclamation with no literal connotations.

fuck me dead with a bargepole!   Another exclamation of surprise and positively no intention of being taken literally.

fuck me for a chocolate duck!   Yet another exclamation without overtones or undertones.

fuck me sideways!   Exclamation, often attracting the response, **not while there's cats.**

fuck truck   Any vehicle used for sexual trysts, often a panel van. ANZ.

fuckwit   Stupid person. ANZ mid C20.

fudge-packer   Active male homosexual.

full as a boot/a bull/a Catholic school/a fairy's phonebook/a fart/a footy test/a goog (egg)/a Pommie complaint box/a seaside shithouse on Waitangi Day/a tick   Very drunk or full of food. ANZ C20.

full of puha   Talking nonsense. Current teenage slang.

full tit   Maximum output, usually from a car.

full up   Exasperated, tired, disgusted. ANZ late C19.

full up to the dolly's wax/the pussy's bow   So full of food one could not eat another morsel; from Victorian dolls having heads of wax and pussies (the four-legged kind) with bows on. ANZ.

full up to the knocker   Boozed, possibly from one of the many meanings of 'knocker' as nose or face.

fun bags   Woman's breasts. ANZ.

funny/silly as a piece of string/a two-bob watch   Humorous or daft. ANZ c1930.

F

funny money party   Disparaging reference to Social Credit political party, which was believed to want to print money when it felt like it.

furburger/furpie   Vagina as object of cunnilingus. ANZ.

furburger and Y-bone   Sexual meal, playing on the notion of a T-bone steak.

FURTB   Replete, as in Full Up, Ready to Burst. ANZ.

futuparu   Rugby football. A cod-Maori word.

fuzzy duck A drinking game, like the Hokonui swindle, in which the offender drains his glass; can be reversed, to the immense amusement of the drinkers concerned.

Gal Blacks Nickname for the New Zealand women's rugby team. Late C20.

gamp Grandad/grandma.

gang Almost invariably one of several motorbike or bikie gangs of mostly young men whose rugged clothing, lurid insignia and macho demeanour are perceived as antisocial, including Black Power, Mongrel Mob, Headhunters and Satan's Slaves. From 1960s.

gangie/gangbang/gangbash/gangsplash Serial female rape. ANZ.

garbage guts Greedy eater. ANZ.

garbiologist A rubbish collector, eg, 'RCA tells us of their local garbiologist.' *New Zealand Woman's Weekly*, 4 October 1965.

gark A nick or scratch, eg, 'That table has a gark in it. Somebody's chisel slipped there.'

gate Mouth, as in, 'Shut yer gate, mate.' From about 1910.

Gawd pickle me nuts! Exclamation, usually of surprise, not a God-bothering request expected to be taken literally.

g'day/g'die/gidday/gudday ANZ versions of 'hello'.

gee whiskers! Euphemistic exclamation of surprise, not 'Jesus!'. Early C20.

geek 1. A look. From Cornish *geek*, an intense look. ANZ from WWI.

2. Studious, unsporty, almost certainly bespectacled and probably a bore. A computer geek is a computer nerd or wimp, American slang for unsporty and unfashionable.

3. Excellent, by reverse teenage inclination.

gekko A look, combining *geek* and *dekko*, a look, from the Romany word *dik*, a look.

gelly/jelly   Gelignite, early C20 here and later elsewhere. A **gellyhead/jellyhead** was initially somebody wobbly from too much inadvertent inhalation of gelignite fumes, broadened to mean an idiot.

Gentle Annie   A steep slope, hill or mountain; used ironically by coachmen from mid C19, possibly inspired by a popular song about missing Gentle Annie in springtime.

gerry   An old person, as in 'geriatric'. ANZ, latter C20.

gertoss   A girl. Teen slang, possibly contracted from 'girl' and 'tosser', a masturbator.

get, do a   Run away, probably in a hurry. ANZ, early C20.

get a boot out of   Gain satisfaction, eg, 'I really got a boot out of that,' as a lawyer remarked of a client who was going straight, *Metro* magazine, March 1989.

get a milkshake   Experience fellatio. Teen slang.

get a shot away   Achieve male sexual release.

get a spark up   Tiddly. From late 1930s.

get amongst it   Enjoy engagement, usually sexual, but can be a booze session or making money.

get down on   To steal. ANZ, mid C20.

get/give the runaround   Treat evasively or mislead, eg, 'Ever know a politician who didn't give you the runaround?' ANZ.

get in behind!   Jocular order to do as you are told, originally barked at sheepdogs to get behind the flock, popularised from 1970s by gumboot Kiwi comedian Fred Dagg.

get in tow with   Keep company, often of the kind that represents a loving couple. Mid C20.

get into   Enthusiastic approach to anything, like work or eating. Early C20.

get it on with   Have sex with, or at least the chance thereof. British 'get it off with'.

get off the grass!   Scornful rejection. 'You become an All Black? Get off the grass!' If you happen to be in the way, there is the addition

and let my mother/wife/lady friend see the races. Mid C20.

get off the train at Green Island/Papakura   Coitus interruptus.

get on it   To set about serious drinking of alcohol. Early C20.

get on with   Be able to be friendly with someone, eg, 'Bunsy gets on with just about everybody.'

get out from under   Extricate yourself from a difficult situation. ANZ.

get out of it   To become stoned on cannabis.

get out of jail   Lucky escape, eg, 'If the All Blacks win this they'll get out of jail.' Stu Wilson on the first test against Ireland, 30 May 1992.

get plunked   Become pregnant, by association with the Plunket Society, which advises parents after the fact.

get real!   Emphatic way of telling someone to be realistic, eg, 'Get real, Daph! That joker's never going to pop the question.'

get rooted!   Rude rejection. ANZ from late C19.

get stuck in/into   To fight or engage vigorously in some activity. ANZ C20.

get the old heave-ho/run   Be given the sack, eg, 'Bill was only there a week when he got the run.' The latter usage seems related to being 'given your running shoes'.

get the willies   Become frightened or very nervous. From US slang *the willies*, vague fear. Early C20.

get to it!   Command to become actively engaged in a task.

get your a into g/arse into gear   Command to start doing something quickly.

get your wool shorn   Get a haircut. ANZ from c1925.

GG   The Governor-General.

gibstopper   Active male homosexual, a crude current play on gib (gibraltar) board, an interior cladding that requires the services of a gibstopper to smooth over the cracks.

giggle factory/house   Mental institution. Mid C20, from Australia.

gink   1. An idiot, which Partridge speculates could be from Scots *ginkie*, a reproach to a woman.

2. A look, in the phrase 'take a gink at', *gink* being British dialect for a 'peep'. ANZ mid C20.

give a pop   To fight; originally to fire a machine gun, among WWI Kiwi soldiers. Kiwis have been giving what for ever since, as in the following entries.

give birth to a politican   To defecate. ANZ.

give curry   To abuse or encourage aggressively, usually in the context of spectators wanting a better performance from a competitive sport.

give her/him a crispie!   Reward someone, from the plain wine-style biscuit studded with sugar, eg, 'Rudders finally got his century. Give him a crispie!'

give her/him a vibrator and tell her/him to buzz off   Tell someone to go away.

give it a burl/go/whirl   An encouragement to try something. ANZ C20.

give it away   Abandon a project, often in defeatist fashion. ANZ mid C20.

give jaro   To scold, a bastardised version of Maori word *wharo*, to scold.

give jute   To tease or criticise adversely.

give me a circle   Please return my call. Teen slang.

give running shoes   The sack. Popularised by Minister of Public Works Bob Semple in mid 1930s.

give the arse   Get rid of someone who is annoying. ANZ, c1950.

give the fence a run   Engage in sex, as the bull intends when he is running along the fence separating him from the cow paddock.

give the go   Reject a suitor or abandon something, such as a place or a job.

glazing   Sleeping with your eyes open, or daydreaming. From 'glaze', eye or eyesight.

glide time   Public service initiative in the 1970s of working flexible hours, transformed by Roger Hall's play of the same name into public servants skiving or slacking.

glory box Prospective bride's collection of linen and other mostly manchester household items readily stored in a trunk. From WWI. ANZ.

gnawing Kissing the way streetkids describe it.

gnawing the nana Performing fellatio, where the 'nana' or banana is the penis. ANZ.

go Ready to start, often in the phrase **it's a go**. From early C20 part of ANZ desire to move forward.

go and dunk your left eye in cowshit Go away.

go and have a roll Go away. ANZ mid C20.

go around/out with Steady relationship. ANZ.

go at a lick/a good lick/full lick Proceed at speed. If you **go for the lick of your life** then it is at the absolute extent of the speed you can muster, eg, 'Bruce took off for the lick of his life, but he wasn't fast enough, the bull caught and tossed him.' Variations of British dialect and American *lick*, a spurt.

go bite your bum! Rude request to absent yourself. Sometimes with the ruder extension **and make sure you leave your tongue in it**.

go bush Go into hiding, usually in rough country, to avoid debt or jail or threat, or simply to get away from hustle and bustle to peace and quiet. ANZ C20.

go dog on To turn nasty on someone. Late C19 ANZ.

go down the toity To fail, 'toity' being toilet, eg, 'Maggie's goalshooting's gone down the toity this season.'

go for a row of shitcans Be in big trouble, eg, 'That's his fourth drink-driving offence. This time Jugsy'll go for a row of shitcans.'

go for an oatie Toilet visit for purpose of defecation. Could be inspired by porridge for brekky or by Captain Oates, whose last words to his tent mates in 1912 were reportedly that he was going outside and 'may be some time'.

go for it Encouragement; eg 'C'mon, Hakky. You've jumped that high in practice. Go for it!' ANZ.

go for the doctor   To bet heavily on a horserace or go as hard as you can, take big risks, usually in some sporting effort. The Irish card game 'forty-fives', played on the West Coast since the goldrushes of the 1860s, included the advice 'go for the doctor'. ANZ.

go for the growler   Approach or engage a woman's genitals. ANZ.

go home and ask Mum if you can go to a wedding   Go away, you wimp.

go hostile   Act annoyed. ANZ since WWI.

go into smoke   Go into hiding. ANZ early C20.

go kiss a cocky's blowhole   A rude way of telling someone to get lost.

go like a marble clock   Reliable, efficient, smooth-running.

go like a power of piss/a shower of shit/shit through a goose   Move fast, eg, 'Once school is out, that boy is off down the lagoon like a shower of shit.' ANZ.

go like a strangled fart   Move slowly.

go much on   Approve of, usually in the negative, as in 'I don't go much on the new car registration stickers.'

go nineteen to the dozen   Travel very fast, eg, 'Once he's in the clear, that winger Berryman goes nineteen to the dozen.' Originally 'ninety to the dozen', from steam engines achieving top performance by pumping out 90,000 gallons for every twelve bushels of coal shovelled in. A Cornish saying that persists here.

go off at   To abuse or scold. ANZ.

go on the swag   To become a tramp.

go out the bush   To proceed into the bush, eg, 'Dad, next time can I come when you go out the bush after pigs?'

go out with   Keep steady company, or courting. ANZ.

go outside and tell your mother she wants you   Dismissive remark.

go the whole nine yards   Giving your all. 'Nine yards' was Royal Air Force slang for 'everything' in the 1970s, according to Partridge.

go through like a packet of salts Achieve something with the rapidity of Epsom salts on the bowels, an ANZ variant of 'dose of salts'. Later C20.

go to the pack To deteriorate, either somewhat or all the way, falling to pieces. ANZ early C20.

go to whoa Beginning to end, 'whoa' being the cry to pause a horse. ANZ.

goatboat Surf canoe or skiff, in surfie talk.

gobstopper A large lolly, for which you paid a penny in 1906. ANZ.

God Squad A clutch of committed Christians, eg, 'Betcha those jokers comin' up the path in grey suits and white shirts are God Squad.' ANZ.

God's gift to women A vain heterosexual. ANZ.

God's waiting room Tauranga, 'because of its high proportion of superannuitants', wrote Richard Long, *Dominion*, 23 September 1991.

Godzone New Zealand. Contraction of 'God's Own Country', which Thomas Bracken thought his best poem.

going jade An army jungle exercise, from the jade colour of Asian jungle, particularly Malaysia and Vietnam.

gold Money.

gold watch Term of high approval, eg, 'You're a gold watch.'

Golden Oldies Veteran rugby players who should know better but cannot resist pulling on the boots to play another team of greyhairs.

Golden Shears International shearing and wool-handling championships held every March at Masterton since 1961.

goldie 1. An impressive object. Probably evolved by 1980s from nickname for a gold sovereign.

2. Recognised with a capital 'G' in the 1990s as nickname of record try-scoring All Black winger Jeff Wilson, also known as 'the Golden One'.

3. A goldfish.

gone pear-shaped Failed, usually a plan or strategy. On 8 March

2003 TV3 commentator Hamish McDonald said 'it's all gone pear-shaped for the Crusaders tonight,' as the Auckland Blues Super 12 rugby rivals thrashed the champion Canterbury team.

gone to billyo 1. Disappeared, gone to a faraway place, where you boil the billy in the great outdoors.

2. Messed up, plans gone awry, the influence of 'Old Billy', the Devil.

goneburger Something departed, defeated or spent, as TV One weatherman Jim Hickey frequently calls a collapsed weather system.

goob/goobie Spittle or snotball. From British dialect *gob*, a slimy clot. ANZ.

good as gold Affirming wellbeing. Mid C20.

good fit, like a stocking on a chicken's lip Neat piece of work; in joinery a well crafted job.

good ink Anything pleasing, as in 'What's the good ink on the latest Blues game?' ANZ c1910.

good leave, a Judicious action, eg, commentator Glenn Turner calling 'a good leave' when Ken Rutherford did not play at a Waqar Younis ball fast and rising outside the off stump, TVOne, 20 February 1994.

good keen man, a Acceptably Kiwi person who can do or fix pretty much anything, a version of the ordinary bloke taken from Barry Crump's 1960 novel title. Is also used sarcastically.

good old Kiwi ingenuity A self-congratulatory comment on New Zealand resourcefulness, eg, Judy Bailey on the TVOne News, 10 August 1989, used the expression about a Christchurch couple with an exclusive contract from the Reserve Bank to destroy used notes, who proceeded to have them chewed up and used as lamp bases.

good on ya/you Well done. Early C20 ANZ.

good one Encouraging phrase, eg, 'That's his sixth ball in a row got past the bat. Good one, Shane.'

good value Worth having or performing well, often in regard to a person. ANZ c1920.

good wicket Desirable state, as in 'We're on a good wicket with this fine weather.' ANZ 1920s.

goodnight, nurse! Irrevocable turn of events, eg, 'Intercept! Goodnight, nurse!' was Keith Quinn's call when the French began their match-winning try late in the test against the All Blacks, 3 July 1994. Originally WWI greeting the soldiers used with gratitude and brought back from hospital, becoming comical or incredulous, and c1920 marking completion. ANZ.

good-oh Moderate approval, ANZ C20.

goody gumdrops/goody, goody, gumdrops Juvenile derision or enthusiasm. ANZ.

goog 1. An egg. From Scots *goggie*, juvenile word for an egg.

2. A fool. Both ANZ C20.

goolie A stone or rock, possibly from juvenile usage of a stone suitable for throwing. ANZ.

goori A dog, from Maori *kuri*. Sometimes used as an abusive word for a person.

gorse-eater/goss-eater Ugly person, usually directed at a female by lower South Island males. Early 1970s.

gorsepocket Mean person, often said to have **gorse in his pocket**.

goss 1. Gorse, usually in the southern South Island.

2. Gossip, as in 'Got any goss?' The ACT party obliges with a newsletter of parliamentary gossip titled *The Goss*.

Grab and Snatch GST, or Goods and Services Tax.

graft Work, usually heavy manual labour. From the British dialect word for performing work, ANZ late C19. Now used frequently in rugby, where a **grafter** is a hard-working if unspectacular player.

Grand Scale Theft GST, or Goods and Services Tax.

Granny Nickname for the *New Zealand Herald* newspaper, supposedly because it is old-fashioned. Early C20.

grape Gang rape.

grape on, have a To be angry or sour at somebody. ANZ early C20.

grapes Haemorrhoids. ANZ.

Grassgrub, The Railcars in Taranaki and South Island, from colour of cars.

graunch Loud grinding, often from failing to engage car gears. Adapted from British dialect word for grinding teeth.

gravel rash Kissing burn on jaw.

gravel-scraper Useless sheepdog.

grease Butter, from British dialect *grease*, rancid butter. Mid C20.

greaser A heavy fall, often in the phrase **to come a greaser**.

greasies Fish and chips usually, but any deepfried takeaway food. ANZ.

greasy A butcher, shearer, rural cook or fastfood cook. ANZ C20.

Great Helmsman Ironic nickname for the bland 1990s Prime Minister Jim Bolger. Originally used of Chinese leader Mao Tse Tung.

greedy guts Glutton. Early C20. ANZ.

green tobacco Marijuana.

greenie A proactive conservationist, unlikely to eat out of tins. ANZ.

grey matter Older people hired by young entrepreneurs to provide the illusion of an experienced operation.

greyhound A very thin roll-your-own cigarette. ANZ.

grog on/grog on regardless Drink persistently. ANZ.

grommet/grummet/grummit Desirable female, from Australian surfie slang for a groupie, evolved from nautical slang for the vagina, by association from the rubber grommet or washer used to screw nuts tight. A **shepherd's grummet** is a sheep.

grommet dude A boy, to today's teenagers.

grot, the The toilet. Mid C20.

grouse Desirable or excellent. Often applied to an attractive woman. ANZ, opposite meaning of British 'to grumble'.

grow another leg Raise one's performance, eg, 'As the season wore on, Tana Umaga grew another leg, just getting better and better.'

growler Vagina. Recent local extension of rhyming slang identifying 'cunt' as 'growl and grunt'. ANZ.

grunds/grundies Underpants, from rhyming with 'undies' from the 1960s. ANZ.

grunt Power, often horsepower, eg, 'Boy, has that souped-up Holden got some grunt.' ANZ from 1980s.

grunter Promiscuous woman or prostitute, from anticipated noise. ANZ c1940.

grunter hunter Pig hunter.

gruts Underpants, a variant of 'grundies' in recent times.

Gumboot City Taihape, self-proclaimed and promoted from the 1980s with a gumboot-throwing competition the Tuesday after Easter. The point of 'Gumboot Day' is to restore pride in a part of New Zealand's heritage.

gumboot tea is ordinary common or garden tea, as opposed to herbal, for example.

gumdigger/gumpuncher A dentist. ANZ.

gumdigger's dog, as mad as/as skinny as/as stupid as/as useless as Very mad/skinny/stupid/useless. In the case of skinny, **a gumdigger's bitch** is an alternative invocation.

gummies Gumboots. ANZ mid C20.

gummy Toothless old sheep. ANZ late C19.

gun Expert or admirable person. Originally a top shearer. From early C20. However, if you are **in the gun** you are in line for something, usually punishment, from British phrase meaning drunk. ANZ.

gunga Vagina or anus. Often used in the derisive suggestion **stick it up your gunga**. Originally military reference to the anus and the phrase 'Bung it in, Gunga Din', which now has the innocent imperative to proceed with something like pouring the concrete. ANZ.

gunty Cool or radical. Current teen slang.

gurgler The plughole, often **down the gurgler**, indicating something is irretrievably lost or a complete failure. ANZ.

gutbuster A mountain trampers know is going to be challenging. From mid C20.

gutless wonder Poorly performed person or thing, eg, 'What a gutless wonder that new number eight turned out to be.' ANZ.

guts, rough as An ugly or dishevelled person, perhaps from a night of excessive drinking. ANZ.

guts-ache Irritating person. ANZ C20.

gutser Greedy person since early C20. However, if you **come a gutser** you have failed miserably. ANZ.

gutsful More than enough, usually **had a gutsful**. From c1920. Australians settle for the singular 'gutful'.

gutsing Shoplifting in the 1990s, where goods are stuffed in gut area under voluminous garment.

gutted Exhausted and/or disappointed. Increasingly used by rugby players interviewed after a game.

gutty Whitebait that has lived in freshwater long enough to no longer have a transparent gut.

gypsy Housetrucker. 1990s.

Hagley by day, Shagley by night Central Christchurch park allegedly changes at night to a place of sexual dalliance.

hair like a bush pig's arse Untidy and unattractive hair. ANZ.

hair oil Worcester or other dark sauce, especially on the West Coast.

hair pie The vagina in cunnilinguist terms. ANZ.

haircut What you give your car when you wind the odometer back.

hairy 1. Rundown or of doubtful value, eg, 'That's a pretty hairy motorbike you're trying to sell, Barry.'

2. Tricky, eg, 'That new maths master comes up with some hairy equations.' ANZ.

hairy dog/goat, run like a Poorly performing ANZ racehorse or motorcar. Mid C20.

hairy legs The joker in the pack of cards.

hairy maclary A female permitting sexual exploration but stopping short of connection.

haka A fuss, eg, 'That toddler does a haka every time you put him to bed.' From Maori *haka*, a demonstrative chant dance.

half a shake Request for someone to wait a moment. Early C20.

half the lies he tells you are not true Jokey way of saying someone is not a complete liar.

half-cut Silly or stupid, as one is likely to be in the C19 British phrase to be half or partly drunk. ANZ.

half-g Large glass or plastic container for beer, which may no longer measure the half-gallon it once did. Mid C20.

half-pie Unimpressive, poorly performed, not properly done.

Possibly from Maori *pai*, good, though 'half-baked pie' is another possibility, particularly as popular in Australia too. Early C20. From mid C20 also means half-hearted. ANZ.

half-rinsed   Fairly drunk. From c1912.

half-time   Break midway through a sporting contest, formerly also the period after the shorts when there was time to buy refreshments before a feature film.

hand in/up   Helping someone, from the assistance often welcomed by those boarding trams or trains. ANZ mid C20.

hand off   Fend off an opponent attempting a tackle in rugby union.

hand that lifts the cup, The/should not be used to shift the gears   Advice not to drink and drive, especially farm machinery.

handle   Beer glass with a handle, usually a pint, eg, 'Pull us a handle of Speight's, mate.' A **half-handle** is a half-pint. Early C20.

handle the jandal   Get a grip.

hangi pants   Hot pants, as in a female adjudged sexually on heat.

hangman   Rough diamond. Partridge identifies as rare in Britain after 1650.

hanguva   Mildest intensive for those who cannot bring themselves to say 'helluva'. The same goes for **like hang**, eg, 'He is a hanguva good player,' to which the rejoinder might be, 'Like hang he is.' ANZ c1920.

happy as a bride without her bloke/a Baptist in a nudist colony/a bastard on Father's Day/a kiwi in a dog kennel/a shag off a rock/a sick eel on a sandspit, etc   Very unhappy in some of the multitude of variations. ANZ.

happy as a dog with two dicks   Ecstatically happy.

happy as Larry   Very happy, though the capital 'L' may be misleading, for 'larry' could be short for 'larrikin' or 'larrie', a British dialect word for a jest, a joke or a lark. ANZ.

happy camper   A person of amiable disposition, desirable when one is camping. Often used to encourage such attitude among children, as in 'Try and be a happy little camper.'

hard case/doer/shot/thing An amusing, exciting and/or resolute man or woman, the 'hard' bit admitting of admiration in ANZ circles.

hard out Extreme effort, eg, 'The Blues went hard out for the full 80 minutes.'

hard stuff Strong liquor, usually spirits. Since late C19 ANZs have been indulging a shot or drop of the hard stuff.

hard word on, to put the An insistent demand for a loan, or sex, or anything considered difficult to ask for. C20 ANZ.

hard yakker Demanding work, usually manual labour. From Aboriginal *yaga*, meaning 'work'.

hard yards, the The progress made up a rugby field by grinding physical effort, often by the unglamorous front row of the forward pack, wearing down the opposition and slowly pushing them back towards their own line.

Harry twice Harihari, South Westland.

hash-me-gandy Sheepstation stew. Possibly a combination of the restrained eater Mahatma Gandhi and/or the meat and egg mince called salmagundi.

hasn't got the brains to give her/himself a headache Not very intelligent. ANZ.

hatchy malatchy, the world of Optimistic view that things are improving, *Holmes* TV show, 11 September 1989.

hatter Loner, from the goldmining era. The loneliness sometimes made such men mad as hatters, who went mad from tanning hats with mercury. ANZ.

have a hairy fit and die bald Extreme rage.

have a squat To defecate and also, female, to urinate. ANZ.

have balls on him like a scoutmaster Large and active balls, as scoutmasters were supposed to have from rampant homosexual predation, in the 1930s perception when the catchphrase was most popular.

have on To confront or to tease. Used in negative when do not wish to confront or attempt something. Mid C20 ANZ.

have one too many   Overdoing the alcohol and showing it.

have possums in the top paddock   Mentally deranged, a variation of Australian kangaroos in the top paddock, or head.

have the goods on   In possession of damaging information, eg, 'The police have the goods on that dealer who's winding back speedos.' NZ c1932.

have the white gloves on   Moving with authority, as traffic police did when directing traffic with white gloves, eg, 'He obviously had the white gloves on — he was waving them through,' said Arran Pene, TVOne, of the opposition not tackling Eric Rush during the All Blacks game against a Scottish Development XV, 17 November 1993.

haven't laughed so much since Granny got her tit caught in the wringer   Grossly amused, from the not unknown event in the days when washing machines had temperamental wringers attached. ANZ.

having a rottie   Very bad mood, after the fierce guard dog breed of Rottweiler.

hay makes the bull fat, the bull makes the cow fat, the cow makes butterfat   Kiwi humorous chiding response to 'Hey!', when polite people say 'I beg your pardon'.

he, I'll go   Expression of surprise or vow of confidence; eg 'If that's not worth a fortune, I'll go he.' Orsman sources the 'he' to the tagger in children's games. ANZ.

head a norwester, can   A good lead or heading dog that can handle the trickiest stock. From the Canterbury norwester, a strong, dry wind. Mid C20.

head down, arse up   Hard at work, eg, 'Bolton's one of those jokers who works flat out dawn to dusk, head down, arse up.' ANZ.

head job   1. Mentally lacking, eg, 'Seth's a head job, couldn't add two and two together.'

2. Ugly enough to need plastic surgery, eg, 'Milt's got a face like a fright, needs a head job.' Both ANZ.

head like a Mini with the doors open   Sticking-out ears. ANZ.

head over turkey Tipping over vigorously; variant of the army catchphrase 'arse over turkey'. ANZ early C20.

head read, need your Indication of doubts about your sanity or sense. ANZ.

head sherang The boss. From Anglo-Indian *serang*, a captain or boatswain. ANZ.

heady Clever, shrewd, full of ideas. ANZ C20.

heap of shit Useless person or object, eg, 'That car is a heap of shit.' ANZ.

heap shit on Abuse or dismiss, eg, 'That critic heaps shit on any local production.' ANZ.

heaps, give her/him/it/them 1. Put or demand extreme effort, as in ramming the accelerator to the floor of the car.

2. To tease or take to task. Both ANZ.

heck and Thomas! Mildest expression of disgust.

hedgehog 1. An orange stuck all over with toothpick skewers of nibbles, usually mild cheddar cubes, pineapple pieces or chunks, and sometimes pickled onions. Mid C20.

2. Radical feminist. Late C20.

heifer A woman; recorded by E.J. Wakefield among early C19 whalers here before elsewhere. A **heifer paddock** is a girls' school. ANZ.

heinous Ugly or bad to a teenager.

hell's bells and buckets of gravy Cute, if pallid, exclamation.

hell's bells and buggy wheels Mild exclamation.

hen cackle 1. A mountain that is easy to climb. From 1930s.

2. Any trifle.

hen's face A steep climb. Mid C20.

hen's teeth, pickled eels' feet, pan petkin pie and Presbyterian custard One of the most elaborately arch answers to the unwelcome juvenile question 'What's for tea?' Popular in lower South Island.

Her/His Ex Short for 'Her/His Excellency, the Governor-General'.

herbs Power, usually motor power, often in the phrase **give it herbs**. Originally oats for horses. Mid C20 ANZ.

here's a go Anticipatory remark, as when spotting the potential for a rugby brawl.

here's looking up your kilt A popular toast. ANZ.

hermit A sheep which has lost interest in being with the flock, as a result of being 'tuted', ie, eating the poisonous *tutu* plant.

he's a bigger ram than a Ramsden rammer rammer Said admiringly of a sexually active male.

hickey 1. Thingummyjig, late C19. Baker reported its use in the South Island, initially spelling it *hiki*, a Maori word one of whose meanings is a charm for raising anything from the water. Baker also offers 'do-hiki', very close to the American 'do-hickey'.

2. A snotball or a pimple. ANZ.

3. A love bite. ANZ.

hiddybugger Unattractive person in current teenage slang.

hide Impudence or shamelessness. Often in **a thick hide** or alleged to possess **the hide of Old Nick**, the Devil. 'Nick' as the Devil was a jocular C16 colloquialism for St Nicholas, patron saint of scholars and thieves. ANZ mid C20.

hide/sink the salami/sausage/sausie/sav/soss/sossy Male intromission of the penis, or more generally, sexual intercourse, eg, 'Fancy a bit of hide the sausage tonight, dear?' ANZ later C20.

hiff/hurf To throw; to 'hiff a goolie' on the West Coast was to throw a stone, Peter Kitchin, *Evening Post*, 1997.

high time Something just this side of overdue, eg, 'It's high time you had yourself a holiday.' ANZ.

highway robbery Excessive charging. ANZ.

Hill, the 1. Parliament buildings, adjacent to Hill Street.

2. High-country mustering, working the hill.

3. Mt Eden Prison in Auckland, despite being in a valley below the volcanic hill of that name.

hillybin Female homosexual by mysterious conjunction of 'lesbian' and 'chillybin'. 1970s.

hinaki Prison. Maori for 'eelpot'. Mid C20.

hiss To tramp rapidly, usually in the phrase **to hiss along**.

hiss and a roar, with a Doing something obviously and/or loudly, with implication that you are maybe overdoing it. Some of the Maori MPs in NZ First entered Parliament with a hiss and a roar, and exited three years later like punctured balloons.

hisser Something welcome or admired, like a hisser of a meal.

hit around, a A social game, often of tennis, eg, 'Let's use the lunch hour for a hit around, whadya say, guys?'

hit it up Behave excessively. ANZ C20.

hit the sack Go to bed. A coal sack nailed to four posts was a cheap pioneering bed, still in use, as author witnessed in the done-it-himself abode of the late Tony Yelash, Ahipara's last gumdigger. The Royal Navy may have called a hammock a sack before or after Kiwis did. Americans also hit the sack. ANZ C19.

hit the spot To have precisely the desired effect, often from alcohol, but from any object of desire, eg, 'Ooh, these oysters/James Lee Burke thrillers/cabsavs from Magill Cellars hit the spot.' ANZ.

hit up for Beg or charge excessively. ANZ early C20.

hit your straps Move or depart quickly. Possibly derived from looking for your swag-straps, which meant seeking another job; or from using reins to encourage a horse to run faster.

hitimi A marble. Developed from 'hit me', the juvenile challenge in a game of marbles.

hit-up A game of tennis or cricket. ANZ mid C20.

hobbles In top form, eg, 'Any French team — if it hits its hobbles on the day — can be impossible to beat.' Alex Wyllie quoted in the *Auckland Star*, 15 June 1989.

hobo Rough person ANZ post-WWI, not necessarily the tramp it means elsewhere.

hobnail express Travel on foot. Mid C20.

hock   Achieve or gain something, like hock the used tennis balls after a tournament.

hock off   Get rid of something without attempting to gain recompense as you would from a pawnshop, eg, 'Let's hock off this pile of old magazines, dump them at the gym, maybe.'

hockey sticks   Hogget chops. Mid C20.

hoe in/into   Vigorous effort, often in regard to eating heartily, verbal attacks such as politicians indulge, manual or mental labours. ANZ early C20.

hoha   A nuisance, eg, from Keri Hulme, 'Somebody come and look after these hoha kids for a change.'

hokianga   A mutton sandwich of doorstop girth.

Hokitika swindle   Pub game involving numbers called in a certain sequence requiring a specified payment, used to purchase drinks.

hokonui   Illegal booze, specifically the whisky made illegally in the Hokonui Hills of Southland.

Hokonui swindle   Drinking game combining elements of chance with the ability to hold your liquor and follow a few simple rules. The deviousness of the caller can influence proceedings. The aim is fun, lots of drinking and seeing who can last the pace.

hold a tangi   Experience problems or setbacks, eg, 'We're holding a tangi with our kiwifruit farm. One more year like the last and we're stuffed.' From Maori *tangi*, mourning.

holding   Having ready funds. Often in the phrase 'Are you holding?' ANZ C20.

holding paddock   Old people's home.

hollow as a bunghole in a barrel   Without credibility or simply quite empty, physically or metaphorically.

hollow log   A dog. ANZ.

hollywood   Suspect or faked behaviour, often in the phrase **doing a hollywood**, popular in competitive play to gain a breather. ANZ from 1960s.

Home   Britain to previous generations, who referred to a Home boat,

H

Home government, Home newspapers. The phrase **gone home** referred to worn-out clothes. C19.

home and hosed   Secure. ANZ mid C20.

home on the pig's back   Easy success or attended by good fortune. ANZ c1910.

homebake   Illegal production often in a home of morphine or cocaine rock from cooking codeine phosphate, often retailed to the street community by organised gangs. Mid 1980s. ANZ.

homer   A new phone you get cheap from a telephone installer. 1980s.

homie   Street kid, adopting black American uniform of back-to-front baseball cap, baggy long shorts, sneakers with laces undone, boombox rap. Teenagers use the word for a variety of meanings involving approval or disapproval. Began in United States as a *homeboy*, one from same place as you and equally adrift in city, hence a friend. Now also used to mean a street kid troublemaker. From 1980s.

homogrips   Sideboards.

honesty box   Unsupervised container for leaving money when you buy goods on offer, often at a roadside fruit stall.

honeymoon tucker   Lettuce alone. Usually in form of a question and answer.

hoo   A bend or kink, eg, 'That track's got a hoo in it.' Mostly South Island usage.

hoodackie   Thingummyjig or object of indeterminate use. From mid C20. Variations include **doodackie/doohickey/hoojacky/howdacky**.

hoodie   A sweatshirt with built-in hood, and its wearer.

hooer   Abusive term, dialect or mock-Scottish for 'whore'.

hoo-ha over the puha   Lot of fuss over nothing.

ho-ohhh!   Kiwi bushman's identification call, a version of 'cooee'.

hook one's bait/mutton   1. Depart, eg, 'As usual Fess only stayed in town the week, then hooked his bait.'

2. Engage a partner in a dance. Both 1920s ANZ.

hool   To drive fast, often **hool along**, as you would perhaps expect hooligans to hurtle. Mid C20.

hoon   Hooligan. **Hoonery, hooning around** and **hooning it up** usually mean wild or irresponsible behaviour, such as driving with squealing tyres and loud revving in a **hoonmobile,** the group so behaving occupying **hoondom**. Post-WWII of unknown origin.

hoop along   Something hoons do, move at a fast clip. Probably from Scottish *hoop*, to hurry.

hooped   Drunk. A mid C20 word perhaps created from the hoops fixed tight around a barrel of booze.

hooray   Farewell. Early C20 ANZ, extended later to **hooray fuck**, which might not be intended as a fond farewell.

hoot/hootoo/hout/hutu   Money, a corruption of Maori *utu*, ransom or price.

hooter   The toilet, whence hooting noises may be heard. In Australia for once it represents the other end, ie, the nose.

hoovering   Consuming everything in sight, as the Hoover vacuum cleaner does. Usually applied to an eager drinker of alcohol.

hooya!   Juvenile cry of derision, ANZ C20.

hop across   Any quick journey, most often a flight to Australia.

hop into   Vigorous attack on person or thing such as a job. ANZ late C19.

hop to it   To act speedily, or the command so to do. ANZ.

hop up and down   Distressed behaviour. ANZ.

hopeye   Hot meat pie, the nation's favourite lunchtime meal.

hophead   Drunkard, or somebody acting silly or wild enough to be thought drunk. To be **hopped out** is to be drunk. ANZ mid C20.

hori   A Maori, usually a male, a translation of 'George'.

horror house   The school dental clinic.

horse bite   Squeezing nastily above the knee, a playground favourite mid C20.

horse cock   Luncheon sausage roll.

hose down   Raining very hard, eg, 'Boy, was she hosing down the day we walked the Routeburn track.'

hose in   To win easily, often in sport, eg, 'The ABs should hose in at the World Cup.' Possibly a variation of 'home and hosed'.

hosed off   Upset. Supporters are usually hosed off at their team losing. Mid C20.

hose out   To comprehensively defeat. Later C20.

hospital pass   A rugby ball passed to someone about to be tackled, anticipating where he will end up. Catholic players also know it as **the Hail Mary pass** because the recipient will probably be in need of prayers. Later C20.

hostie   Airline hostess. ANZ.

hotdog   Batter-covered saveloy on a stick, usually with tomato sauce trickling from the top. Local variant of the American frankfurter in a bun, which is also served here, except it too is a saveloy, though it's called an 'American hotdog'. Later C20.

hotten up one's copper   Consume warm food or hot tea. C20.

House of Pain   Carisbrook rugby ground in Dunedin.

house of parliament/parliament house   Public toilet — where all the big pricks hang out. ANZ mid C20.

House of Taine   Carisbrook rugby park, in tribute to All Black and Otago captain Taine Randell prominent there for over a decade.

how about giving your feet a party and inviting your dress down?   Your dress is too short, my girl.

how are you, now you're all right?   Greeting that is not necessarily facetious or ironic.

how much would you charge to haunt a ten-room house?   Indication you think someone ugly.

how would you be?   Hello.

howleybags   Nappies or knickerbockers, hopefully for different reasons.

how's it goin?/how's she goin?/how ya goin?   A greeting. ANZ.

how's your bally knees/belly, knees and things? A friendly enquiry about your health.

how's your belly where the pig bit you? An enquiry about the health of your stomach.

how's your big wheel? An enquiry about the health of your heart.

how's your father A fight between rugby players, eg, 'A little bit of how's your father in that scrum'. Keith Quinn on *Sportsnight*, TVOne, 3 July 1990. He attributed to D.O.C. Williams on a tour of South Africa in 1970 this sexually innocent meaning for what usually refers to sex.

hubberlush Desirable female. Variant of 'hubba hubba', from the mid 1930s.

huck off, fairy legs Go away, you unattractive person.

huckery Unwell, unattractive or unpleasant. You could feel huckery, and you could see someone you regarded as huckery. Could be evolved from the Maori *pakaru*, ruined, via its corruption as 'puckeroo' and then 'huckeroo'.

Hughie 1. God, often in the phrase requesting rain, 'Send her down, Hughie.' ANZ early C20 among shearers needing rain, later among trampers defying rain.

2. Mt Egmont/Taranaki, god-like site of much rain.

hui-hopper Someone who spends all his/her time going to meetings or, in Maori, *hui*.

hula The hull appendage — Team New Zealand's innovative but ineffective sheath around yacht to defend America's Cup. January, 2003.

hulahaka A person of mixed Maori and Pacific Island descent. 1990s.

humdinger Anything attractive, such as a humdinger of a footy match, adapted from American airmen reference to fast aircraft. ANZ.

hump To carry a load, from when the swagman **humped his bluey**. ANZ.

humpy The hump-backed whale.

humungous   Huge, eg, 'Snow just caught a humungous wave.'

huntaway   A sheepdog that comes in from behind. ANZ C20.

hurl   To vomit. ANZ.

hushytuttut   On the booze.

hutch   Crutch, from shearer's rhyming slang.

hydraulic sandwich   A liquid alcohol lunch.

hydraulicing   Raising price artificially or theft, both involving the lifting qualities of a hydraulic jack, seen in unscrupulous real estate agents and used-car salespeople and in warehouse and wharf thieves. Mid 1990s.

hydroglycaemic as a newt   Drunk. A variant of 'pissed as a newt', inspired by an MP in the early 1980s claiming he was rendered tipsy by one beer on an empty stomach.

I beg your parding, Mrs Harding, my chicks are in your garden eating all your cabbages Elaborately juvenile apology for a burp.

I didn't come down in the last shower Firm indication not to be considered a fool or naive. ANZ version of the British Navy's 'didn't come up in the last bucket'.

I don't give a fat rat Indication of supreme indifference, eg, 'I don't give a fat rat whether Fitzy plays or not, we will still win.'

I might as well speak to me bum – at least it talks back Protest at being ignored.

ice Spotless, eg, 'This room is ice. Nothing on the floor, no Barbie dolls, no rubbish.'

Ice, The Antarctica.

Ice Blacks National men's hockey team from 1998.

ickem Soft animal manure. Possibly an extension of 'icky', meaning sticky and unpleasant.

identity/old identity A person, usually one associated with a particular locality, or considered a dag or a wag or something of a character. Coined by E.B. Cargill in the Otago Provincial Council when he said settlers should endeavour to preserve their old identity amidst all these 1860s new goldrush identities. Popularised by Charles Thatcher in his goldfields balladeering about 'the old identities', the settlers there before the 'new chums' arrived on the goldfields.

if brains were dynamite, he/she wouldn't have enough to part his/her hair Someone lacking in the brain department.

if bullshit was music, you'd have your own orchestra Response to hearing a load of rubbish. ANZ.

if bullshit was rubber, you'd fly to the moon You are talking rubbish.

if it moves, shoot it; if it doesn't, chop it down! Glum conservationist view of the way sportsmen and bushmen destroy native flora and fauna.

if it rained palaces, you would get hit on the head with the knob off the dunny door Very unlucky person. ANZ.

if looks could kill . . . Reaction to a frowning face, often intended to jolly somebody out of a moody, sometimes with the addition **. . . I'd be dead**. ANZ.

if that lump on your shoulders ever comes to a head, someone should squeeze it One way of expressing dislike.

if the missus of the house caught a mouse in her blouse would she rouse? By Jove she would! Parental reaction to being pestered by children.

if you can't be good, be careful Advice to take precautions, usually with sex. ANZ.

if you don't help yourself, nobody else will Advice to be self-reliant. ANZ.

if you fell into a barrel of tits, you would come up sucking your thumb Unlucky person.

if you fell off the Arahura/Aratika/Maori/Tamahine, you'd come up with a mouthful of fish Lucky person, in the unlikely case of someone falling off an interisland ferry.

if you had a brain, it'd be lonely You are stupid.

if you had another brain, you could start a rock garden Dolt!

if you had a shit, your head would collapse You are truly a stupid person. ANZ.

if you laughed, your face would crack Morose person. ANZ.

if you think that, then you've got another think coming You are wrong.

if you were side-on, you'd be invisible A thin person.

if your brains were barbed wire, you couldn't fence a dunny You are stupid. Pre-WWII.

if your brains were shit, you wouldn't need any toilet paper No visible means of intellectual support.

if your head was full of dynamite, it wouldn't blow your hat off You are thick!

if you've got it, flaunt it Make use of your physical charms. ANZ.

iffy Anything of dubious value or likely to be risky. Buying a secondhand car off the side of the road could be iffy. ANZ c1920.

Iky Ikamatua, West Coast.

I'll be eating ducks while you're chasing feathers Defiant boast that you will be more successful one day than somebody who is doing better than you now.

I'll fry your lips Warning to be quiet, hopefully a jocular one.

I'll hand it to him/I've got to hand it to him Expression of approval, perhaps reluctant; eg 'I've got to hand it to that forward pack, I never thought they could hold out the Blues for an entire half.'

I'll kick your bum and make your teeth bleed Threat, hopefully jocular.

I'll punch your teeth down your neck until you fart them out A dire threat.

I'll punch your teeth so far down your throat you'll have to stick a toothbrush up your arse to clean them A very dire threat. ANZ.

I'll see you right Promise to look after somebody, usually with some financial assistance, eg, 'No worries about the mortgage, bro. I'll see you right.'

I'll trim the knots off you Promise of a thrashing; *trim* is an old word for thrashing.

illegal Tegel Any game bird shot out of season or any protected bird you should not be eating, such as the kereru, weka or muttonbird; after a well known brand of frozen chicken.

I'm not your bum boy I am not your servant.

I'm up stream with the trout Indication of intended imminent departure, with a caution not to enquire where.

improve, on the Successfully recuperating. ANZ early C20.

in a shit In sulky or petulant mood. ANZ.

in deep shit In big trouble, eg, 'We're in deep shit with spreadable butter sales to the bloody Brits.'

in for your chop Vigorously working to get your share, or possibly more. From the divvying up of the sheep's carcase, from c1920. ANZ.

in like Flynn Swift and successful, usually sexual. From reported sexual exploits of Australian actor Errol Flynn. ANZ.

in one ear and out the other Accusation of being inattentive, usually directed exasperatedly at a child, eg, 'If I've told that boy once I've told him fifty times not to eat peas with his knife. Never listens. In one ear and out the other.' ANZ.

in smoke In hiding, concealed. ANZ early C20.

in the dogbox In disgrace, eg, 'Pete's in the dogbox with Madge after coming home pissed last weekend.' ANZ.

in the poo In trouble, eg, 'Monty gambles too much, he's always financially in the poo.' ANZ.

in the shit In trouble, eg, 'Looks like we're in the shit with this MMP carry-on.' ANZ.

in to win Attitude or intent to compete hard, not just to turn up for the fun of it or to merely play the game, eg, 'The All Blacks are in to win every game they play.' Mid C20.

in two shakes of a dog's hind leg Promise not to take long, eg, 'I'll be there in two shakes of a dog's hind leg.' ANZ.

in you go, says Bob Munro Expression of encouragement. No person of that name recorded in this context, suggesting it is merely rhyming slang. Mid C20.

in your dipper! Defiant expression, eg, 'You want me to support Cullen on this super tax pool? In your dipper!'

Indian giver One who gives a gift and later asks for it back. ANZ.

indigenous cringe Deferential towards other cultures, a variation of the cultural cringe ANZs have recognised since Australian A.A. Phillips coined it in 1950.

influence in the right quarter   On the contrary, an ironic appreciation of a menial job such as its origin in latrine duty among WWI Kiwi soldiers.

Inland Robbing-you   Inland Revenue Department.

Internet Island   Stewart Island, traded on the Net by people who never set foot there; a cyber land-grab.

Invergiggle   Invercargill.

Invincibles, The   The 1924 All Blacks, who won every game on their northern hemisphere tour.

IQ of a grapefruit   Identification of low-wattage in the brain box from *Boots 'n' All*, TVOne, 15 June 1992.

Irish confetti   Gravel.

Irish curtains   Cobwebs. ANZ. The English version is 'Irish draperies'.

Irish merino   Wild pig.

iron lung, wouldn't work in an   Lazy person. ANZ.

iron out   1.To fix something. Probably from ironing out wrinkles. ANZ c1930.

2. To attack so successfully you flatten someone.Thus **ironed out,** exhausted or knocked senseless by fists or booze. ANZ mid C20.

iron undies   Any female or her garment adjudged difficult to penetrate or remove by coarse and frustrated males, including roll-ons, cycle shorts, Spandex tights, witch's britches, corsets, girdles, easies. ANZ.

Island chow mein   Corned beef and vermicelli, a Pacific Island food combination.

it/she couldn't drive a nail into a piece of balsa wood   Poor quality car.

it's a go!   All agreed whatever can proceed, eg, 'Despite the teething troubles with MMP, I reckon now it's a go.' ANZ.

it's a goer   Something ready and/or fully able to proceed, eg, 'I wouldn't say the NCE non-exam is a goer in those performance-driven private schools.' ANZ.

it's a little bit over   Reassuring remark from butchers and greengrocers and anybody else selling you more than you asked for.

it's snowing down south   Your petticoat is showing.

it was in Baghdad that you were in your dad's bag   Your father was over there when you were conceived, but was your mother? More simply, you're a bastard. WWII.

I've been doing this since your arsehole was the size of a shirt button   I am more experienced than you, with the implication that you should know your place and not criticise your betters.

I've got a carbuncle on my pollywonkle   Facetious response, usually implying that it was a stupid question.

I've nearly bust my foofer/foofoo valve   Indication that you have overdone the physical activity. The 'foofoo valve' was a mythical gadget blamed for breakdowns in the Royal Navy early last century. ANZ.

I've read about you on jam tins   Indication of doubt and suspicion of being deliberately misled. I don't believe you, you are kidding me.

I've seen better heads on a bumful of boils   You are hideously ugly.

I've seen better heads on a glass of beer   You are plain ugly, my friend. ANZ.

jack A look, usually when you take or **have a jack at**.

Jack Nohi A nosey parker, combining a 'jack' or look with the Maori adaptation of 'nosy', from Maori *kanohi*, the face.

jack of Rid of something annoying.

jack up 1. To organise, such as jacking up a date for the evening. Since about 1930.

2. To support, as in jacking up a retaining wall.

3. Increase something, as in jacking up the price of fruit.

4. Organise deceit, as in jacking up a coalition deal. Opposite of British meaning of collapse or destruction.

jackberko A Central Otago quail, from the sound it makes.

jackyjacky The red-billed gull, a version of Maori *tiakiaki*.

Jafa Aucklander, in the acronym 'Just Another Fucking Aucklander'. 1990s.

jag To get on someone's nerves. Late C19.

jagged Worn out, usually from hard tramping.

jagging Social visit, perhaps combining 'gad', gossip and 'jag', a spree.

jake, she's Reassurance that everything is fine. Early C20 ANZ and America, possibly Scottish dialect *jake-easy*. Elaborated ANZ in **she'll be jake, jakaloo/jakerloo/tray jake**, the last playing on French *très* meaning 'very'.

jam and butter it! Mild exclamation.

James Burke Act of male masturbation. Not the British TV presenter, but rhyming with 'jerk'. ANZ.

jandal Thong or flipflop, a spongy plastic or rubber sandal that businessmen Morris and Antony Yock adapted from the *geta* or wooden Japanese sandal they saw in 1957. In 2003 the Kiwi jandal was declared a fashion icon internationally, with consequent rise in cost.

Jap Japanese or sika deer, among deerstalkers.

Jap crap Cheap and nasty goods from Japan post-WWII, still in occasional use.

jar Pint, jug or handle of beer. ANZ since 1920s.

jawjab Conversation. Teen 2000.

jay 1. An easy victim, a variation of US meaning of a fool.

2. The Vietnamese jungle to Kiwi troops there in 1960s, sometimes **deep jay**.

jaybee A ship girl, from 'jungle bunny', Australian slang for a dark-skinned person.

JC/Jesus Christ bird Any seabird appearing to walk on water, like the skipjack and the white-faced storm petrel.

jelly tip A Maori redneck, from the chocolate icecream with tip dipped in red jelly. *Dominion*, 5 October 1993.

Jennycide Tough social implications of Social Welfare cuts imposed by then Minister of, Jenny Shipley, 31 March 1991.

jerkin the gherkin Male masturbation. ANZ.

JGE Just gay enough, meaning someone heterosexual but not too much, acceptable socially to gay community.

jif To clean, usually in reference to the bathroom, from the cleanser 'Jif'.

jigger Hand-operated railway line trolley used in line maintenance. Early C20.

jigger board/stick The flat piece of wood axemen fit into the log they are cutting to stand on during competition.

jingling johnnies Sheep shears; a shearer was a **jingling johnny** from c1870. ANZ.

jink To cheat; from taking all the tricks in the card game forty-fives.

About 1920. Now more likely to indicate a tricky manoeuvre on rugby field.

job in a spirit level factory, a   Mildly derisive reply in lieu of the difficulty of explaining what you actually do.

Joe Blakes   The alcoholic shakes. Rhyming slang with 'snakes'. ANZ.

Joe Blow   An ordinary bloke. ANZ.

joes, the   Depression or nerviness, ANZ early C20.

Joes, The   Any religious order containing St Joseph's name, such as the Sisters of St Joseph of Nazareth and the Sisters of St Joseph of the Sacred Heart. The former were **Black Joes**, the latter **Brown Joes**, latterly **Old Black Joes** and **Old Brown Joes**.

john   1. Policeman, from rhyming slang 'John hop/cop' or a play on *gendarme*. ANZ. More than one cop are **the Johns**.

2. Chinese man, from goldfields habit of identifying all such as 'John Chinaman'. ANZ.

3. Penis, shortened form of 'John Thomas'.

John Dory   Signature, possibly rhyming slang for 'your story'.

joint   Brothel from 1930s.May have been brought by Irish immigrant girls.

jointie   The person who puts up and takes down sideshows, from 'joint', a carnival.

joker   A bloke. ANZ from C19, from British word for a merry fellow.

journo   A journalist. ANZ c1940.

judas   The sheep that leads the others to slaughter in a freezing works, named after Christ's betrayer.

judder bars   Haemorrhoids.

jug   An electric kettle for boiling water for tea or coffee. You **put the jug on**. From mid C20.

jumbo   Buttocks, from c1945, from the elephant of that name at London Zoo in early 1880s.

jumbuck   Silly person, originally a sheep. From Aboriginal word for a white mist.

jump-start   Get a vehicle with a flat battery started using cables attached to another vehicle's battery, or by pushing or running the vehicle until the engaged gear turns over the motor.

jumper   A cardigan in C20, but originally a goldminer's shirt, usually blue.

jumping spider   A cave weta.

jungle hour   Riotous domestic period around 5 until 6 pm, when young children go into feeding frenzy and object to bath and bed. Latter C20.

junket around   Act tiresomely, act the fool. ANZ C20.

junket trumpet   The penis, in the context of its sexual employment.

just a mo/sec/tick   Plea for a little more time, employing diminutives of moment and second, sometimes reduced to **half a mo/tick**, sometimes varied to **hold on/hang on a mo/tick**. ANZ.

just around the corner/down the street   Very close, in a variety of contexts. Good times, for instance, are said by politicians to be just around the corner. ANZ.

just not on   Indignant objection, eg, 'Dropping his daks at his sister's wedding, that's just not on!' ANZ.

just quietly   Confidentially matey remark, as in 'Just quietly, Joel is a creep.' WWI. ANZ.

just the berries/she's berries   Exactly what is wanted, perfect. Berries connote testicles.

just the shot   Precisely what one wants. ANZ c1918.

justin   Half-gallon container of beer, just in case you run out.

kai A meal, from Maori for 'food'.

kai kart Piecart or fast food takeaway that may or may not include kina with the chips.

kaitaia Takeaways or meals-on-wheels, the kai or food you take away on tyres, a splendid crosslingual pun.

kakapo-cuddler Extreme conservationist who puts flora and fauna before people. 1990s.

kapai Good, often used as expression of approval, from Maori *pai*, good. Probably popularized by the good-feeling song 'Haere mai, everything is kapai.'

kapaiburger Fresh white bread bun filled with beef pattie, slice of lettuce, onion ring, maybe beetroot, tomato sauce and mayonnaise made with condensed milk, possibly first served at Putaruru c1970.

Karitane yellow Dirty yellow colour, referring to infant excrement; related to Karitane Hospital, where Sir Truby King established his first Plunket hospital to care for infants and their mothers.

kauri, in the Remote areas, like the parts of Northland where kauri once flourished.

Kea Kiwi Expatriate Associate, one of those New Zealand businesspeople linking up on the Internet for mutual benefit. TVOne News, 9 February 2003.

keep a dog and bark yourself Someone overdoing activity unnecessarily, even duplicating work, not leaving it to the designated person or person most suited to do it, eg, 'The Prime Minister seems determined to administer personally every portfolio in the Cabinet. Can't understand why she keeps dogs and barks herself.'

keep your legs together Advice to young women not to make themselves sexually available. ANZ C20.

keep your powder dry Advice to young men not to let drink spoil their sexual performance. Possibly a hangover via Western movies from when musket troops were invariably advised to keep their powder dry.

keep your shirt on Don't lose your temper. ANZ C20.

keepsies Playing marbles for keeps. From mid C20.

keg A vessel containing beer, delivered to parties along with a pressurised gas valve. Students in particular engage in a **keg party** and compete in a **keg race** to consume the most beer in the shortest time, referred to as **kegging it up**. ANZ, from start of C20.

Kelliher art Dismissive phrase for chocolate box paintings of New Zealand landscapes, from the Kelliher Art Prize. Sir Henry Kelliher, Dominion Breweries founder, required entrants to paint a 'realistic or natural representation' of our country. The award ran from 1956 to 1977.

Kelly Brown's A party, after the long-running TV ad of recent years inviting everybody to the home the Browns had left to go on holiday.

kero Kerosene. ANZ from 1930s.

kerosene cowboy Noisy jet over Ohakea Air Force base in lower North Island. 1990s.

ket Electric kettle.

kete-carrier A Pakeha promoting Maori rights or hardline conservation designed to keep people out and flora and fauna in. Often used contemptuously by freemarketeers. 1990s.

keyboard plaque Build-up of dirt and gunk on a computer keyboard.

kia ora G'day; Maori meaning 'good health'.

kick for touch/kick into touch Back off from a potential confrontation, resign from conflict. From the rugby union action of kicking the ball across the sideline, often to get out of a threatened defensive situation.

kick her/it in the guts 1. Expression of doubt; eg 'Ya reckon there's gold in that creek. Kick her in the guts, mate. I didn't come down in the last shower.'

2. Advice to be more aggressive, perhaps use brute force to get an activity or machine underway.

kick him where his mum never kissed/missed Disciplinary prescription, usually aimed at the testicles, sometimes the buttocks. ANZ.

kick like a run cow A violent blow such as one received from a run cow, one not leg-roped in the milking bails.

kick on To continue, often successfully; for example, a 1500–metre runner may surge through the field, kick on and win the race.

kick up bobsidie Cause trouble by being aggressive, making a lot of noise.

kiddo A girl or boy, from late 1880s. ANZ.

kidney buster/crusher/rider/rotter/sweater A frameless backpack that bounces on the kidneys of a tramper.

kidney pie Insincere praise, from the Antipodean habit of kidding or teasing or deliberately misleading for the fun of it. ANZ early C20.

kidstakes Nonsense or a paltry amount. Possibly from a small bet such as a kid could make. ANZ C20.

kin oath/k'noath Rude reassurance, short for 'fucking oath'.

kindy 1. Kindergarten, from 1950s. ANZ.

2. Suburb where young people train to be gang members.

King Country spanner Bottle opener.

king fleece/mate/tide/tree, etc Any object rated tops, though not always with approval, eg, 'She was a king tide last night. Thought the house was going to get swept away.' ANZ early C20 began with cattle/sheep/wool king, used with reluctant admiration and then reversed in other uses, often ironically.

king hit Knock down or maybe knockout blow, c1920, and latterly any sudden misfortune. ANZ.

Kipperland Britain, where kippers of cured herring are popular for breakfast.

Kiri Te Kumara One of several new national dishes, along with **Curry Te Kanawa** and **Kiwi Te Kanawa**, a kiwifruit mousse, all celebrating opera star Kiri Te Kanawa, who said in late January 2003 that Sir Edmund Hillary was the most famous New Zealander, but she is the other one.

kiss-crust Two loaves of bread baked in the same tin and pulled apart when done.

kite-flying Potential political policy presented to the public to test its acceptability. ANZ.

Kiwi A New Zealander, named after the flightless native bird that is the national icon of our identity here and abroad. Started probably by Australians, with characteristic putdown by the kangaroo nation of the smaller transtasman cousins, to identify New Zealand soldiers in WWI.

kiwi, a definition: A nocturnal creature that eats, roots and leaves, or eats roots and leaves. The comma makes all the difference between the sly Kiwi seducer and the shy threatened native bird which has become our national nickname.

Kiwi Ferns National women's rugby league team.

Kiwi fruit A New Zealand homosexual.

Kiwi green Cannabis grown in this country.

Kiwi mafia New Zealanders gravitating into support groups when overseas.

Kiwi style The way New Zealanders are expected to behave, which is modest, resolute, resourceful, no boasting.

Kiwiana Popular New Zealand culture, such as the children's toy Buzzy Bee. Leighton Carrad claims to have originated the word in 1956, using it on Art Union tickets he bought. Check on www.kiwiana.co.nz.

Kiwidom Any typically New Zealand situation, such as afternoon tea featuring plates of pikelets, asparagus rolls, pavlova with kiwifruit topping and tea and beer.

Kiwified The integration of immigrants to be indistinguishable from the average Kiwi person.

Kiwi-ism   A phrase that could only be from New Zealand, such as 'up the booai'.

Kiwiland   New Zealand.

Kiwispeak   The way New Zealanders use words distinctively.

knock about/around   An object known to be handy, if you could just find it, eg, 'My shoes are knocking about somewhere.' From mid C19.

knockabout   Handyman. A sheepstation worker from c1875, expected to turn his hand to many tasks. ANZ.

knock across   Encounter casually, eg, 'We're sure to knock across some of those drag queens if we just hang about K Road long enough.' Late C19.

knock back   To reject; a **knock-back** is a rejection. ANZ C20.

knock down   1. To drink alcohol greedily or live indulgently. From 1850s.

2. To introduce somebody, in the compound form **to give the knockdown** From US.

knock for a row of shitcans   Guaranteed to impress, eg, 'The new first five is going to knock the lot of you for a row of shitcans.' Mid C20.

knock it on the head   Curt demand to be silent, eg, 'Knock it on the head, will ya. There's a kid tryin ta sleep in the next room.' ANZ c1920, from killing a snake.

knock off   To score sexually with a woman. ANZ early C20.

knock over   Kill a man or any other creature. ANZ C20.

knock/trim the corners off   Refine crude aspects of someone's character or behaviour, eg, 'It's about time someone knocked the corners off that girl, she'll never get a job covered in tats and with that attitude.' Early C20.

knock the drawingroom/sittingroom out of   Make someone physically tougher. From mid C20.

knock the wool out of his/her head   Help someone think more clearly. Early C20.

knock up 1. To make something readily, such as a batch of scones.

2. To wake somebody.

3. To get somebody pregnant. All ANZ.

knocks like a ten-ton lorry Sexually aggressive woman.

knocker Punctual, in the phrase **on the knocker**. ANZ mid C20.

knuckle-up A fist fight, probably barefisted. From mid C20.

koala-shagger An Australian.

komaty Dead. From the beginning of Te Rauparaha's famous haka, *Ka mate*.

kotanga Car aerial, a pun on 'coathanger', which is sometimes twisted out into a diamond shape and employed as an ad hoc car aerial.

K Road Karangahape Road in Auckland city.

kumara cruncher A Maori.

Kummykummy Land Taranaki, where the *kamokamo* or marrow flourishes. Late C19.

L&P   Lemon and Paeroa, a popular soft drink made originally from Paeroa mineral water.

ladies a plate   A covered plateful of savoury or sweet food women were expected to contribute to a gathering, while the men brought flagons of beer and maybe bottles of sherry for the ladies. From 1930s.

lady's leg   Liqueur bottle, from the shape of its neck as much as any male expectation.

lady's waist   Small, tapered glass or its alcoholic contents, from the male choice for women in lounge bars earlier C20.

lagerphone   Informal musical instrument constructed of bottle tops loosely attached to a broom handle for banging and shaking. A play on xylophone. ANZ mid C20.

la-la land   Bemused zone where somebody drugged or boozed or heavily tackled resides.

lamb-brained   Weak or stupid, eg, 'That's a lamb-brained notion you have, cross-leasing a section that small.' ANZ.

Lambton Quay Caucus   Political opinions voiced on the street below Parliament by groups of opinionated men. Mid C20.

Land of Fungus   Taranaki, where a fungus was harvested for Oriental uses late C19, attracting envy and derision.

Land of the Long Black Cloud/Long White Shroud/Wrong White Crowd   Jocular variations on 'Land of the Long White Cloud', the popular translation of Aotearoa.

land with your bum in butter   Excessively lucky. ANZ.

lanny   Land-Rover, a 4WD vehicle.

larrikin A thug or a high-spirited youth. British dialect adopted extensively ANZ from 1860s, the activity of such youth being **larrikinism**.

lash An attempt, usually in the phrase **to have a lash at**, while **a lash to leg** is any violent or sudden action, from cricketing term. ANZ early C20.

later'z Goodbye, as in 'see you later'. Current teen slang.

laugh on the wrong side of your face Crying, or miserable, eg, 'If that brat keeps pulling her pigtails, he'll soon be laughing on the other side of his face.' ANZ.

laughing gear The teeth or mouth. Barry Crump invited viewers to 'wrap your laughing gear around this' as he handed over a fish in a 1987 TV ad. ANZ.

lay a cable Void the bowels. ANZ.

lay an egg 1. Make a fuss, eg, 'No need to lay an egg, we'll have your electricity back on in a minute.' ANZ c1920.

2. Void the bowels. ANZ.

layby Item secured by a deposit, different from hire purchase in that no interest is paid, but the item is not uplifted until the full cost is handed over. Popular arrangement with department stores. ANZ c1925.

leather lady Possum after a train or vehicle has flattened it.

leatherjacket Various rough-skinned fish, notably *kokiri*.

left-footer A homosexual. ANZ.

legend Excellent. Current teen slang.

leggie A leg break of the cricket ball, or a slow bowler who specialises in leg breaks. ANZ.

legs like a Tokoroa forest Very thick, very hairy legs.

legs on your belly A crawler, who needs legs on the belly in order to express servility. Mid C20.

lekker/lekkers Electricity.

lemon-lipped Demonstrably irritated.

lemon squeezer Former Kiwi army hat that looked like one.

length The penis, particularly when tumescent, eg, 'Get your length in last night, Jock?' ANZ.

Les Miserables Bastards! The French, notably after they have gnawed an All Black hooker's ear and when they were testing the bomb at Mururoa and blowing up the *Rainbow Warrior*. Phrase employed on banner in Wellington demonstration, July, 1995.

let the hare sit Advice to relax.

lezo/lezzo A lesbian. ANZ c1925.

lick An ice-cream, from the teen 1960s.

lick at the cat and a run round the table Frugal meal.

lie down and I'll fry you an egg Sarcastic response to an unreasonable request.

lie like a flatfish Lie extravagantly, further enhanced with additions such as **on Riverton Beach**.

lifestyle block Rural land acquired by wealthy urbanites as a hobby farm.

lights on, nobody home A somewhat caustic way of saying somebody is dim or mentally deficient. ANZ.

like a daisy in a bull's mouth Tasty morsel.

like a dog golloping tripe Noisy sexual activity.

like a dog lying on a bag of nails Unhappy.

like a fart in a bottle/fit Agitated state. ANZ.

like a fart on a curtainpole In a hurry.

like a hawk in an onion sack Very uncomfortable.

like a hooer at a christening Confused state.

like a maggot on a hot plate Fidgety.

like a mushroom – kept in the dark and fed on shit Not kept informed and not happy about it. ANZ. **A member of the mushroom club** indicates someone excluded from what is going on.

like a pimple on a pumpkin Insignificant. ANZ.

like a rat up a drainpipe Quick moving, often in pursuit of sexual gratification. ANZ.

like it's going out of fashion Very fast, eg, 'That joker spends money like it's going out of fashion.' ANZ.

like kissing your sister Dull, eg, 'That second test was dead boring. Like kissing your sister.'

like old molls at a christening Loud chatter, with 'moll' meaning simply a woman, not the British meaning of a prostitute.

like pushing butter uphill with a hot needle Not easy.

like pushing shit uphill with the end of your nose Not easy and not pleasant.

like shagging a bag of nails Unpleasant sexual intromission.

like shit to a blanket Sticky and unpleasant.

like shitting in bed and kicking it out with your teeth Gross.

like talking to a brick wall Somebody not listening. ANZ.

line A flirtation, in the phrase **to do a line with**. Early C20 ANZ.

lip like a motherless foal Sulky.

lippie Lipstick. ANZ since c1930.

lips are sealed, my I can keep a secret.

lips like string Lips clamped thin in anger or distaste.

liquid amber Beer. ANZ.

liquid laugh A puke. ANZ.

liquid lunch Alcohol only. ANZ.

little beaut/bewdy/ripper Excellent person or thing. ANZ.

little house, the The toilet. ANZ.

Little Italy Island Bay, Wellington, because of its strong Italian community.

little lady, the The wife.

little pigs have big ears Warning that children may be listening. ANZ.

littlie An infant. ANZ.

live in a good paddock Comfortable lifestyle or eat well, or both. Mid C20.

live off/on the fat of the land   Enjoy a comfortable life. ANZ.

live off/on the smell of an oil/oily rag   Very frugal living. ANZ from mid C19.

Log, the/Log o' Wood   The Ranfurly Shield, interprovincial rugby trophy named after the much admired turn-of-the-century Governor of New Zealand, the Earl of Ranfurly. The **log holder** is the rugby province currently holding the shield.

log of wood   Stupid or lazy person. ANZ.

logs, the   Lock-up or small prison made quickly from logs, a goldrush necessity in the 1860s.

lolly   A sweet; shortened form of 'lollipop', used ANZ from mid C19. A **lolly scramble** is a tossing of lollies to a group of children, or the political promise of goodies to a supposedly corruptible and probably naive group of voters, quite different from **chucking/losing/tossing your lollies**, which means to vomit, **doing your lolly**, which means losing your temper, or a **lolly night**, the expectation of sexual fulfilment on pay day. **Lolly water** is a soft or insipid drink. The **lolly boy** originally sold lollies along with icecreams and peanuts and popcorn off a wooden tray round his neck at the cinema. He has come to mean the person who carries and fetches for his boss, as some politicians have done. If you are **caught with your hand in the lolly jar** you have been exposed while profiting surreptitiously.

long acre/paddock   The verge, where animals get free grazing. ANZ.

long drop   A basic outdoor toilet over, or simply a hole, in the ground.

long john   1. Outdoor dunny, where longjohns or heavy underwear had to be divested. ANZ.

2. Oblong loaf of bread.

long pig   A human, originally in cannibalistic context.

long tall streak of weasel piss   Lanky person. ANZ.

long time looking at the lid   Dead for some time.

long-distance call on the big white telephone   Vomiting into the toilet bowl. ANZ.

looks like a one-armed taxidriver with crabs Very busy. ANZ.

looks like a one-legged man at an arse-kickers' party Uncomfortable. ANZ.

looks like the back end of a cow Ugly.

looks like the scum off a Chinese pisspot Scungy-looking food.

looks like two ferrets fighting in a sack Large person's rear.

loopie A tourist, who travels in a quick and maybe foolish loop and then is off. A dismissive term popular in the South Island.

loosie Loose forward, or the open side and tight side flankers and number eight at the back of the scrum in rugby union, compared to 'the tight five' forwards.

Lotto The weekly national lottery, which it is a contraction of.

lounge bar Private bar in hotels, where ladies were allowed before the 1970s, when they were not permitted in the public bars.

love you to bits! Expression of lighthearted fondness, casual farewell or desire for extreme intimacy.

love your work I like or approve of you, used as a greeting or farewell. Current teen usage.

low as shark/whale shit About as unacceptable as a person can be. ANZ.

lower than a coalminer's fart Despicable.

luck of a Chinaman Very lucky, enjoying good fortune, sometimes implication you do not deserve it.

lug-punch A natter with a friend. *Lug* is Scots for ear.

lunatic soup Alcohol. ANZ.

lunch box The bum. To **open your lunch box** is to fart.

lungbuster Cigarette.

lurk A sham or smart plan or cushy job, often in the phrase **on a good lurk**. ANZ early C20.

lusty Attractive person. Teen slang.

lux To vacuum, short for the Electrolux vacuum cleaner. With a particular attachment you can **lux the venetians**.

mad Fashionable, to a new millennium teenager. Last century it tended to mean amusingly angry, as in following examples.

mad as a maggot Very silly or eccentric. ANZ.

mad as a meataxe Very silly or angry. ANZ.

mad-dog To pester persistently, as offspring are wont to with a busy parent.

maggot pack Meat pie.

maggot magnet/taxi Sheep.

maggoty Unwell or irritable. ANZ c1915.

magic sponge, the The sponge full of water applied to injured rugby players with astonishing restorative results. ANZ.

magic word, the The required comment, usually the word 'please', eg, 'You don't get a sweetie until you say the magic word.'

magpie A thief. Originally WWII Kiwi soldiers referring to somebody taking their tobacco or soap or whatever without asking.

Magpies, the Hawke's Bay provincial rugby team, from their black and white playing colours.

maimai Any makeshift shelter, often a duckshooters' hide. From an Aboriginal word *mayamaya*, a bark hut, but not in use in Australia. Duckshooters usually have a flask of **maimai coffee**, which includes brandy or whisky to lift the early morning spirits.

Main Trunk The main railway line between Auckland and Wellington, and once its continuation from Picton south.

Mainland, the The South Island.

mains The main course after entrée and before dessert. Late C20 ANZ and US.

make a box of   Make a mess of something. ANZ.

make a break   1. Run from the police. ANZ early 1930s.
   2. Cut through the opposition in a game of rugby.

make a kai   Prepare a meal, among central North Island forestry workers.

make a sale   To vomit.

make your marble good   To improve your position, as you attempt to do in the game of marbles. ANZ c1925.

makings   Roll-your-own materials, the loose tobacco in a pouch with cigarette papers. ANZ and among wartime allies.

makeover   Product-driven improvement to house and garden. From 1990s.

mallowpuff Maori   Maori perceived as soft on maoritanga or less than committed to Maori culture, from the biscuit that is brown on the outside and white within. From 1980s.

malt sandwich   Glass of beer.

mana-muncher   Maori tribal infighter over assets, from 1990s increase in Waitangi Treaty claims.

mango   Kiwi $50 banknote, from its orange colour.

mango tackle   Head-high tackle.

mangy   Mean-spirited. ANZ.

Maori   Dismissive adjective in non-Maori use for anything perceived as below strength or poorly performed. Some examples follow, most of them offensive:

Maori cannon   A billiards, snooker or pool shot that has gone astray and cannoned into the balls not being aimed at.

Maori chief   Kiwi fish which looks as if its head has been tattooed.

Maori carving   A frown.

Maori Day   Waitangi Day.

Maori foreplay   Are you awake?

Maori holiday   The day following payday.

Maori huntaway   A stone used to move sheep.

Maori kisses   Kiwi biscuits using cocoa, milk, butter, flour, sugar and baking powder.

Maori Magna Carta   Treaty of Waitangi.

Maori overdrive   Coasting your car downhill in neutral gear.

Maori porridge   Boiling volcanic mud, much to the distress of tourists who believe everything they are told.

Maori pyjamas   Marijuana.

Maori roast   Fish and chips or a pie and a jug of beer.

Maori screwdriver   Hammering the screw in with a hammer.

Maori season   Maori permitted to catch trout any time they like.

Maori sidestep   Barging straight into somebody.

Maori splice   Any quick and effective way to save hours of work, like splicing an eye in a wire rope.

Maori strum   Defined by Neil Finn as 'that chinga chinga pub sound,' *Noisy Neighbours*, TV2, 26 November 1992.

Maori time   Easygoing, unconcerned about time.

M

Maoriana   European ceramics featuring Maori imagery, such as a cute little marae version of a weather-cottage, popular in the 1950s and 60s for the tourist trade.

Maori-bashing   Most of the above examples, and any criticism of Maori perceived as unfair.

maorihead   A tall swampgrass.

Maoristan   A self-declared Maori state, c2000.

mare and foal   Bankroll.

mares' nest   A ladies' bar. Mid C20.

marrowbone country   The high country where the weather cuts to the marrow.

massive!   Exclamation of considerable approval. ANZ.

matagouri mermaid   A sheep as the object of a lonely shepherd's fanciful love interest.

match-farming   Burning off land. Mid C20.

match-happy   A farmer overly keen on burning off land.

mate Companion or partner, often used affectionately in the phrase **me old mate**. From earliest days of settlement. Reached epidemic proportions in ANZ rugby league circles and now butt of comic exaggeration, notably in a TV biscuit ad exploiting the name. Like 'bloody' before it, overuse will ensure its decline.

mate's rates Cheaper charges to friends. ANZ.

mateship Male bonding ANZ style.

Maussie Maori Australian.

max, to the Supreme effort or ultimate experience, short for 'maximum', eg, 'Every sport he had a go at, man, he took it to the max.'

Max Blacks National men's Cricket Max team.

may as well be caught for a sheep as a lamb If you are going to do something dodgy or illegal, commit yourself to doing it properly. ANZ.

McJob A low-paid service industry job, such as at McDonald's fastfood outlets.

MDO A sickie, as in **Maori Day Off**.

meadow cake Cow pat. ANZ.

meatbeater Male masturbator.

Meccano set The Mt Eden Prison scaffold, still used by those in favour of its return or as an example of obsolete gallows humour.

member of the Wandering Hands Society A man or woman who fondles another sexually without asking, often **WHS**. ANZ.

mermaids The police at weigh stations, because they are 'cunts with scales'. ANZ.

metho/metho king Methylated spirits addict. ANZ.

Metho Methodist. ANZ.

mic-a-mic Scrub, possibly Maori *uki-uki*. From c1870.

michael/mickey/mickeydidi The vagina, from obsolete English word *mick*, female genitals. Thus **michael-muncher/minge-muncher**, a cunnilinguist. ANZ.

Mickey Do/Doolan A Catholic and/or an Irish person, for the common name of Irish folk, and their likelihood to be Catholic. Early C20.

midair passenger exchange   Collision between planes in flight.

Middlemore pass   Rugby ball passed to a player about to be crunched in a tackle that could well put him out of the game and into Middlemore, an Auckland hospital.

mighty totara   The mostly Maori term of respect for someone; when Prime Minister Norman Kirk died in office in 1974, it was said the mighty totara had fallen.

milkshake   1. Marble of a milky complexion.

2. A dose of bicarbonate of soda to enhance a racehorse's performance.

millionaire's salad   Nikau palm heart, a delicacy.

mimi hill   A comfort stop, from Maori word *mimi*, to urinate.

mince   How ship girls describe jumping ship-to-ship. 1980s.

mince about   To lurk. 1980s.

mind your own beeswax/duckhouse/fowlhouse   Mind your own business. ANZ.

mint   Teenage adjective of approval.

minter   In prime condition, very collectible.

Minto bars   Police long batons, from use during the 1981 anti-Springbok Tour protests to control crowds led by John Minto, spokesman for HART (Halt All Racist Tours). Play on two popular confectionery lines, Minties and milky bars.

miserable   Mean with money. ANZ from mid C19.

miserable as a shag on a rock   Forlorn or depressed. ANZ.

miseryguts   A complainer. ANZ.

mish   Hard work, an abbreviation of 'mission' in the sense of something being a mission.

MMP   Make More Politicians/Mega-Mix Puzzle, jokey versions of Mixed Member Proportional Representation, the new New Zealand political system in 1996.

M

mo   A moustache. ANZ late C19.

mob/mobster/mongrel   Member of the Maori Mongrel Mob gang.

mockamock/mockie   The *makomako* or wineberry tree.

mocker   A woman's dress since 1930s. ANZ.

moistie   A desired woman.

mollyhawking   Pinching fish somebody else has caught, the way mollyhawks like to.

Mondayitis   The blues at the beginning of the working week. ANZ.

mong   Mild term of abuse, abbreviation of **mongrel,** which can be a stronger term of abuse.

Mongy   Mongrel Mob gang member.

monkey man   Bank manager who provides your mortgage and represents the monkey on your back. Mid C20.

monkey oyster   Rock oysters found in mangrove swamps, where they appear to be climbing their hosts.

monkey suit   Dinner suit with collar and tie. ANZ.

monte/monty   A sure thing, or something superlative. A tipster will assure you a racehorse is a monty, while you might call somebody who has helped you a monty. Derived from the three-card monte trick in a card game imported from America with the goldrushes. ANZ.

Monzter, the   Disapproving nickname for Te Papa, from the initials 'Museum of New Zealand' and its brutal bulk and superbrutal cost of over $300 million.

mood adjuster   A few beers.

Mooloo   Pantomime cow mascot of Waikato provincial rugby team.

mopey as a wet hen   Glum and aimless. ANZ mid C20.

more arse than class   More energy or luck than intelligence or style, but doing well, eg, 'That new bantamweight has more arse than class.' ANZ.

more cheek than a fatman's arse   Impertinent person.

more front than Milne's   1. Cheeky.

2. Large-breasted woman. Both refer to Auckland's Queen Street department store of yore.

more jungletime than Tarzan   A soldier who has served a long time in the front line; army slang from Asian service.

more money than a bull can shit   Very wealthy.

more strife than a pregnant nun   More trouble than something is worth.

morning glory   Tumescent penis first thing. ANZ latter C20.

mossie/mozzie   Mosquito. ANZ.

mother and father of   The ultimate. Author recalls being threatened as a boy with 'the mother and father of all hidings', and that was long before Saddam Hussein threatened the mother of all wars. British version is 'the father and mother of …', perhaps because traditionally father came first over there.

Mother Cameron's weed   St John's wort, but nobody knows why.

mountain goat   A 4WD taking skiers to the summit.

mountain mop   The plant *Dracophyllum traversii* which Canterbury trampers use to clean pots and billies.

mountain mutton   Venison.

mountain oysters   Sheep's testicles, a delicacy for some.

mountain trout   Early settlers' name for the *kokopu* or cockabully, *Galaxias fasciatus*, a small freshwater fish.

Mount Cook flea   A Southern Alps cave weta that leaps about, unlike its lowland counterparts.

mousetraps   Slices of bread dressed with grated cheese, tomato and such and grilled in oven. Developed from nickname for cheese, which is used to bait mousetraps.

mousetraps in your pocket, to have   Mean with money.

mouth like a torn pocket   A gossip or plain ugly mouth. ANZ.

mouth like a yard of elastic   A gossip.

mouth like the inside of a Pommie's jockstrap   Rank, fuzzed taste from too much booze the night before. ANZ.

move out To develop. Most seasons a new All Black like Chris Jack moves out or expands his game.

moving/shifting the goalposts Changing the rules or objective unfairly in favour of the person doing the changing, from rugby union, eg, 'Inland Revenue keeps shifting the goalposts on what you can claim on expenses.'

mower's blight Ringbarking or killing trees by careless use of a motor mower or similar machinery.

mud dog Unattractive person.

muddy The monk fish, not easy to cook. If done properly a gourmet favourite, as restaurant columnist Des Britten wrote in *Dominion Post* of 18 January 2003, 'but as temperamental as Russell Crowe on the ran tan'.

mudguard Bald head, sometimes with the accompanying phrase **shiny on top, all shit beneath**.

mudguts Fat person. ANZ.

mudhook A hand, maybe of the randy variety, c1915.

Muldoonism Authoritarian and often vindictive style of politics practised by Robert Muldoon, first as Finance Minister 1967–72, and then as both Finance and Prime Minister 1975–84.

mullety A sailor of the mullet boat class, originally for mullet fishing with a broad beam for shallow water work.

mullock Rubbish or nonsense, and **to poke/sling mullock** is teasing or jeering. **To mullock over** is to mock or to shear badly. From 1860s goldmining. ANZ.

multi Multi-millionaire. Popular in Auckland.

mum and dad Mad; a rhyming slang acronym and perhaps a Freudian explanation for madness.

munga/munger/munja Food or a rest break to have a smoke. Army slang, possibly derived from French *manger* or Italian *mangiare*, to eat. Rations among WWII soldiers were **the munja party**. ANZ.

munted Destroyed, defeated, wiped out. A *munt* was an insulting Afrikaner word for a black person, but more likely from Welsh word for 'ugly'. A **munter** is a fool and **munting** can mean ugly.

murder house   School dental clinic. Mid C20.

muso   Musician, usually of the rock music variety. ANZ.

muster an easy beat   Enjoy a comfortable job, originally army use.

mutant   Idiot; popular with teenagers.

mutton   Penis. ANZ.

mutton dagger   Penis. ANZ.

mutton puncher   A shepherd.

muttoner   A deadly punch that renders recipient as lifeless as mutton.

muttonfish   Paua.

muttonflaps   Woman's genitalia.

muttongun   Penis. ANZ mid C20. Orsman speculates freezing works origin.

my arse is a red cabbage   Reassuring phrase, eg, 'If that is not true, my arse is a red cabbage.'

my bloody oath/my colonial oath!/my oath!   Exclamations of affirmation. ANZ.

my heart pumps custard   Sarcastic pretence of sympathy, eg, 'I hear Smithy's down to his last six mill. My heart pumps custard.'

My Vehicle Disappeared Instantaneously   Jokey version of MVDI, Motor Vehicle Dealers Institute.

my troubles/worries!   Exclamations of concern. ANZ.

mystery parcel   Meat pie.

nail   Rustbucket of a car.

nail your hide to the dunny door   Threat of a thrashing, eg, 'If that kid spits one more time on the floor, I'll nail his hide to the dunny door.' ANZ.

naked lady   Pink lily.

nappy valley   A new suburb where young couples having babies predominate, like the Wellington suburb of Newlands in latter C20.

nana   Head, popular in the phrases **to do/lose one's nana**, to lose your temper. ANZ later C20.

narg   An Indian.

nark   To annoy, be annoyed, be annoying or a spoilsport. ANZ early C20.

nasty   Vagina. Possibly emerged from juvenile use of 'nasty' to mean 'naughty' transferred to the use of 'naughty' to mean sexual intercourse. ANZ.

Nat   Member of the National Party.

naughty   Sexual act. Mid C20 ANZ. The iconic Aussie ratbag cartoon character Barry 'Bazza' McKenzie influenced the 1960s generation of young ANZs, including a young John Clarke on his OE in London appearing in the first McKenzie movie, and nothing preoccupied McKenzie more than **having a naughty**.

NBG   No bloody good, eg, 'NBG to that idea, Frosty. You'll have to come up with something better if you want to keep your job.' ANZ.

nearly   is a frequent Antipodean condition of almost reaching an unfortunate state, often in the course of relating an anecdote featuring the narrator. Some examples are **nearly died laughing/**

fell flat on my face/fell over backwards/had a fit/had a heart attack/had a pink fit/had kittens/jumped out of my skin/pissed myself/pissed myself laughing/shit myself/wet myself/went down the tubes/went for a burton Eg 'Sir Les was so funny I nearly died laughing.'

neat as/neat, eh?/neato Pleasing. 'Like my jumper? Neat as, eh?' Local variants of US 'neat', for anything impressive to teens, popular ANZ from later C20.

neddy Racehorse. **Off to the neddies** is off to a day at the races. Late C19 ANZ.

need a good kick up the arse/bum/Khyber/quoit, etc In need of backside disciplining, eg, 'That Pycroft brat needs a good kick up the bum before he gets completely out of control.' ANZ.

Nelson huntaway A rock rolled down a hill to move sheep instead of using a huntaway, the mustering dog. Early C20.

nervous as a newborn kitten in a room full of Rottweilers Very nervous.

nervous burger Cigarette.

nest of sparrows flew out of me arse, a Expression of deep sexual gratification.

nester The rabbiter's little dog, often a Jack Russell terrier, sent down holes to find rabbit nests. Also baby rabbits still in the nest. 1930s.

never say die till a dead horse kicks you Admonition never to give up.

new chum New arrival. From the goldfields, where it was a dismissive term for a greenhorn. ANZ.

new chum's gold Fool's gold.

New Zealand green Locally grown marijuana.

New Zild New Zealand, particularly the way we pronounce it.

next bloke, the Average person, eg, 'I did find the wallet, officer. Fair go. I'm as honest as the next bloke.'

Nga bush Nga Puhi tribe.

Ngati The prefix of a Maori tribe attached for entertaining reasons to any number of local identities such as the following:

Ngati Blow Ngati Porou tribe.

Ngati Cappuccino Café patrons.

Ngati DB Maori beer drinker, from the brand name of Dominion Breweries, one of the two dominant brewers in the country.

Ngati Drongo Not our tribe, eg, 'Those Ngati Drongos are claiming the moon.'

Ngati Irish Waikato tribe, in recognition of their taste for debating injustices they have suffered.

Ngati Pakeha NZers of European descent.

Ngati Walkabout D Company 'was known as the Ngati Walkabout'. *New Zealand at War*, TVOne, 9 May 1995.

Ngati We-Were-Here-First Defensive bach-owners.

nice one Term of approval, mostly by young people, popularised by children's TV presenter Stu Dennison with his catchphrase 'Nice one, Stu'.

nick, in good In fine fettle, of people and machinery. Popular ANZ phrase from old English word *nick*, good physical condition.

nick, in the Nude. ANZ mid C20.

nick away/off To depart, quickly and/or surreptitiously. 'Nick off!' is a command to go away. From English 'nick', to steal. ANZ.

nick out 1. Leave quickly.

2. Claim a wicket in cricket, often by persistent, nagging bowling. Both ANZ, late C19.

nick over Visit a neighbour or friend for a short time.

nickel spinner A bullet used to shoot fish, a play on the fisherman using a spinner as a lure. Mid C20.

nicker A pound note in pre-1967 imperial currency.

night's but a pup, the Early still, too soon to stop whatever. ANZ C20.

ningnong Idiot. ANZ c1960 variation of English 'nincompoop' and 'nignog'and possibly 'ning-nang', a worthless horse.

Nippon Clipon   The Auckland Harbour Bridge, from the Japanese-made outer lanes added later.

nips on, to put the   To ask for a loan of money. You can also **put the nips in**, or **the squeeze on**. From what you do with pliers or nippers. ANZ c1908.

no beg pardons   Full and vigorous and often aggressive commitment, often in sport. ANZ early C20.

no brain, no pain   Teasing consolation to someone who has suffered an injury, usually to the head. ANZ.

no brain surgeon   Not too bright, eg, 'The kid's hard-working and reliable, but he's no brain surgeon.'

no fear!   Expression of refusal or lack of agreement. From 1860s here, elsewhere later.

no flies on you   You are clever, probably in relation to not attracting flies on a hot day. However, if you are freckly, you can also attract **but we can see where they've been**. ANZ mid C19.

no sense in sticking your nose in butter if you have to eat dripping the rest of your life   Discouraging advice against dressing or acting above the station in life you are condemned to.

no time/no time flat   A little time confidently asserted, as in 'I'll finish this kitset construction in no time flat.'

no troubs/worries   Reassuring remark. 'No worries, mate, we'll make it.' ANZ later C20.

no wucking furries   No fucking worries, I can handle it.

nobbler   Dram or measure of spirits. C19 ANZ.

nobody home   Not very bright or not concentrating, often with blame implied, as in 'The winger ran straight round the fullback, who just stood there, like there was nobody home.'

noggin   A glass of beer, possibly from the word meaning 'head' in Britain, and a poured beer is expected to have a head of froth. ANZ.

nohi   Unacceptably inquisitive. Contraction of 'Jack Nohi'.

no-hoper   A failure, either person or racehorse. ANZ mid C20.

North Cape to Bluff   Complete coverage of the country.

nose, a bit on the   Protesting unfairness. ANZ 1940s.

not!   Decisive rejection, the ultimate shorthand sentence, often responding to some expressed or implied perception, as in Wellington car numberplate 'BMWNOT'.

not a dog's show   No chance, eg, 'You haven't got a dog's show of jumping two metres.'

not give a rat's arse   Total indifference. ANZ C20.

not have a bar of it   Total rejection. Early C20.

not know from a bar of soap   Totally ignorant of. ANZ early C20, updated as **not know from a bottle of detergent**.

not know if you're punched, bored or countersunk   Confused. From carpentry terms.

not know your arse from a hole in a flowerpot/a hole in the ground/your elbow   Confused or naive or plain dumb, eg, 'Since he changed to a heavier bat, that opener is hopeless, doesn't know his arse from his elbow.' ANZ

not much chop   Unimpressive. A backfiring car could be considered not much chop. ANZ.

not the full quid   Mentally disadvantaged, from when a 'quid' was a pound note. ANZ.

not to call the King your uncle/not to call the Queen your aunt   Declaration of independence.

not too foul   Quite nice, eg, 'This low-cal beer's not too foul, eh?'

not worth a cracker/a cuntful of cold snow/a pinch of possum shit/a row of shitcans/a tin of fish/two knobs of goatshit   Some of the ways in which something is declared useless. ANZ.

nuddy   Euphemism for nude, often in the phrase **in the nuddy**. ANZ mid C20.

nuggeting   The application of black boot polish to male testicles for male ANZ bonding reasons, from the Australian Nugget brand of boot polish.

nuky Manuka scrub.

number 8 1. A thick-gauge fencing wire used for many quick fixes, including in joke to indicate an ad hoc solution, as a doctor suggested to a patient he might use after an operation came unstuck. A **number 8 man** is one proficient in ad hocery. Not to be confused with:

2. The forward at the back of the rugby union scrum.

nut, the The rugby union ball.

nut out To lose your temper, as in losing control of your nut or head.

OB Outer board, the softer wood borer leave their tracks in, which they do not in heartwood.

O'Briens Boots, after the Christchurch firm that made good solid workingmen's boots.

Ocker An Australian.

octopus clamp A sure grip. From 1930s champion wrestler Lofty Blomfield's celebrated hold.

Oddity, The The *Otago Daily Times* newspaper nickname, from its initials 'ODT'.

OE Overseas Experience, which young Kiwis get, often on a working holiday. John Muirhead coined the phrase in the early 1970s and friend Tom Scott popularised it in his *Listener* column.

off like a bride's nightie/a larrikin's hat in a high wind/a robber's dog/a whore's drawers, etc Swift departure. ANZ mid C20.

off they go, says Bob Munro The mysterious Bob Munro again, this time signalling the start of something, like a race or the divesting of clothes preparatory to sex.

off your face Stoned, usually on marijuana, but also booze and other drugs. ANZ.

off your onion/saucer/tile/top/trolley Insane, in just some ANZ phrases where a substitute for the head is what you are off. C20.

offside 1. In someone's bad books, often in phrase **get offside with**.

2. Ahead of the play in rugby, thereby guilty of an infringement, and probably the origin of the word. Mid C20.

offsider Assistant. Rugby coaches often have them, as do chefs. Originally in C19 the bullock-driver's assistant who worked the right side of the team. ANZ.

oh, bloody good, whacko, Pup! Exultant exclamation. From Kiwis in WWII at some achievement such as downing an enemy plane.

oh how many cows live in Otaki? Ohau, Manakau, Levin, Otaki – chanted quickly. Great Aunt Bea has more: **Ohau can I cross the River Ohau? Waikanae not get across? Otaki a boat and Oroua across, as a Manawatu's done before.**

oil, the/the dinkum oil/the good oil/the real oil/the right oil The right or true information. ANZ C20, from oil prospecting.

old chum/hand Experienced person, originally one with early settler experience that made him superior to the new chum. ANZ mid C19.

Old Country, The The place immigrants here left behind, usually British Isles. ANZ.

Old Dart, The The Old Country, from British dialect pronounciation of 'dirt'. Often referred to London. ANZ late C19.

old man flood The highest flood. Late C19.

old man manuka The toughest manuka log a sawyer has encountered.

old Maori's beard A lichen trailing off tree branches in the early settler days of 1840s, but now more often the outlawed introduced *Clematis vitalba* with its beard of seeds.

on appro On approval, meaning on trial with no obligation to purchase. ANZ.

on board 1. Prepared to join or already part of the team, cooperating with others, eg, 'Clem's on board for the next America's Cup.

2. Fully aware, often used in negative for someone **not on board**, someone not in command of all faculties, eg, 'Clem's not on board these days, in fact, he can't even remember how to tie a standard reef knot.'

on it/the bash/the scoot Drinking spree. ANZ C20.

on side In a desirable or at least satisfactory position, eg, 'We're on side with the neighbours either side of us.' From rugby, where players are penalised if they stray 'off side' at kickoffs and when a player punts.

on the bones of your arse/bum   Destitute or ruined, eg, 'The national lacrosse team's on the bones of its bum. It can only go up from here.' ANZ.

on the burst   Rugby union players advancing successfully through the opposition.

on the outer   Excluded from the group, ostracised, eg, 'Ever since Barbara blabbed to the teacher, she's been on the outer.' From 1950s, perhaps from an 'outer' in WWII, a wound that allowed you out of the war. Early in C20 it was a term for a binge. ANZ.

on the road   Out of work. ANZ C20.

on the trot   A sequence, originally in two-up. ANZ.

on the turps   Boozing heavily, on turpentine if you are desperate. ANZ from 1930s, when some were that desperate.

on the up/up and up   Improving health following illness or injury, eg, 'How's that flu? On the up?' ANZ.

on with   Involved intimately or hoping to be. ANZ.

on your ear   1. Drunk, c1910.

2. Something easily accomplished, c1920, eg, 'That kid can do the most complicated computer games on his ear.'

once more round the gasworks   Call for one more effort.

one brick short of a load   Mentally challenged. ANZ.

one for the pot   Literally an extra spoonful of tea leaves, often in the phrase, 'One for you, one for me, one for the pot.' Figuratively, to promote extra generosity. ANZ.

one for your duckhouse roof   A setback or snub. Derives from the Australian habit of chalking up a score on the duckhouse roof or wall, denoting a delay or defeat. Out of use there since c1910, according to Partridge.

one look is enough   Indication that you are not impressed, or highly impressed, eg, 'One look was enough, I bought the car on the spot'.

one out of the box   An outstanding object or achievement, such as a spectacularly fine day. Contraction of American *out of the band box*, a new item. ANZ 1920s.

one sheep to the acre 1. Steamed currant pudding that is very short on currants, from the consumer's perspective, often in a boarding school context.

2. Not very bright person.

one-dayer A cricket match played in one day, usually between countries, also known as an ODI or One Day International.

one-eyed trouser snake The penis. ANZ c1960s.

oodle Money. Partridge suggests from oodles of boodle. ANZ mid C20.

oozle 1. To obtain illicitly or by scheming. From WWI troops. Orsman sees a combination of 'ooja' and 'wangle'.

2. Meandering term among trampers from 1930s.

op shop Opportunity shop, selling secondhand goods cheaply. ANZ.

OP's Other people's cigarettes, usually requested by someone giving up cigarettes and not having any on them but desperate at the sight of another person smoking. ANZ.

open out 1. Bad behaviour.

2. A game of rugby that becomes free moving.

open slather No constraints, a free-for-all. Maybe Irish *slighe*, access. Early C20 ANZ.

open the books Making an organisation or business available for public examination. Originally an accounting phrase, since the 1980s used by opposition politicians on the government's economic position once they get elected.

open-collar workers People who work at home and most likely communicate by computers.

orange roughy Person or machine with orange hair or colour, or a machine in poor condition, popular in the 1990s, when the fish of that name reached its production peak.

ordinary bloke/joker The only partly apocryphal average Kiwi full of modesty and resourcefulness, if not smugness.

Oriental Parade The well-to-do of Wellington, who live in the ritzy inner suburb of Oriental Bay, eg, 'Cable Street New World is a well-known gathering place for the well-to-do, or Oriental Parade.' The *Dominion*, 4 July 1995.

Oscar Cash, from rhyming Oscar Asche, who was an actor in early C20. ANZ.

Otahu sidestep No sidestep at all, but a battering ram approach to taking the rugby ball forward, eg, 'Otahu sidestep – straight into him.' Graham Lowe, *Aussie League on Two*, 10 April 1994.

Other Side, the Australia, from c1880.

Otira tunnel Sexually available woman on the West Coast, which you enter through the Otira tunnel.

OTR On the rocks, as in ordering a Scotch whisky, 2002.

OTT Over the top, eg, 'That new actor on *Shortland Street*'s OTT, darling.'

our muttons Some person or thing highly regarded, eg, 'Tana should've been captain years ago. He's just our muttons.'

out of it Drunk or drugged to the point of stupefaction. ANZ.

out of your cap Lost your temper. *So You Think You're a Good Driver*, TVOne, 18 December 2002.

out of your tiny mind Your stupidity comes from your impressively small mind.

out of your tree Drunk or demented or both. ANZ.

out on its/your own, like a country dunny/shithouse Alone, morose, or unique, but not necessarily admirable. Early C20. ANZ.

out the back The toilet, eg, 'Sorry, madame, but at this bach you have to go out the back.' ANZ.

out to it Unconscious from excessive alcohol, or heavily asleep. ANZ.

over the fence Unreasonable, greedy, outrageous, akin to being beyond the pale; perhaps a reference to hitting a cricket ball over the fence for six. NZ late C19, elsewhere later.

over the shoulder boulder holder Bra. ANZ c1935.

overstayers People staying here illegally after work permits expired; usually Pacific Islanders.

oxygobblers Old people, as perceived by callous kids, as people gobbling up oxygen and little else.

OYO Own your own, usually a self-contained flat.

Oz Australia.

pack, to go to the   To deteriorate, as seen in many public buildings in order that they may be demolished without much protest. Another way of 'going to the dogs', when a pack is the hunter's or musterer's dogs. ANZ early C20.

pack a sad   Displaying a deficiency or sulking. From the building term for a warp or sag in a wooden structure.

pack of bludgers/deros/drongos/no-hopers/prunes, etc
Unimpressive group, eg, 'Look at those jokers all wearing floppy hats. What a pack of prunes!' ANZ.

pack shit   1. Nervous, if not terrified, to the point of soiling your pants. ANZ.

2. Talk nonsense.

packet from Paris   A baby, probably arriving by stork. ANZ C20.

packie   The person controlling pack-animals.

paddock/pasture lice   Sheep.

paddy batch   Great batch of scones, after an Aussie rugby league player; also the nickname of recent New Zealand star cricket batsman Mark Greatbatch.

Paddy's apples   Potatoes, the Irish food for all meals. Early C20.

Paddy's lucerne   Weed-infested paddock. ANZ early C20.

Paekakariki Express, The   All Black fullback Christian Cullen, who comes from Paekakariki, whence restored steam train expresses venture venerably up the North Island several times a year, where local newspaper the *Paekakariki Expressed* takes on Transit New Zealand with the same flair Cully commands on the footy paddock.

pai/pie on   Good or right, eg, 'That new stretch of fencing is pai on.'

Maori *pai*, good, *pai ana*, suitable.

pain in the puku   Irritating person. Maori *puku*, stomach.

pair   Breasts, eg, 'What a pair on that sheila!' ANZ.

pair of bastards on a raft   Poached eggs on toast. C20.

pair of spectacles   Successive ducks in cricket. ANZ.

Paka-Asia   Pakuranga, an Auckland suburb with 1990s increase in Asian residents. Quoted in local *Evening Standard*, 8 November 1995.

Pakeha   A non-Maori New Zealander. A Maori word of indeterminate origin referring to Europeans generally.

Pakeha time   Rigid time-keeping.

Pakehatanga   The culture of non-Maori or Pakeha New Zealanders, sometimes with the implication that there isn't much of it.

paki/pakihi   Bald patch on a man's head, from Maori word *pakihi*, a bush clearing.

Palmie   Palmerston North.

Panama Road boys   Rugby league lads from a strong league area, Otahuhu; Panama Road is adjacent to the Auckland suburb, in Mt Wellington.

park your puku   Command to be seated.

Parnell shout   Paying for oneself. The phrase lingers from when the Auckland inner suburb was poor but proud, before its makeover as a trendy place to live and eat. In early C20 **to go Parnell** was to pay your share.

Parrie   Paremoremo prison.

parrie   The paradise duck.

part up   Pay for, eg, 'Part up your share of the holiday.' Late C19 ANZ version of 'part'.

party line   Name for sharing your telephone connection with a number of others, in the days before direct dialling.

pash on/pash up   Vigorous kissing and cuddling, with the passion or **pasho session** not necessarily extending to sexual intercourse. ANZ mid C20.

passion-busters Unromantic knickers, originally issued to female members of the Second New Zealand Expeditionary Force during WWII; the term is generally used for any undergarments considered an unreasonable barrier to male lust.

Pat Malone On your own, ANZ rhyming slang C20. Often somebody is **on one's pat**, with not even Malone for company.

patch Gang insignia sewn onto jacket. From 1970s with additions such as **to be patched** or **to patch up** for receiving membership; **a patched member** is distinguished from a 'prospect' who is still earning his patch, and any member is subject to **depatch**, to lose membership.

patio over the playground Big belly. Often used in the phrase **you can't play with the toys if there's a patio over the playground**.

patsy Jar or jug of beer. From Patsy Riggir, former queen of the local country music scene, whose surname sounds like the rigger or squarerigger, a nickname for the obsolete half-gallon jar.

Patu Squad The 1981 anti-Springbok Tour protesters' nameplay on the Red Squad, the more notorious of two squads of several hundred police created for crowd control, issued with the then new long batons, riot shields and helmets. The Patu Squad issued themselves with motorcycle helmets and the shields of righteousness. From Maori *patu*, a weapon.

pav Pavlova cake, named after Russian ballerina Anna Pavlova who toured New Zealand in 1926, the cake appearing the next year in the jellied shape of a tutu, a few years later converting to meringue, with Australians claiming first dip on that recipe. The **pavlova brigade** cooked competitive pavs in the mid C20 heyday of the meringue cake. Now **pavlova** also means snow, according to Jim Hickey, TVOne Weather, 2 October 1989.

pavs and savs Pavlova and saveloys, traditional Kiwi party fodder.

pay through the nose Excessive charge, eg, 'If you want one of the new top-of-the-range BMWs, you pay through the nose.' ANZ.

PC Politically correct, the right way to behave at present, eg, 'Tim is one PC Pakeha, always has to say kia ora when he meets you.'

pea, pie and pud Piecart serving of mince pie with mashed potato and peas sloshed over with gravy. Pat Lawlor recorded its desirability in his juvenile diary of early C20 Wellington.

peabrain Small of intellect, eg, 'That peabrain never manages more than four-letter words in Scrabble.' ANZ.

pearl/pearler/purler Excellent person or thing. British dialect *purl*, to go head over heels, by way of a severe blow or 'purler'. ANZ from mid C19 for a fall physical or metaphorical, evolving the next century into admiration of whatever.

pearl diver The station hand charged with picking wool from dags underneath the woolshed.

peas in the pot, calling for snot Juvenile chant at prospect of having to eat peas. Mid C20.

peasouper Teetotaller in the 1890s.

peewee Small marble.

peggy square A knitted or crocheted blanket square, sewn with others to make a rug, popularised in the 1930s by Peggy Cook. Became a popular gift for the soldiers away at war.

pelt back To be beaten; teenage Kiwi slang variant on Australian meaning to be thrown from a horse.

pen and ink A drink in ANZ rhyming slang mid C20.

penguin A nun in the C20 days when the religious habit was reminiscent of a penguin. ANZ.

Perfume Point Places on the coast where the smell of sewage spoils the scene.

perishable, the Any goods train carrying perishable foods, usually fruit and vegetables.

perk A perquisite or extra benefit informally attached to pay. ANZ.

perkbuster A campaigner against excessive perquisites or informal expenses, notably MP Rodney Hide, out to right wrongs as vigorously as the FBI's crimebusters and Hollywood's Ghostbusters.

perv/perve/pervy Lustful staring or the person who does so. Short for 'pervert'. ANZ mid C20. A **perv show** is a strip show. ANZ.

phat Fashionable, in its fashionable spelling among young people.

physio Physiotherapist or what he/she does. ANZ.

PI Pacific Islander.

pick To guess or predict, eg, 'I'm picking Dim for dux.' ANZ C20.

pick up the ball and run with it Show initiative, as originally William Webb Ellis did with a soccer ball to invent rugby, nowadays more likely to be a finance minister and unlikely to be as felicitous as the first occasion.

pickled eels' toenails and jujubes Answer to a littlie wanting to know what is for dinner.

picnic A problem. You may be intending to picnic on an island but if the weather turns nasty on the yacht there, it could be **no picnic**. ANZ late C19.

piecart Caravan with hinged side-door through which fastfood is dispensed. Often located near a railway station or bus terminus. From 1920s.

piepicker The freezing works employee with the unglamorous job of picking the wool out of the pile of odoriferous sheepskin.

pie on Everything is fine. Maori *pai*, good, and probably from phrase *e pai ana*, it is good, eg, 'She'll be pie on if we can finish loading before dark.' Early C20.

pig Flagon of beer.

pig an' pakeha A hangi or feed of pork and potatoes.

Pig Islander New Zealander, from the land Captain Cook peopled with pigs. Bestowed by Australians.

pig out To eat excessively. ANZ.

pigeon A branch falling on bushworkers like a lumbering native pigeon. Mid C20.

pigeon's milk Good liquor, eg, 'Orrhh, fine drop of pigeon's milk, me old china.'

Piggy Nickname for Prime Minister Robert Muldoon, coined by Steve Whitehouse in a mid 60s student revue at Victoria University of Wellington.

pigroot Any steep hill or track traversed by wild pig.

pig's arse/bum/ear Exclamation of doubt and derision. ANZ.

pig's Christmas parcel Arsehole.

pig's poop and treacle Crude response to asking what's for dinner.

pigs/little pigs in a blanket Oysters rolled in bacon or sausages coated in potato mash.

pigshit, treacle and fried worms Another answer to the dinner query.

pigskin country Land it's preferable to ride on horseback, maybe including masses of pigfern, but after British slang 'pigskin' for a saddle. Hence, **riding pigskin** for rural horseback riding.

piker Somebody who opts out of an activity, usually a drinking bout, eg, 'Mike proved a piker again, didn't come to the party.' **Piking on** your mates disappoints them, because you have not arrived. To **pike out on** your mates is to depart, perhaps in the sense of being rendered unconscious by excessive booze intake. From these meanings comes the general sense of somebody contemptible. ANZ, from British dialect *piker* for a tramp or gypsy.

pikkie A picture, a photograph. The plural 'pikkies' is the cinema. ANZ.

pill Rugby ball.

pillion pickup/pussy Girl on the back of a motorbike, from the 1950s when her driver was called a milkbar cowboy after his entertainment destination.

pillow-biter Male homosexual. ANZ.

pimp Telltale. ANZ, originally used by children. C20.

ping Penalise, usually a referee decision in rugby signalled by the ping of the ref's whistle, popularised by commentator Earle Kirton from 1989.

Ping An Asian, later C20, from perceived high pitch, singsong tone of voice.

ping off Release a missile, usually a stone, from a shanghai or a beebee gun or something more lethal, eg from Glenn Johnston: 'We went out the bush and pinged off a few bunnies.' Word may derive from the sound, what Partridge calls an echoic coinage.

pinhead Fool, for a pinhead could scarcely contain many brains. ANZ early C20.

pinnie pains Menstrual pain, from the days when the flow was contained by pads pinned for safety.

pipi-picker Flash shoe, probably pointed.

piss Beer, ANZ since early C20.

piss all over Defeat easily. ANZ.

piss awful Unpleasant.

piss down Torrential rain. ANZ.

piss easy Exceptionally easy to achieve.

piss elegant Think yourself the height of fashion, do you? ANZ.

piss in Act of easily achieving. In the Super Twelve final the Blues pissed in.

piss in someone's pocket Ingratiate yourself. ANZ C20.

piss in the hand Something that is easily achieved.

piss in/into the wind Not making much progress. ANZ

piss on regardless Determined drinking, ignoring consequences.

piss on someone from a great height Give someone a very hard time, eg, 'That bastard who conned all those pensioners out of their savings deserves to be pissed on from a great height.' ANZ C20.

piss up large Drink long and hard.

piss weak Inadequate.

pissed as a fart Very drunk. ANZ.

pissed as ten pigeons under a mockamock tree Very inebriated, as pigeons become from feasting off the *makomako*, the wineberry tree.

pissed out of your brain Totally intoxicated. ANZ.

pissed to the eyeballs Full of booze. ANZ.

pisser The pub. ANZ.

pissfart Insignificant person or fiddling around, eg, 'How about we stop pissfarting about and finish this drain.' ANZ.

pisshead Persistently heavy drinker from early C20 here, elsewhere later.

pissing it up against the wall Wasting your money or resources.

pissing razorblades Painful urination, from an infection. ANZ.

pissy-eyed Drunk. ANZ.

place where the big nobs hang out Men's toilet. ANZ.

placer A lamb whose mother has died and it has adopted a stone, bush or other object as a mother substitute. ANZ C20.

plain as a pikelet Unprepossessing appearance; eg 'That new actor in *Shortland Street* is as plain as a pikelet.'

planny A man-made forest, usually of exotic trees, short for 'plantation'.

plastic fantastic 1. Revolutionary all-plastic hull designed by Bruce Farr for the yacht KZ7 in the Kiwi challenge for the 1987 America's Cup.

2. Credit cards. At Christmas a lot of us **thrash the plastic**.

plastic tiki culture The trivialising of Maori culture by sales of cheap plastic Maori artefacts.

play doctors and nurses Juvenile sexual exploration between sexes. ANZ.

play the field Go after all possibilities, often in sexual sense, eg, 'Tom enjoys playing the field too much to ever settle down to marriage.' ANZ.

player Person, usually female, available for sex. Mid C20.

plonk Any alcohol, usually cheap and nasty. Originally a dire port sold by the quart. Phrase probably brought back by soldiers from WWII France, where *vin blanc* or white wine would have been a new experience for most of them. ANZ.

plug A good, steady horse, one that plugs along. Late C19 ANZ.

plum The new customer as the car salesperson sees him or her.

plum jam A lamb, in the rhyming way of shearers.

plunk a baby Give birth, a tribute to the Plunket Society's dedication to all Kiwi newcomers. Variations are **to get plunked**, **get trubied**

after Plunket founder Sir Truby King, and **get karitanied** after the founding place of the society outside Dunedin. **To be plunked** is to be pregnant. A **plunket shield** was a contraceptive sheath, playing on the name of the premier local cricket trophy.

pluot A new fruit marriage of apricot and plum, encountered at a wayside stall outside Napier on 14 December 2002, the seller adding these were the best keepers she had bred. Delishimo!

pluty Well off and/or assuming superiority over the rest of us ordinary Kiwi jokers. The plutocracy are found still in suburbs such as Fendalton, Remuera and Kelburn. ANZ from turn of C20.

pogger To meander. 'An interesting perambulation with no rhyme or reason,' according to city council town planning officer Marilyn Ager quoted by Jack Leigh in his booklet *Exploring Auckland on Foot*, 1977.

point the finger at To accuse, often of criminal activity. ANZ.

point/poke percy at the porcelain To urinate. ANZ mid C20.

poke a stick at, more than you can Supply exceeding demand. Too much of anything, like cricket or rugby at the end of the long seasons. ANZ.

poke in the eye with a burnt stick, better than a One way of suggesting gratitude for something that is perhaps less than wonderful, but better than nothing. ANZ.

poke through on the rails A last-second racehorse win by flashing down the inside next to the rails. ANZ c1930.

poked Very tired, eg, 'I've been on a yacht in Cook Strait all day and I am utterly poked.' Adaptation of 'poke', fuck.

pokie Poker machine. Australian from 1980s.

pole To steal. A **poler** is a thief, **to pole on** is to bludge. ANZ early C20.

politico A politician, but possibly carrying the attitude reflected in politicians always coming bottom of any occupational popularity poll. ANZ mid C20.

pollie A politician. Originally US.

Polly Polynesian.

Pom/Pomeranian/Pommie   A person from Britain. May have developed in early C20 century from children rhyming 'immigrant' with 'pomegranate', or from rhyming 'Tommy', the word for the British soldier. **Pommie-bashing** is usually verbal abuse. A **Pommie bastard** is a term of cheery abuse popularised by cartoon Ocker Bazza McKenzie. ANZ.

pomcholygaflasma   Amazing! As indeed is this nonsense word.

po-mo   Post-modern, a literary conceit. Late 1990s, used in *Sunday Star-Times*, 2 February 2003.

Pond, The   The Tasman Sea.

pong   Stink. Maori *puhonga*, stinking.

Pongo/Pongolian   British person. British soldiers in WWI had a forage cap resembling that worn by the dog Pongo in a Punch and Judy show, earning the nickname 'Pongo' from the navy. In WWII adopted name for English servicemen, thereafter for any British person.

pony   Small glass of beer, 140 ml. ANZ.

poo palace   Homosexual bar.

poo pusher   Active male homosexual.

poof/poofter   Male homosexual. Probably from a poof, a soft cushion seat, or the sound of a puff of wind, or a woman's powder puff, all aspects of character attributed by macho Anzacs to male homosexuals, along with limp wrists and mincing manner. General derogatory term for any person more arty and less sporty, or seen as softened by wealth and privilege, like those who live in Pauanui. ANZ C20.

Poofanui   Pauanui, dismissively called in 1990s by those who can't afford to buy into this luxury North Island beach resort.

poorman's whitebait   Shredded potato.

poos and wees   A mild expression of disgust or disapproval, eg 'That's the second year in a row Jill's forgotten my birthday. Well, poos and wees to her too.'

poozling   Scavenging in derelict buildings for recyclable items. Whimsical without known origin.

pop A try or chance at something, when you **give something a pop** or **have a fair pop** at something, eg, 'Reckon I'll give acting a pop.' ANZ 1920s.

popular as a piepicker at a picnic/the pictures Very unpopular, as you would expect smelly wool-floor scavengers to be at your picnic.

POQ Piss Off Quick, before you get a **BSA**, a Bloody Sore Arse. ANZ.

porangi Mentally ill. Use of Maori word for such condition, widely applied to anybody temporarily daft or weird.

Porirua briefcase Portable sound system. 1980s.

pork pie A bad bruise, eg, 'You know, Hughie, in Otahu we call a pork pie a haematoma on the leg.' Graham Lowe to Hugh McGahan, *Aussie League on Two*, 19 March 1993.

Porkalofa Aucklander.

Porklander New Zealander.

porridge pot An active mud pool in volcanic areas of Central North Island.

Port Craig cocktail An egg, Worcester sauce and meths, from remote Southland location.

possie Hiding place and/or useful position, originally Gallipoli dugouts. ANZ.

possum Dear, eg, 'Hello, possum, how's tricks?' Barry Humphries popularised this usage through his alter egoine, Dame Edna Everage.

possum popper Professional possum trapper.

poster A kick at goal which fails from bouncing off either goalpost.

pot 1. An attempt to kick a goal in rugby.

2. To throw a stone, shortened version of pot-shot.

3. To inform on. Latter two ANZ C20.

pot-stirrer Anti-establishment activist, like many a protest leader, causing trouble by stirring up the muck at the bottom of the establishment pot.

potato   A Polynesian, brown on the outside, white within.

potato/potatoes, to have your   To be ruined, a version of 'goose being cooked'.

poultice   A large sandwich using all available ingredients, like an American dagwood.

pound to a pinch of goatshit – and you hold the stakes in your mouth   Confident bet, extending the English phrase 'pound to a pinch of shit'.

Pressbutton/Pressie   A Presbyterian. ANZ C20.

pressie   A present. ANZ.

pricey   Expensive. ANZ early C20.

pricker   Angry or disliking, in the phrase **to get the pricker with**. ANZ c1930.

prickhead   Mild term of abuse that can be affectionate.

priest   A club to stun fish.

pro/probie   1. Probation officer, though the employer has switched from Probation Service to Community Corrections.

2. A prohibition order, preventing someone coming within a certain distance of someone else, usually because of violent actions.

probie   Trainee for a 'white' gang.

Procesh   University students' annual procession, possibly from the way it is pronounced by its participants after a boozy journey through town on satirical floats.

proddy dog/proddyhopper   Protestant to Catholic kids mostly. ANZ.

professor   Excellent, among teens today.

prospect   Trainee for a 'black' or Maori or Polynesian gang, a prospective member.

prowl-car   Police car on patrol. ANZ.

prune   Silly person.

pub pet   The two-litre plastic bottle of beer.

puckeroo   To ruin. Maori *pakaru*, broken. Other spellings include **buckeroo, pukaroo, pukaru, pukeroo** and **pukkaroo.** If you are

puckerooed you are totally tired, as in 'buggered'.

pug of neatsfoot Cup of tea. The pug was the English housekeeper's parlour, neat's foot is a pale yellow oil of similar shade to tea, made from cattle bones and used to dress leather.

Pukatawhino 'Buggered if I know.' You have to say it quick. Often a response to the question 'Where is Waikikamukau?', another placename that can be slowed, to render 'Why kick a moocow?' The usual response to that was, 'Because it kicked me.' Keri Hulme offers her childhood variant: 'Wheatawhakaue?' Answer: 'Pukatawhainau!'

pukeko A gawky fellow, long-legged like the swamp bird.

pukunui Big tummy.

pull/put over a quickie/swiftie Deceive with some clever or dishonest move. ANZ.

pull finger Hurry up. Local version of 'pull your finger out'.

pull someone's tit Tease or make a fool of.

pull your head/neck in Mind your own business. 'Pull your woolly head in — the woodpeckers are flying low,' was the advice to Kiwi troops in Korea. ANZ c1930.

pulpie A pulp-and-paper mill worker.

punch out/over To beat someone up.

punch out a dark one/a nougat/a steamer To defecate. ANZ.

punch someone's lights out Beat somebody badly enough to render them unconscious or unable to see, the lights being the eyes, or the internal organs, perish the thought.

punga The penis.

punter A pickpocket's assistant with the job of distracting the target.

push a turd uphill with a toothpick Very hard work.

push shit uphill Hard work. It becomes nigh on impossible if add **with a pointed stick/a rubber fork**. ANZ.

pussy-knitting Reflections in puddles, the way wool can look after a kitten has played with it.

pussy power Power of the female sex to control men, with sex.

put a horn on a concrete post Appreciation of a properly completed task, everything being there, such as a slap-up meal with all the trimmings.

put a red collar on Cut a beast's throat, usually a sheep. Mid C20.

put a ring around that An affirmation of certainty, such as putting a ring around the name of Chris Jack at lock for the All Blacks in 2003. From circling or ringing an important calendar date. Mid C20.

put across a beauty Doing something smart, eg, 'Tana and Pita put across a beauty of a scissors movement and Pita went in under the sticks without a hand on him.'

put an iron on your shoulder Place yourself in debt.

put away your John Banks Don't use your cellphone here! Early 1990s reference to then Minister of Police John Banks accused of using his cellphone on a flight.

put in Betray, work well, contribute or simply propose. You could put in a slack worker to your boss, put in a good day's work, put in for a present for a fellow worker leaving, or you could put in for a raise. ANZ c1925.

put into broodmare's paddock Be made pregnant.

put one across/around/over/past To deceive somebody. ANZ.

put one on To punch or simply confront. ANZ.

put the cat among the kereru Local version of putting the cat among the pigeons, or generating trouble.

put the shits up Frighten someone. ANZ.

put you crook Mislead or reduce someone's status. From c1930.

put your kicking boots on Achieve accuracy, from goal kicking in rugby.

QFRTB   Quite full, ready to burst; that is, belly very full of beer. ANZ.

quad   Four-wheel motorised farm bike that has replaced the horse. Rural TV personality and weatherman Jim Hickey referred to a 'farm quad' on TVOne News, 16 December 2002.

Quaky Isles, the   New Zealand, being earthquake-prone. Barry Humphries made a short film of New Zealand which shook throughout its duration.

quarter acre, the cult of the   New Zealand preference from pioneering times for every family to have a quarter acre to put their house on. Austin Mitchell satirised it in his 1972 book *The Half-Gallon Quarter-Acre Pavlova Paradise*.

quarter-loaf   South Island version of a half-loaf of bread.

Queen City   Auckland, after its main street.

Queen Street bushie/cocky/farmer   City dweller with a farm.

Queen Street from Christmas, doesn't know   Confused or stupid.

Queen Street Yank   Flashy dresser and probably loud with it, the way WWII American servicemen were perceived walking up this central Auckland street.

queer   Mentally unsound, eg, 'He's a bit queer in the head, that new boy.' ANZ c1925.

queer as a quacking quail   Very peculiar.

queerie   Simpleton or homosexual.

quick quid   Money readily acquired. There's no longer a quick quid to be made from kiwifruit. A 'quid' was a pound note from c1920 until a pound became two dollars in 1967, but the quid-ity lingers as verbal liquidity. If you **make a quid** you are earning money; if you are **not the full quid** you are deemed to be mentally defective; **for quids** is something desired above dollars, eg, 'I wouldn't miss that new production of *Carmen* for quids.' ANZ 1920s.

quick smart   At once, on the double, eg, 'C'mon, lads, let's have the chairs stacked quick smart.' ANZ.

quickie   A swift sexual experience, eg, 'Feel like a quickie, tonight, dear?' ANZ.

quiet, a   A glass or so of beer or other alcohol on your own.

quiet, on the   Secretively or confidentially, eg, 'On the quiet, I reckon those duckshooters are working the reserve.' From 1860s here, elsewhere later.

quince   Wimpy, effeminate person. **To get on somebody's quince** is to annoy them. ANZ c1920.

quite a few   A lot, actually, eg, 'Had quite a few beers last night.' ANZ.

quite nicely   Pretty nigh perfect, eg, 'That'll do quite nicely, girls, the table settings are fine.'

quizzy   Overly inquisitive. ANZ C20.

quoit   Backside, perhaps because it is a hollow ring. To **go for your quoits** is to run fast. ANZ early C20.

rabbit   1. A young woman, eg, 'Joel's making a fool of himself, going out with a rabbit at his age.' ANZ c1920.

2. A Rastafarian prospect.

rabbit on skates, as daft as a   Very silly. Mid C20.

rabbiter's breakfast   A durry and a dump, or a cigarette on the loo.

rabbiting   Causing a rugby ball to be carried illegally across the try line by a second movement. Mid C20.

rabid   Angry. 1960s teen slang. A girl could be rabid about mislaying her frosted pink lipstick.

race off   To seduce. ANZ 1960s.

racehorse   Thin cigarette you rolled yourself. ANZ since 1930s.

rack off!   Go away! ANZ 1970s.

rad   Fashionable. Short for 'radical'.

radical!   Exclamation of mock horror. 'No knickers under his kilt. Radical!'

rad-les-sep-fem   Radical lesbian separatist feminist, the creature that sweeps into establishment male nightmares like Brunnhilde and her Valkyries.

radio with pictures   Television, from the man who introduced it into our community in the early 1960s, Director-General of Broadcasting Gilbert Stringer.

Rafferty's rules   No rules whatsoever, from a boxing reference to a rough house. Extends to lack of honour and restraint, particularly in politics. Rafferty's rules could be said to apply in the first MMP Parliament. Not an Irish name but from a British dialect variation of refractory, variously spelled 'raffatory/raffertory/refatory/reffatory'. ANZ early C20.

rag   No good. Juvenile 1990s slang.

rage   Wild time or wild party, which can be **ragey** or a **rage up**. A **rager** is a party animal or drug binger who likes to rage all night. ANZ 1980s.

raincoat   Condom; its perceived lack of appeal indicated in the phrase **taking a shower with your raincoat on**. ANZ.

raining harder than a cow pissing on a flat rock/raining like a drunken dog   Teeming down, the way it was every day in January 1989 in Auckland.

raise my rent!   Exclamation of surprise, eg, 'Ben's won the double again. Well, raise my rent!'

raisin   Old person.

rajah   The erect penis. Mid C20.

ram down your throat   Something forced upon you, eg, 'Old Foxie's always trying to ram Shakespeare down our throats.' ANZ.

ram it up your bum   What can be done with something unwelcome, eg, 'Old Foxie can take his Shakespeare and ram it up his own bum.' ANZ.

randy as a bitch on heat/a bushed billygoat/a drover's dog Panting for sex. ANZ.

random   Weird person or behaviour to a teenager today.

rangatira   Leading citizen or magistrate in earlier days, now informally of anybody important. Sometimes used ironically, eg, 'Ever since he made prefect, Ronnie's been coming the rangatira, trying to boss everybody.' From Maori for chief.

Rangitoto Yank   Aucklander, implying brashness of those who live on the land around the young volcanic island of Rangitoto.

raped on   A put down, to a modern teenager, eg, 'The new maths teacher must have raped on everybody in the class in the first week.'

rapt   Ecstatic, or at least pleased. Short for 'enraptured'. ANZ 1960s.

rare/scarce as frog's feathers/hen's teeth/rocking-horse shit Extremely uncommon. ANZ. From C19 US 'scarce as hen's teeth'.

rark   Hoon around in a vehicle.

rark up Stirring up, or the act of scolding severely, or simply an argument; 'The new FOL president did his best on the *Holmes* show to rark up the trade union position.' Unknown origin. 1990s.

Raro A Rarotongan, sometimes any Pacific Islander. Early C20.

rash, all over someone like a Tiresomely attentive, often sexually.

rata flood The 100-year variety, though they seem to come every few years these days of global warming. George Hall recalls Lower Hutt folk called all big ones by this name.

ratbag/ratter 1. Nasty, eccentric, unreliable, troublesome, uncouth or worthless person, likely to exhibit **ratbaggery** or unacceptable or eccentric behaviour, eg, 'Every afternoon he hogs the pool table. Typical of his ratbaggery.' This condition could also, depending on the context, mean

2. Engaging rogue or unconventional fellow, often an **old ratbag**.

The first meaning extends to mental instability in those who **have/ get a rat (in the garret)**. This condition could require a visit to the **rathouse/rat factory** or psychiatric hospital. Unless you are just drunk and hallucinating or **in the rats,** which could provoke someone to **give you rats** or a scolding. If you **rat on** someone, you fail them or betray them, often to the police, or abandon, in literal and figurative senses, eg, 'In the 1970s there was a trend for priests to rat on their vows of celibacy and get married, but they had to leave the priesthood.' Both ANZ early C20.

rat double Small bets for small returns on horseracing. Mid C20.

ratch/ratshit Feeling horrible from booze or ill health, or person or object such as food or machinery attracting disapproval as incompetent or unpleasant. A ratshit attitude is one you deplore, as in a surly teen who lives in squalor, who for his or her part **doesn't give a ratshit**, or does not care at all. ANZ.

rate of knots, a Travelling fast. ANZ from mid C19.

ratfuck Cause excessive harm, eg, 'Drug dealers often ratfuck each other, not just on deals but even enticing rivals into boobytrapped marijuana plantations.' 1990s.

rations Sexual entitlement, often used negatively in **cutting your rations**.

rat-on A sexual erection, eg, 'Despite vows of chastity, priests find nature provides them with inadvertent rat-ons.' Possibly from the vigorous action of a rat up a drainpipe. 1990s.

ratstail Rotten weather.

rattle your dags Shaking someone up to get on with it. Allegedly from the noise of uncrutched sheep dags or excrement-coated hindquarters flapping together as a sheep moves. From early C20, in an apparent further mix of the British dialect word for dirty hindwool on sheep and the Australian rhyming habit with 'dag' and 'wag'. The combination entwined comprehensively in the phrase **the dags do not wag the sheep**, meaning that the rank and file do not control the leader, a variation of the tail not wagging the dog. Thus **dag-rattling** when a leader reminds followers of how they should behave, something the Prime Minister of New Zealand has been required to do way too often. ANZ.

rattletrap Rundown vehicle, eg, 'Can you credit this rattletrap getting a warrant?' ANZ.

ratty Silly, stupid or slightly eccentric. People get **ratty on/over** when infatuated with another person or project, like those gluttons for punishment who crew America's Cup yachts. Here late C19, elsewhere later.

Razor Gang, the The Cabinet Expenditure Review Committee of the 1980s, the scourge of bureaucratic employment in the days when Roger Douglas was axing public service jobs. The succeeding National Government maintained the Razor Gang through the 1990s.

razz To jeer. Probably from giving somebody the raspberry. ANZ c1890.

razzy roostered Pleasantly surprised, eg, 'The way young Cutler's got the farm up and running in just a few weeks, why, I'm razzy roostered!'

ready A swindle or dodgy activity, eg, 'That lawyer's not to be trusted, he's pulled more than one ready with client funds.' ANZ C20.

readymade, a A cigarette made in a factory, from mid C20, overtaken in use by the older British Navy 'tailormade'.

rearend loader Active male homosexual.

ream The anus, what preceding entry is interested in, as opposed to America, where it is what he does to it. From mid C20.

reck Rubbish, eg, 'That exam was reck, man.' Teen usage.

red-fed Left-wing agitator or somebody who is difficult about workplace conditions. From the nickname for the NZ Federation of Labour, established in 1909 to represent workers' interests.

red sails in the sunset Menstruation, often a male lament at it interfering with sexual activity. ANZ.

reef fish Foreign exchange dealers and other highrisk-taking speculators who dart about unpredictably like reef fish; attributed to Hon. David Lange. 1990s.

rego Car registration. ANZ.

rellies Relatives. ANZ.

remit Branch directive for consideration by central executive.

remittance man British person supported Down Under by a family remittance of money to keep him here. ANZ late C19.

Remmers Remuera, an Auckland suburb.

Remuera rocket/shopping-basket/tractor/taxi 4WD vehicle, late 1990s Auckland, named after the upmarket suburb and its denizens driving to the local mall or school a vehicle made for crosscountry conditions, a case of the genteel underemploying the grunt. The Toyota RAV is known as the **Remuera Attack Vehicle**.

rep A rugby footballer representing a team or province. ANZ late C19.

retread Worker back from retirement, like a tyre that has been retreaded for another working life. ANZ mid C20.

rev up 1. Put life into something, such as a party or an alcoholic beverage, eg, 'This punch needs a rev up. I'll get the vodka.' ANZ.

2. Make somebody feel anxious or try harder, eg, 'That flanker's slacking, about time the coach gave him a rev up.'

Richard Cranium A silly person; elaboration of 'dickhead'. ANZ.

ridie   Controller of a sideshow, maintaining machinery and servicing customers.

rig   Shark. Ministry of Agriculture and Fisheries prefers the spotted dogfish/pioke/gummy shark/smooth hound. Mostly South Island name.

ringbark   1. To circumcise.

2. A worn-out person is **ringbarked.**

3. To fart; ring is old slang for the anus.

ringbolter   Stowaway, from play on 'bolthole' and the 'ringbolts' used on ships for tying ropes to the jetty, up which the ringbolter can travel.

ring-in   A substitute or somebody invited in to make up the numbers, often in a sporting contest. Originally ANZ early C20 for a horse illegally substituted in a race.

riotpack   Carton of wine or beer. 1980s.

rip   To annoy, as in the once popular phrase **wouldn't that rip your ration book**, from the days when you needed an unripped ration book after WWII to purchase essential food items. ANZ 1920s.

rip into   Engage vigorously, the way Super Twelve forwards enter a scrum. Often fisticuffs or a severe reprimand; the former meaning originated in ANZ late C19.

rip, shit and bust   A vow to make a huge effort, from the constipation context. Mid C20.

ripper!   Exclamation of approval. ANZ late 1970s.

RITP   Rip into the piss, which is an invitation to drink up.

roadhopper   A hitchhiker to be found beside the road, hopping like a grasshopper from one car to the next.

roadroller   A bushman or itinerant worker, maybe a country bumpkin. Early C20.

roarer   A creek in full flood.

Rob's Mob   Supporters of late Prime Minister Rob Muldoon, perceived as ordinary blokes.

robber's dog, in like a   Keen or prompt. ANZ.

rock chopper   Roman Catholic, perhaps from initials. ANZ.

rock college   Prison.

rock your socks off   Something that will surprise or excite you — what DJs promise the music will do for you.

rocket fuel   Available alcohol mixed in a softdrink bottle by adolescents aiming to get drunk quick. 1990s.

rockhopper   Coastal fisherman. ANZ c1930. Here can also mean a tramper who has to cross rivers and swollen streams.

rod-walloper   Male masturbator. ANZ.

Rogernomics   The free market reforms of Finance Minister Roger Douglas in the mid to late 1980s.

roll/roll-your-own   Cigarette rolled by hand. ANZ 1920s.

roll over   1.   Give up. Pity help any rugby team that rolls over. From the submissive posture dogs adopt. ANZ.

2. Give up somebody else, in sense of implicating your mates or colleagues, not unknown among those the police take into custody and perhaps do a deal with.

rooster   Person. Amiably meant, often qualified as 'old' or 'odd'. From mid C20.

rooster one day, feather duster the next   The up and down of life, particularly for performers and politicians. ANZ.

roostered   Worn out, often sexually.

root   Sex, the doing verb or the done noun, eg, 'I want to root you' and 'He/She was a good root.' ANZ from early C20.

root, hog or die   Pioneering vow to make every effort.

root more, eat more, drink more piss!   Police Red Squad chant as they dealt with anti-Springbok Tour protesters in 1981, from the acronym 'RED' for Red Squad.

root my boot!   Exclamation of surprise.ANZ mid C20.

rooted   Exhausted from whatever. ANZ mid C20.

rooter   Sexual enthusiast.

root-faced   Humourless.

root-rat   Active heterosexual.

ropeable   Extremely angry. Late C19 ANZ.

ropehead   Rastafarian or pertson sporting deradlocks.

rort   1. Scam, like the dubious welfare claims the authorities are trying to stop.

2. Something exceptional, often a party, called also a **rorter**.

The first meaning came across the Tasman in 1980s, and is generally about political chicanery but, before that, was used to mean sexual intercourse or the female object thereof. Derived from British 'rorty', splendid, rowdy or coarse. ANZ.

rotary hoe   Right oh, a cute way of agreeing with somebody.

Roto-Vegas   Rotorua. *Fear and Loathing in Roto-Vegas* was rated a top Maori film, along with *Four Hangis and a Tangi.*

Rottenrua   Rotorua, from the pervading rotten-egg stink of sulphur.

rottie   Rottweiler breed of dog. 1990s.

rough as/rough as a bag of files/a dog's or pig's breakfast/a goat's knees/a soujee bag/bags/boots/guts/houses/sacks Uncouth, crude or untidy; some of many versions from late C19 ANZ. A soujee bag was made of coarse material and was what Indian flour came in during C19. Teens now use the shortened version 'rough as'. ANZ.

roughie/roughy   1. Difficult sheep to shear, difficult sheepdog, out-of-control cattle, poorly performing racehorse, poorly qualified people or a job poorly done. Early C20 ANZ.

2. Quick and crude sexual bout, or any other somewhat rugged encounter, person, animal, or situation, such as a poorly told joke. Latter C20 ANZ.

rousie   Rouseabout or shearing shed hand in C19, from British dialect word for a rough, active person, reverting somewhat in C20 to mean any menial worker. ANZ.

rousie's chewing gum   Sheep dags, the muddy, excrement-coated wool which forms around the sheep's hindquarters.

rubber guts   Someone lacking intestinal fortitude. Originally the

German naval shell from the Kiwi point of view in WWI.

rubbish To dismiss or scorn, ANZ early C20.

rubbity The pub, as in 'rubbity-dub' rhyming slang. C19. Other spellings include **rubby/rubberdy/rubbidy/rubbidy dub/rub-a-dub/rubblededub**. ANZ late C19.

rubydazzler Something superb. Early C20 variation of 'bobbydazzler'. ANZ.

rugby, racing and beer Accepted definition of New Zealand leisure pursuits mid C20, at least for males.

rugger bugger Rugby fan or rough player of the game. ANZ.

ruly Excellent, as in the popular extension **she rules** or **it rules**.

rumpty Anything excellent, including sexual, sometimes **rumptydooler**. ANZ variation of 'rumtitum' from early C20.

rumptypumpty A bout of enthusiastic sex, eg, 'Fancy a bit of the old rumptypumpty tonight, dear one?'

run/trot, a bad/lean/rough or good Period of misfortune or good fortune, often a bad trot but a good run. From a trot sequence of two heads in the game of two-up, with more words for a bad run/ trot indicative of the game's usual outcome. ANZ.

run around like a blue-arsed fly/a headless chook Erratic behaviour, often manic, like a blowie buzzing a dead sheep. ANZ.

run like a hairy goat/stink Both mean to move either very slow or very fast. ANZ.

run rings around Defeat easily. ANZ early C20.

runner Worth considering, eg, 'Helen Clark might say he was never a runner for Cabinet.' 1990s.

rustbucket Decayed car. ANZ latter C20.

Rusting Tower of Visa, The Bank of New Zealand Wellington headquarters, rust apparent during lengthy construction period stalled in latter 1970s by a spat between the Boilermakers Union and confrontational Prime Minister Muldoon.

ruth Vomit, often in the phrase **cry ruth,** the word expressing the sound of the action. ANZ latter C20.

Ruthanasia   Policy of savage cutting back of state benefits by Minister of Finance Ruth Richardson, specifically her bill to reduce welfare benefits by $780 million from 1 April 1991, reported in *Time* magazine, 22 April 1991.

Ruth's Rottweilers   Treasury officials keen to do her slash policy on state benefits. 'Ruth's rottweilers must not be allowed to dictate terms to the ultimate disadvantage of all.' Dr Ian Shearer, Dean of Auckland Technology Institute, *Dominion*, 20 June 1991.

R

sack rash 1. Scarring from vigorous activity in bed.

2. Ugly person.

sailer Loose branch, one that will sail in the next high wind. A logging term. Mid C20.

sale To vomit; usually you **make a sale**.

salmon day, a A work day wasted swimming against the current of problems and getting nowhere.

salubrious Fine weather among trampers, for whom **salubing** is sunbathing, and a **salubrium** a rest in the sun. Mid 1930s.

same as your tongue and a little older than your teeth My age is none of your business.

Sami Samoan.

sammie Sandwich. ANZ.

Samoan steroids Ground taro root, staple food in Pacific Islands cuisine.

sandwich short of a picnic Mentally disadvantaged. ANZ.

Sandy Hookers Nelsonians, specifically local musterers, from living near Farewell Spit.

s'arvo This afternoon, as in 'See ya s'arvo.'

sausage jockey A woman with a reputation for riding men sexually.

sausage sizzle Selling barbecued sausages in a slice of bread, usually for $1 as a fundraiser. Latter C20.

sausie/soss/sossie A sausage, or a penis.

save a match and buy a farm Adage encouraging thrift.

save it Keep it to yourself, I don't want to know.

save your breath to cool your porridge   Conserve your words or energies, they are not required. ANZ.

save your money and buy a pie   Decline of loan request with admonition to go feed yourself instead of trying to feed off others.

saw and say nothing   Hold your counsel. From sawmilling.

saw off me legs and call me tripod!   Exclamation of surprise.

sawdust sandwiches   Hard rugby practice indoors, usually in a sawdust-floored gym. Coach Frank Walker explained Wellington's win over North Harbour, in the *Evening Post*, 14 August 1995: 'I think it's those sawdust sandwiches they eat.'

sawing wood   Snoring.

sawyer   The tree or bush weta, c1880, from the scraping sound it makes with its legs suggestive of a bushman's saw.

scaler   Someone who steals, especially from his mates or from a prostitute whose favours he has enjoyed. From British dialect *scale*, to depart hurriedly. ANZ.

scaly bloke   Thin man, from 1930s Depression.

Scandy   A Scandinavian.

scarfies   Dunedin students, from the scarves they wear at rugby games.

Scarfieland/Scarfyville   Dunedin. 'It meant putting in a few nights without booze in Scarfyville.' Marc Ellis, *Evening Post*, 8 March 1993.

schlong   Penis, perhaps pretend Yiddish. ANZ.

schoolie   Sexy schoolgirl.

scissors, the   Rugby back movement where two players cross and pass the ball at same time, one continuing as the dummy runner while the other swoops in to score a try, if it works according to plan.

scoat dog   Undesirable person, to a teenager.

scoaty   Ugly.

scody/scady   Something admirable, or not admirable. Street slang, deriving from skateboarding. 1990s.

scoffler/scoofler/scoofter/scuffler   A wild pig.

scone   1. Head, which is roundish like a scone. ANZ.

2. To hit somebody on the head. Orsman suggests from British dialect *scon*, hit with flat of the hand. However, Partridge alludes to 'sconce', crown of the head, used among Kiwi servicemen in WWII in the phrase **do your sconce**, lose your temper. Nowadays it tends to be **do your scone**. **Off your scone** means you are mad. **Suck your scone in** is advice to stop talking nonsense or mind your own business. **Use your scone** is advice to act sensibly. All 1940s ANZ.

scone dough isn't properly mixed   Dim-witted.

scone hot   Superb, eg, 'An uninjured Chris Cairns is a scone hot cricketer.' ANZ 1920s.

scone in the oven   Pregnant; variant of the bun.

sconegrabber   A toddler.

scoot   Drunken bout, usually in **on the scoot**. ANZ 1920s.

Scotch mist and duck under the table   Answer to 'What's for tea, Mum?'

Scotchman's/Scotsman's grandstand   Non-paying view of a sporting event, often from advantageously placed building or foliage. Sometimes the controller of the unofficial stand will charge a fee for its use.

Scotchman's/Scotsman's shout   Entertainment paid for by parties indulging, though they wouldna object if you paid more than your share.

Scottytanga   Otago folks' alleged predilection for borrowing without asking.

scrag   Anything inferior. A poorly performing new team in a competition could be **scrags**. In forestry a **scragging area** has been cut already and has remnants to work. Derived from **scragends**, the poorest cuts of meat. Whaling term C19 for remnants, from British dialect word for useless leftovers. Possibly linked to 'scrag', neck. ANZ.

scrapers   Your feet when you are running away and **take to your scrapers**. From Anglo-Irish *scraper*, foot.

scratch cat   Woman of ill temper. From early C20.

scratchie   Lottery ticket from which you have to erase the top layer to reveal the potential prize. 1990s.

screwy   Crazy, from 'a screw loose'. Early C20; elsewhere later.

scrog/scroggin   The dried fruit, nuts and chocolate that provide a high energy snack when tramping.

scrub   1. The bush, ANZ C19.

2. To reject, as a player might be scrubbed from the All Blacks. ANZ 1930s.

scrum   An all-in tussle, like the political scrum we see every three years. From the rugby scrum.

scull/skull   Drink alcohol fast, from Scandinavian toast *skol*.

scunge   To beg or borrow, as with cigarettes.

scungy   Dirty person or place, such as a student flat. From Australia c1920, possibly mixing 'scurvy' and 'gungy'. A **scungebucket** is a derived term of abuse.

scunner/skunner   Any strong dislike, from Scottish and Irish dialect *scunge*, sly person and slinking behaviour.

seagull   Casual, non-union wharf labourer who, like a seagull, was on the wharf waiting for scraps — of work, not food. From 1930s. Used now for a scavenging loose forward in rugby.

seagull's breakfast   Traditional bushman's breakfast of a yawn, a piss and a look around, with the addition of a walk on the beach.

Sealord Bonefishery   Nickname for Maori-controlled Sealord Fisheries.

section   Plot of land to build on that has been getting smaller as its cost rises.

see a star about a twinkle   Need to urinate. ANZ.

see you in church/court/jail   Goodbye indeed. ANZ 1930s.

see you in the soup, bring your own spoon   Warning of hard times coming and expect to look after yourself. ANZ.

seed beast   Compulsive male masturbator.

seedless raisin Married man with no children; of army origin.

seen better heads on a glass of beer Not an attractive person. ANZ.

seen better legs on a billiard table Thickset and unshapely legs. ANZ.

seen more pricks than a dartboard/pincushion Promiscuous person. ANZ.

sell out Vomit. ANZ.

sell the horse Bar game where the one who guesses the number written down collects the pool of money, a version of 'sell the pony' or tossing to see who buys the drinks. Early C20.

semi/semis The semi-final of sporting competition. ANZ.

send up gutless Make fun of.

seppo Angry, as in septic.

seppo nuts Troublemaker.

septic Angry; **go septic** is to get angry.

septic tank Any person or thing that is regarded poorly and with which it rhymes, like a Yank and a bank and a wank. ANZ 1970s.

serve, a A foul blow in rugby; often cited by commentators in rugby league matches, from old British verb 'serve', to wound or injure. Possibly carries echoes of the serve of tennis and the work of a waiter in an ironic fashion, for the phrase is often presented as **serving up**. ANZ.

sesh A session, especially smoking marijuana, but also gossiping. Teenage use late 1990s.

sesqui, a An incompetent mess, muddle or failure. From Wellington City Council's sesquicentennial celebrations in 1990, marking 150 years of Pakeha settlement in New Zealand with millions misspent on entertainment that pleased virtually nobody. Spin-off phrases that did not linger were **dry as a sesqui**, which could be the condition of your throat or wallet; **away with the sesquis**, which was even less well performed or focused than somebody 'away with the fairies'; **get a good sesquiing**, to be exploited comprehensively.

session A period of drinking alcohol. ANZ mid C20.

set against/on A strong objection, eg, 'Caleb has a set against all Mormons.' ANZ early C20.

set alight Start or energise, eg, 'The mayor set alight the fundraising for the stadium with her launch speech.' From mid C20.

set in a crack To resolve something quickly or be well placed, like somebody who held on to his Brierley shares through the crash and is now set in a crack. From late C19, when whips were in skilful use.

set like a jelly Well placed, ready to go.

sexo Randy person. From mid C20.

shackledragger An Australian, from the shackles worn by early convict residents.

shade To be slightly better than somebody, eg, 'Justin shaded Byron for the halfback position.' ANZ C20.

shagger's back Sore back from excessive shagging or sexual intercourse. ANZ.

shagging wagon Van or stationwagon where shagging is conducted. ANZ c1965.

shagnasty Salutation or greeting, as in 'G'day, shagnasty, how's it goin?' Originally British for an unpopular man.

shake An earthquake, from earliest times.

shake 'n' bake suburb A new suburban area built quickly from kitset and composite materials, referred to in *NZ Listener*, 26 January 2002.

shake your shirt Apply yourself, as when a labourer removes his shirt. With an exclamation mark, 'Get a move on!'

Shaky Isles, the New Zealand, land of earthquakes. ANZ.

shame Excellent, in the reverse habit of today's teenagers.

shandygaff 1. A mongrel sheepdog, from the word meaning a mix of beer and gingerbeer or lemonade.

2. Poor performer, such as a weak government.

shanghai/shangie Catapult. Although the New Zealand version tends to be a single strip of rubber cut off an innertube, with a slingshot purse attached to house the hurled stone, the word

S

appears to derive from the Gaelic *seangan*, a cleft stick, as in the conventional British catapult with rubber attached between the prongs. The act of being shanghaied or kidnapped and forced to crew a vessel appears to have come later. Mid C19 ANZ.

shanty A pub, nowadays tending to refer to remote rural establishments. From the goldfield days of tent hotels. ANZ.

shark biscuit Surfboard or boogie board, a small inshore surfing board — and not entirely jokey, for shark have been known to take an exploratory bite out of these fish-shaped polystyrene objects.

shark 'n' shavings/taties Fish and chips, the fish often shark.

shat/shat off Angry or depressed. ANZ c1945.

shave Shorn young man, of the sporty rather than tattooed skinhead kind. Late1990s.

she A substitute for 'it' in popular phrases such as **she'll be right/ she's apples/she's jake/she's right/she's sweet**, all assurances that everything is fine. ANZ latter C19.

sheepcocky Sheep farmer on a modest scale. ANZ late C19.

sheep king/baron Wealthy sheepfarmer, ANZ latter C19.

sheepo Shepherd, specifically the musterer of sheep into pens, from the cry employed. ANZ early C20.

sheepshagger An Australian, to rude New Zealanders, and vice versa. The shagging component refers to a sexual predilection for sheep. ANZ.

sheepshit for brains Unpleasantly jocular suggestion of low intelligence.

sheep's back, living on/off the Relying on wool to sustain income handsomely. ANZ 1930s.

Sheffield blight The elimination of vegetation by axe or slasher; from the fine steel of Sheffield.

sheila Woman or girl, probably from common Irish name Sheila, Gaelic *Sile*.

shellacking Severe beating, verbal or physical, on the field or down the back alley. ANZ.

shellshock Alcoholic spirits. ANZ mid C20.

shepherd's grummet A sheep as an object of shepherd's desire.

shepherd's shandy Glass of water containing a sheep dag.

shepherding Deliberate interference with players who could apprehend the ball-carrier in rugby. Originally referred to a golddigger who had become a squatter and was aiming to keep others off his claim.

she's all wool and a yard wide Fat woman. ANZ.

she's on 1. A woman regarded by male as available for sex.

2. Anything that is going to happen, such as a bet or a game, eg, 'Reckon she's on for tomorrow if the weather holds.' ANZ.

shick/shicker/shickered/on the shicker Drunk. From the Yiddish word *shiker*, to be drunk. ANZ 1880s.

Shield, The The provincial rugby trophy the Ranfurly Shield, which requires the **shield holder** to play **shield matches** which usually generate **shield fever** among the supporters of both the holder and the challenger, to be compared with the now obsolete gift of another governor, the **Plunket Shield**, for provincial cricket teams.

shift To move house, from late 1920s. If you **shift along** you are moving yourself, and speedily, often used as advice to a slowcoach.

shingle short, a Mentally challenged. From mid C19. ANZ.

shirtlifter Homosexual, right back to convict days, when a shirt was the only clothing issued. ANZ.

shit a brick!/shit a brick and fart a crowbar Extreme exclamation. ANZ c1925.

shit a brick and build a house Exclamation, often at unexpected good luck, eg, 'Shit a brick and build a house, he's in for three tries in the first half!'

shit all over Beat easily, eg, 'In recent years the Canterbury team has shat all over the opposition.' ANZ.

shit, eh? Expression of ironic astonishment, eg, 'Anton's back in the All Blacks. Shit, eh?' ANZ c1945.

shit-features Ugly person.

shit for brains Stupid person, eg, 'When it comes to any eye–hand coordination, Monty's got shit for brains.' ANZ.

shit in Win easily, eg, 'Wellington will shit in against Wairarapa Bush.'

shit in your own nest Ruin or do something to your own disadvantage, eg, 'Sacking half her Cabinet is just shitting in her own nest.' ANZ.

shit of a thing Something unacceptable or unpleasant, eg, 'Shit of a thing losing three quick wickets in the ten minutes before lunch.' ANZ.

shit oh dear/oh dearie oh Exclamation of regret, if not lamentation, eg, 'Bowled for a duck first ball in both innings — shit oh dearie oh.'

shit on the liver Bad-tempered, eg, 'The way that mayor always snaps in public, you'd think he had shit on the liver.' ANZ.

shit oneself/one's pants Disconcerted by fear or anger, eg, 'Thought I'd shit meself when all these bikies surrounded me at the lights.' ANZ.

shit out of Missing something, maybe luck, eg, 'Bowled by a rank full toss on 99. Poor Stephen was shit out of.'

shit-puncher/stabber/stirrer Aggressive male homosexual. ANZ.

shit sandwich Male homosexual act.

shit show, not a No chance. ANZ

shit someone off Annoy someone, eg, 'It really shits me off when you come round banging on the door at two am for no good reason.' ANZ.

shit tacks Afraid, eg, 'When that rottie came at me, man, I was about to shit tacks.' ANZ.

shitfish The *parore* or blackfish, because it is purported to prefer sewer outlets.

shithead Objectionable person. ANZ early C20.

shitty A really vile mood. Displaying such can be to **crack/pack/throw a shitty**, eg, 'Old Nort really packed a shitty when someone let his cows out again.' ANZ late 1930s.

shivers! Mild exclamation. ANZ.

shivering like a shag shitting razorblades Wind-chill factor, eg, 'One more minute in this damn maimai and I'll be shivering like a shag shitting razorblades.'

shoemaker The white-chinned and other species of petrel, from the tapping noise they make when at home. **Westland shoemaker** is the Westland black petrel.

shonky Dodgy or unsafe, as in pyramid salesmen or the rotting walls of new houses. Crossed the Tasman in the 1980s, identified by Orsman as probably derived from 'shonk', abbreviation of *shonicker*, an offensive name for a Jew.

shook on Attracted to someone or something, usually used in the negative of being **not too shook on**. From a past participle of 'shake' in the dim distant past. Latter C19 ANZ.

shoot in Put in jail, eg, 'Pat was shot in for brawling in the street.' From 1910.

shoot off/through Depart hastily, often leaving behind someone in trouble, eg, 'Jack shot through once he heard Mabel was preggers.' ANZ early C20.

shoot your bolt Male sexual ejaculation. ANZ.

shooting blanks Man failing to fertilise a woman.

shooting bunnies Farting.

short arms and long pockets Mean person.

short fuse/wick Quick tempered.

short of a sheet of bark Mentally deficient. ANZ.

short of change Mentally limited. ANZ.

shortie Undersized and thus illegally harvested crayfish.

shot full of holes Drunk. WWI soldiers.

shot to the eyeballs Very drunk. ANZ.

shotty 1. Shotgun.

2. Excellent, to a teenager.

shoulder surfing Reading people's PIN number over their shoulder at an ATM machine, with a view to stealing the card and using the number later. Late 1990s.

shouse Lavatory, diminutive of 'shithouse'. ANZ mid C20.

shout Round of drinks, maybe a free one, or a treat. From the need to shout to have your order heard. No need when it is the **house shout**, when the barman treats you to a free drink. ANZ mid C19.

shove under To kill; **shove underground** is simply to bury, whether or not you killed the body first. ANZ late C19.

shovel it! Expression of disgust or disbelief, suggesting what you can do with your bullshit.

show A chance. Another egalitarian expectation from the goldfields, eg, 'Give us a show, will ya, I've only had three lots of practice darts.' ANZ.

show a point to To swindle or deceive. Late C19. Now more likely to be **show a trick to.**

shower, I didn't come down in the last Rejection of ignorance or gullibility. Indignant claim to know more than one is credited with. ANZ C20.

shrapnel Small change. WWI soldiers referred thus to French currency, full of holes as if hit by shrapnel. ANZ.

shrewdie Clever person or clever behaviour, often in the phrase **to pull a shrewdie**. ANZ early C20.

shrimp Small and/or wimpy person. ANZ.

shufti A look. WWII soldiers from the Arabic *safa*. ANZ.

shunt 1.Dismissal. Many civil servants got the shunt during government restructuring. ANZ.

2. Ensure a horse does not do well, in order to have its weight reduced in future races. ANZ.

shut the gate Indicative of an unassailable situation, usually a team with an unbeatable lead. 'When the Blues passed 50 with 10 minutes to go and Natal had only three points on the board, it was shut the gate.'

Siberia   The General Assembly Library, the far end of Parliament where Opposition MPs are consigned.

sickie   A day off work, maybe sick, maybe not, almost certainly the latter when a test match is on and large numbers of mostly male staff **take/throw a sickie**. ANZ mid C20.

sicko   A person who is mentally ill or masquerading as such or a particularly unpleasant criminal or psycho, eg, 'That joker arrested for stabbing his stepdaughters — man, he is some kind of sicko.'

sidecars   Foolish passenger leaning out car window while driver goes as close to parked cars as he dares without damaging the passenger.

sideways   Suicide. A euphemism suggesting you are not leaving this world front-on.

sifting   Taking it easy, eg, 'It's great sifting around at the bach weekends.'

silent policeman   The concrete bump or judderbars that slow down traffic. ANZ mid C20 combination of the American 'silent cop' and the English 'sleeping policeman'.

silly as a square wheel/a two-bob watch/a wet hen/a Woolworth's watch   Very silly indeed, 'bob' meaning the imperial shilling. ANZ mid C20.

Silver Ferns   National Kiwi netball team, after insignia worn on uniform.

since Adam was a cowboy   A metaphoric means of indicating a long time ago. Less popular variations include **since Dick Seddon was a boy/God made little green apples/God gave chickens teeth/Jesus had the measles/Jesus played fullback for Jerusalem**. ANZ in most cases.

sink   Imbibe alcohol. Footy teams have been known to sink a few beers after a game. Early C20 use here before elsewhere.

sink the boot in   To kick opponents, too common in games of rugby. Can be used metaphorically, as a politician does verbally to an opponent. ANZ.

sinking lid   A 1980s policy of reducing public servant numbers by not replacing those who leave by choice or by demise.

siphon the python Male urination. ANZ mid C20.

sit down and I'll feed you tomorrow Be quiet and patient.

sit on my face Request for cunnilingus, or just being crude rude. ANZ.

sit on one's arse Being lazy. ANZ.

sitting on your Ngatis On horseback.

sit up like Jacky Behave well or confidently, like an organ grinder's monkey, which was often called Jacky. ANZ.

six axe-handles across/across the acre/arse/bum Large person, particularly in the buttocks. Although six is favoured, two, three and four are also employed. ANZ.

six-day bike rider Seventh Day Adventist. Mid C20.

sixty-nine! Shearers' warning: ladies approaching, stop swearing.

skate 1. Disappear or depart quickly, in the phrase **do a skate**. ANZ c1925. To **go for a skate** is: 1. Get into trouble.

2. Take a fall, literally. Both mid C20.

skatie Skateboarder. Latter 1990s.

skerrick, not a Not even the smallest amount. From a Yorkshire dialect word for a small fragment. 'Can't help you, mate. I haven't a skerrick on me.' ANZ.

skin a rabbit Undress a child.

skin is cracking, my Dry from lack of booze and feeling an intense desire to remedy this deficiency. 1930s.

skinner Empty or broke. If the pub has no beer it's a skinner. From mid C20.

skinnier than a gumdigger's dog Gaunt.

skinny as a match/rake/yard of pump water Very thin indeed. ANZ.

skinny Girl or young woman. ANZ.

skins 1. Cigarette papers, thin as dried onion skin.

2. Shaven-headed neo-Nazis, short for skinheads.

skite   To boast, which a skiter does when he is being **skitey** or boastful. British dialect *bletherskate*, a boaster. ANZ late C19.

skitebook/skitetape   An actor's CV or best moments in print or on video tape for job applications. ANZ.

skizziest   The best. 1960s teen slang.

slab   Twenty-four pack carton of beer. ANZ 1990s.

slabby   Timber worker, from handling slabs of timber.

slack   Anything a teenager does not care for, eg, 'That maths teacher is so slack, we haven't learnt a thing.' ANZ.

slackarse   Lazy or tired. ANZ.

slanter/slinter   A trick, often a mean one, often in the phrase **to work a slinter**. ANZ mid C19.

slap on the wrist with a wet bus ticket, a   Light punishment that scarcely fits the offence. Jim Anderton said so in May 1997 of a mild Parliamentary Privileges Committee decision about an alleged assault on John Banks by Winston Peters.

slapsie/slapsie-maxie   A taxi, rhyming slang. Mid C20.

slather   To scold, eg, 'His parents say the boy has a hypo condition with some fancy name, but I reckon he just needs a good slathering.' From British 'slather', to thrash, also used more literally here in a **slather-up**, a brawl, and more figuratively in **slathered**, drunk. ANZ from c1920.

sleep in the ditch   Kiwi soldiers' name for *slivovitz*, the potent plum brandy the locals plied them with during their early 1990s peacekeeping role in Bosnia.

sleep in the dogbox/under the house   In disgrace, usually of a domestic kind, like coming home drunk and threatened with such treatment, or the threat implied. ANZ.

sleep in the star hotel/starlight hotel/star and moon hotel Open-air sleep.

Sleepy Hollow   Nelson. From mid C19.

sleep with Mrs Green   Another open-air sleep.

sleever   Drinking straw. Mid C20.

slimmie A girl.

sling A tip, bribe or bonus. ANZ 1930s.

sling off at To jeer. ANZ early C20.

sling the billy Prepare a cup of tea, from the process of hanging a billy over a fire to boil water for tea. ANZ 1870s.

sling the dirt To gossip nastily about someone. From 1930s.

slipper Boot, eg, 'A pity to see the Cardiff team captain put the slipper in.' Keith Quinn, All Blacks vs Cardiff at Cardiff Arms Park, 15 October 1989. ANZ.

SLOB Established lawyer, as in 'Senior Lawyer On the Bar/Bench'. Mid 1990s.

slog down To gulp booze. From C20.

slop back Guzzle booze or **slops**, beer. ANZ from 1920s.

slowcoach A person who moves slowly or is lazy. ANZ.

slug Exorbitant price applied. ANZ c1920.

slumgullions and barmolic Nonsensical response to the question 'What is for tea?'

slusher/slushy Assistant sheepstation cook. ANZ c1910.

slutdust The dust that is swept under the carpet or bed instead of removed.

sly grog Illicitly sold liquor from earliest days of European settlement. Reached a pitch during the middle decades of C20, when some areas voted dry, banning liquor, and liquor was not for legal sale after 6 pm, provoking both the **six o'clock swill** and the subsequent **sly-grogging**. ANZ.

slyballs Dismissive term for a male.

smacked bottoms on toast A threat and a promise to a rowdy kid.

smacker The mouth. ANZ early C20.

smack-up A fight, c1906. To **smack up** is to attack. **To be smacked up** is to be defeated in a fight or to be wounded.

smart arse Obnoxious fellow, not at all clever, who may **smartarse around**. ANZ 1930s.

smart fart   A know-it-all. From 1930s.

smarty   Impertinent person, usually a child. ANZ early C20.

smell, hang around like a bad   Lurking nuisance who is unaware when his or her company is not wanted. ANZ.

smell like something crawled up your arse and died there   You stink. ANZ.

smell like the back end of a brewery horse   Very smelly. ANZ.

smeller   Objectionable person. Late C19.

smoke   To leave. To **go into smoke** is to go into hiding, where you are **in smoke**. If you say something far-fetched or induce disbelief, you are **like smoke in a wheelbarrow.**   ANZ.

smokepole   A cigarette.

smoker   Pink, musky-tasting little lollies originally intended to mask cigarette smoke on one's breath, but curiously popular in their own right.

smoko   Refreshment break for workers. From late C19, when a break usually meant time to smoke a cigarette. The refreshment area was called a **smoko room** or **smoko shed**.

smooge/smooze   To kiss and cuddle, flatter or show affection in an overdone fashion, from British dialect *smudge*, to kiss. Politicians are perceived as a bunch of smoogers. ANZ.

smoothieboots/smoothiechops   Ladies' man, an extension of British 'smoothie'. A **smoothiepuss**   is a pretty woman.

snag   1. Sausage. **A few snags short of a barbie** is somebody not all there in the brain department. Possibly from the British dialect *snag*, a morsel. ANZ mid C20.

2. Person or thing giving you a tough time, from 'snag', an obstacle. You can have a snag of a day at work, when nothing is going right. ANZ.

snag-toothed barrister   The thorny native plant, bush-lawyer, playing on the 'snag-catcher', the dentist.

snaky   Bad-tempered. Australian, early C20, as are any other 'snake' composites that moved across the Tasman to this snake-free nation, notably **snakeproof**, said of any tight-fitting trousers that would deny a snake a leg-up. Somebody running fast and maybe unevenly is said to **go like a cut snake**.

snap-and-snarl The wife.

snare To win or seize, as one might snare a snarler or sausage. ANZ late C19.

snarf To gobble up food.

snarked off To be upset.

snarler Sausage, which snarls when frying. ANZ mid C20.

sniffer Police device for detecting alcohol on driver's breath. Early 1990s.

snigged home To be wrapped up or pulled into place. From logging term 'snig', to drag a log.

snitch on/get or **have a** is to take a dislike to, from the reverse meaning of a 'snitch' as someone who informs against you. Someone **snitchy** is ill-tempered or difficult, but a **snitcher** is an excellent person or thing in its mostly juvenile use as well as a grudge, dislike or something you take offence at. Origins unknown. ANZ early C20.

snob The last sheep in the shearing pen. A play on 'snob', cobbler (ANZ C18), who employs a last.

snobshop Exclusive private school where for large fees children are trained to regard themselves as socially superior to the public school product. From the English 'snob', anybody with an exaggerated respect for social position, particularly their own. From mid C20.

snodger Excellent person or thing. ANZ 1920s.

snore-off A short sleep. ANZ early C20.

snork Baby. From British dialect word for a piglet. ANZ C20.

snorter Hot day. A **ringtail snorter** is an exceptionally hot day or any other exceptional thing. ANZ C20.

snothead Unattractive person, or mild term of abuse.

snotlog Custard square. ANZ.

snout on, have a Bear a grudge or resent someone, a variation on looking down your snout or nose at someone. ANZ early C20.

snow Dismissive term for a blond lad, or a Polynesian. From mid 1930s, ANZ.

snowbirding Pilfering women's undies off the clothesline.

snowrake Play a trick on a callow lad. A South Island shepherd extrapolation from the term for getting sheep out of snow, maybe sending the new boy to collect the snowrake. Mid C20.

snozzler Exceptional person or thing. ANZ from mid 1930s.

snufflebuster Spoilsport or wowser, one who works to rid the world of those who are snuffy, or drunk. The British 'snuffle' referred to a person taking you to task. ANZ.

snuffstick A cigarette, which can snuff, or kill, you.

so low he/she couldn't parachute out of a possum's bum Despicable. ANZ.

so mean/tight he/she couldn't pass caraway seeds Mean with money.

so mean/tight he/she wouldn't give a rat a railway pie/piss on you if you were on fire/sell you the steam off his/her shit Memorably mean with money. ANZ.

so mean/tight you couldn't pound a toothpick up her/his arse with a pile-driver/screw anything out of her/him with a post-hole borer up her/his bum Astonishingly mean with money. ANZ.

so thin you could cut your finger on its/his/her spine A starved animal or anorexic person.

so thirsty I could scull the cap/scab off a can of beer Urgently desirous of alcoholic refreshment.

soap the geyser Increase potential by some input, eg, 'C'mon, yous jokers, Martin's just lost his job. Let's soap the geyser, help the family out.' From the practice of adding soap flakes to tourist geysers to encourage volcanic activity.

SOE Sold Off Everything, more usually called state-owned enterprise, observed on a wall of the inner Wellington suburb of Brooklyn, 10 August 1990.

sole charge The only teacher in a rural primary school. From mid C20.

sonk To hit, a variation on socking someone.

sook/sookie A wimp or a crybaby, as weak as the calf it originally referred to. The British dialect word *sook* was a version of 'suck', a pet name for a calf. ANZ 1920s.

sool Set a dog on somebody, from the British dialect *sowl*, for a dog seizing a pig's ear. ANZ mid C19.

sooner A nervy horse that is too eager. ANZ C20.

sore toe, done up like a Overdressed, and makeup overdone. ANZ mid C20.

sort A person, often **a good/bad sort**. ANZ 1920s.

SOTW Start Of The Weekend. Steve Parr, *Sale of the Century*, TVOne, 1 September 1989.

sounds like a billygoat crapping in an empty kerosene tin A raspy voice.

southerly buster Southerly storm, specifically the savage south wind that periodically whips Wellington for several days, causing the wreck of the *Wahine* interisland ferry in 1968. Referred to by Wellington-born writer Katherine Mansfield. ANZ.

spanker Disc of dried cow dung used as a play missile by rural kids, eg, 'We had fights with cow spankers. I'd love to have those days back climbing trees and throwing spankers.' Andrewina MacArthur on her Wellington childhood. Derives from 'cow-spanker', an Australian dairy farmer.

spare me days! Long-suffering exclamation, eg, 'God spare me days, do you have to keep making that racket!' ANZ early C20.

sparkie An electrician. ANZ.

spaz A weird person, from 'spastic', the uncontrollable muscle spasms seen in cerebral palsy victims. ANZ.

speaking into the big white telephone Vomiting into the loo. ANZ latter C20.

spear tackle Driven by two opponents headfirst into the turf, penalised as a dangerous tackle. ANZ.

spear the bearded clam Intromit the penis. ANZ latter C20.

spell   A short period of work or play. Rugby has two spells or halves. ANZ late C19.

spew   Emotional outburst, in phrase **to have a spew**. ANZ.

spiel   Fast chat, maybe to spin a line of salesman's patter. ANZ c1870.

spieler   Gambler, con man, a crafty fellow. From German *Spieler*, player. ANZ late C19.

spin   Luck or fate, in the phrases a **crook/rough/tough spin** for a bad time and **fair spin** for a good or successful time, neither achieved unless you try or **give it a spin**. From the act of spinning the two coins in the game of two-up. From WWI. ANZ.

spine-bashing   Sleeping or resting, originally on your bunk or stretcher to WWII Anzac soldiers, much more desirable than parade-ground bashing.

spit, the big   Vomiting. ANZ mid C20.

spit the dummy   Display petulance or be defeated or in some way removed from an expected position. Paul Holmes on TVOne newsbreak 8 June 1995 promoting an upcoming item about a politician resigning from his party said 'another National MP spits the dummy'. From what an infant does preparatory to exercising lungs. ANZ latter C20.

splash the boots   Urination by a male, and expected fallout. ANZ latter C20.

sport   Casual form of address, eg, 'G'day, sport, how ya keepin?' Early C20 ANZ neutralising of British notion of a good sport or a bad sport.

spotties   Measles, mid C20.

spotty   1. A black-spotted reef fish easy for children to catch. Late C19.

2. A spotlight, often used to fish for flounder.

spreader   A blanket; used by whalers here before it was recorded elsewhere.

spud   1. A potato, recorded by E.J. Wakefield as whaling slang here in 1845 before it appeared elsewhere. Possibly derived from a three-pronged fork of this name ideal for digging up spuds.

2. Pregnant; corruption of Maori *hapu*.

spud-barber   The potato peeler, originally in the army, WWI.

spunk   Sexy-looking person, who is said to be 'spunky'. From word for semen. ANZ.

sputnik   Orange skewered with nibbles on toothpicks.

squashed fly biscuits   Dried fruit between two biscuit squares.

squattocracy   Wealthy sheep farmers who assume aristocratic status. ANZ mid C19.

squeal like a stuck pig   Shrill shrieking.

squeeze a lemon   Female urination. ANZ.

squib   A failure, or a cowardly or frail person, from 'damp squib', a small firework that fails to ignite. ANZ early C20.

squiz   A look. Less emphatic than the British dialect word meaning to examine something critically, eg, 'Mind if I take a squiz at your lecture notes, Jonesy?' ANZ early C20.

staffie   A Staffordshire bull terrier. 1990s.

stag   Anything useless, eg, 'She's a stag of an edge-trimmer, mate, time to get a new one.' From rural meaning of an improperly castrated ram. C20.

stairdancer   Hotel or office thief, from 1950s. Later used elsewhere.

stairway to heaven   A run in a woman's stocking. ANZ.

stand around like a stale bottle of piss   Idle and maybe mopey. ANZ.

stand out/stick out like a country shithouse/tits on a bull   Obvious or conspicuous. ANZ.

starter   Ready to give something a try, eg, 'I'll be a starter for this bungy-jumping caper.' From the one who starts a horserace. Mid C20.

starve/stiffen/stone the crows!   Exclamation of surprise. ANZ mid C20.

staunch   Loyal, as gang members are required to be to the death. 1990s.

stayer   1. Someone who endures, usually in a drinking group, maintaining good mateship and liquor control.

2. A racehorse sure to last the distance. Both ANZ.

steal the show Unexpected star turn — like several New Zealand medium pace bowlers in test cricket over recent seasons. ANZ 1930s.

steam Cheap and very nasty liquor, ANZ early C20. Originally methylated spirits on its own or mixed with a modifier such as cheap, fortified wine or, as Joan Monahan recalled seeing in Victoria Park, Auckland in *NZ Memories*, December/January 2003, meths mixed with tea and called **steam-boats**.

steamroller Extra fat roll-your-own cigarette. Mid C20.

steelie A steel ball-bearing used unfairly in the game of marbles, shattering glass and clay opponents. ANZ c1920.

steinie A small bottle of Steinlager-brand beer.

step out/step outside Invitation to fisticuffs, usually outside the house where there is more space to engage, and less risk to the family furniture. ANZ.

stewed bugs and onions Another response to the question, 'What's cooking?'

stick Mate, eg, 'G'day, stick, ow's it goin' then?' Maybe a contraction of 'stickman'. ANZ.

stick it up your arse/cunt/ginger/gunga, etc Dismissive remark. ANZ.

stick like snot to a wall Loyal. ANZ.

stick to your ribs Hearty meal usually involving a lot of meat. ANZ.

stick up 1. To credit goods to your account, from mid C19 hotel habit of chalking drinks ordered on a slate you have to pay later.

2. Hasty erection of the construction kind, likely to be identified as jerrybuilt. From early C20.

sticker 1. Hunter's knife for sticking pigs.

2. Traffic ticket from mid C20, when it was stuck with glue to the windscreen, now folded under the windscreen wiper.

sticky Sweet dessert wine. ANZ 1990s.

stickman An active heterosexual. A recent movie played on the other meaning, a pool player.

sticks, the 1. The provinces or remote rural area. Mid C20 ANZ, originally US.

2. The rugby goalposts. ANZ C19.

stick-up 1. Robbery, requiring hands be raised off possible weapons; and derived meanings of robbing a bank, demanding money, or stopping somebody. ANZ mid C19.

2. Recently, a delay in traffic, without necessarily any overt physical threat involved, though that is increasingly likely on Auckland and Wellington motorways.

stickybeak To snoop, or somebody who does so, or is just inquisitive. ANZ 1920s.

stiff Unlucky, but often meant ironically, usually with addition as in **stiff cheese/cheddar/kumara/luck** Bad luck. Originally Australian for penniless; unlucky in ANZ early C20.

stiffie/stiffy Erect penis. ANZ.

stink Any person, situation or object considered unpleasant, used without a preceding article, eg, 'That movie was stink.' Juvenile usage latter C20, now general.

stinker Hot, humid day. ANZ C20.

stinkie Small clay marble, lowest in the marble pecking order, seen to stink in the sense of being inferior.

stinko Drunk. ANZ.

stinkpot Mild term of abuse, often indicating a person is offensive. ANZ.

stipe Stipendiary steward, a racecourse official employed to enforce rules. ANZ C20.

stir 1. Trouble, or the act of encouraging or stirring up trouble, for which reputation you can be scolded as a **stirrer**, often in a political context. If you are a nasty or mischievous trouble-maker you are a **shit stirrer**, but if you **stir shit out of** you are chastising a troublemaker or anybody else you deem deserves it. Mid C20 ANZ.

2. Party; eg 'Great stir you had last night.' Latter C20 ANZ.

stir the porridge   Man having sex with a woman after another man has, often in pack sex context. ANZ.

stir the possum   Cause trouble, eg, 'Tank goes to every election meeting he can, just to stir the possum.' ANZ.

stir the pot   Cause trouble.

stockie   Stock or reliable bowler in cricket and, more recently, also a stockcar driver. Latter C20.

stocking   Extortion, bullying, standover tactics by youth gangs on other children.

stoked   Excited, very pleased, or drunk, eg, 'Jim's really stoked he won.' ANZ surfing slang from late 1950s.

stone   ANZ intensive, often with addition, such as **stone cert**, a betting certainty. Adaptation of British 'stone broke' for penniless. The **stone end** is the dead end.

stone me!   I am surprised. ANZ.

stone the crows!   Another expletive, ANZ from mid C19.

stonewall   Frustrate parliamentary business with lengthy speechmaking and points of order. From 1875, Australia 1880, over a decade before the English used it to indicate boring defensive batting in cricket.

stonker   To defeat, as many a rugby team was by the kicking boot of the late Don 'The Boot' Clarke. To be **stonkered** is to be exhausted, outwitted, defeated, drunk, in dire trouble. May derive from British dialect *stonk*, a play in a game of marbles. From WWI. ANZ.

stop off   To cease, eg, 'Stop off the psychobabble, will ya, Prof? We've heard it all before.' From c1880.

story/the story   Correct information acknowledged, sometimes commended, eg, 'You've checked everything three times, Charlie, and that's jake. Story.' Fred Dagg liked this one word when it saved many. Mid C20.

stoush   A fight. In context it can be an appreciative reference to an outstanding, hard-fought rugby game, or a memorable fight in a game of rugby or in politics. From British dialect *stashie* or *stushie*, a quarrel. ANZ.

straggler   A sheep that has wandered and missed the muster. From mid C19.

straight off the turnips   A country bumpkin. From 1930s.

straight wire, the   The truth, guarantee it. ANZ late C19.

strain the potatoes   Male urination. Mid C20 ANZ.

streak   A very thin person, often extended to **a streak of weasel piss**. ANZ.

strength of it, the   The importance of something, or its reliability or extent. ANZ early C20.

stretcher case   1. Somebody crazy enough to warrant being stretchered off to a psychiatric hospital.

2. Somebody playing a game regardless of a serious injury, or somebody who has just received a serious injury. ANZ.

strike me bloody hooray/handsome/lucky/up a gum tree
Exclamations of surprise. ANZ C20.

string, the   The seam of a cricket ball, used by bowlers to create deviation, eg, 'I'm starting to hit the string more than I used to,' the newly successful Firebirds (Wellington) medium fast bowler Ash Turner told *The Dominion Post*, 27 January 2003.

string along   To deceive or kid or tease. ANZ c1920.

stripey   Unconvincing, as in streaky. Late C19.

stroke   An achievement, often either **a good stroke** or **a bad stroke**, eg, 'That was a good stroke appealing against the light so the fast bowler could catch his breath.' Late C19.

stubbie   Small bottle of beer. ANZ.

stubbie short of a six-pack   A bit dim. ANZ.

stuck in/into   Engage with gusto. It can also mean to attack verbally or physically, which often involves rugby forwards. ANZ, mid C20.

stuff   To defeat comprehensively, to be **stuffed** is to be ruined or exhausted, eg, 'That five setter really took it out of Jason, he looks utterly stuffed.' ANZ. However, **to not give a stuff** is to not care at all, eg, 'Who gives a stuff how many Helen has in her Cabinet, so long as she gets the job done.' This flexible combination of sexual euphemism and the image of vigorous stuffing of material like wool into bales and plastic into furniture is evoked in many C20 phrases such as the following:

stuff about Muck around, procrastinate, exemplify muddle. ANZ.

stuff and butter it! Exclamation of exasperation.

stuff and butter me! Exclamation of surprise.

stuff it up your jumper! Get lost! Do what you like. ANZ.

stuff off! Go away.

stuff-up A major mistake. ANZ.

stumered Ruined, perhaps financially, for a stumer was a dud cheque. Often used in sporting or gambling contexts. ANZ mid C20.

stunned Drunk. ANZ c1910.

stunned mullet, like a Stupid or dazed. ANZ mid C20.

stylie Teenage exclamation of approval. Contraction of 'stylish'.

sub A replacement player in a game of rugby. ANZ.

subbie A subcontractor. ANZ from mid C20.

subs Crumbs in a drink you share. Little submersibles. Teenage cognition.

suck off into the sunset! Go away.

suck the arse out of a durry Smoke a roll-your-own cigarette down to the last gasp. ANZ.

suck-holer A toady. ANZ.

suff Enough, as in 'sufficient'. From c1880.

suicide fish The frostfish, from its tendency to be found in numbers on beaches.

Sulphur City Rotorua.

sun shines out of your arse Said to somebody who rates themselves highly, or of somebody rated highly. Parents might be said to think so of their offspring. ANZ.

Sunday dog   Lazy mustering dog. ANZ 1930s.

Sunday driver   Irritatingly slow driver. ANZ.

Sunday shearer   Lazy shearer.

sunnies   Sunglasses. ANZ.

super   1. Superannuation paid by government to those 65 and over. ANZ.

2. Superphosphate fertiliser from 1920s, super in its job of bringing high country land into pasture production from aerial topdressing. ANZ.

Super Twelve   Rugby competition between 12 conglomerate provincial teams from South Africa, Australia and New Zealand.

superpompidious   Excellent.

supersnagative   First rate.

surf 'n' turf burger   Fish and meat burger.

swag   Backpack of the tramp, who is known as a **swagger/swaggie/ swagman**. To become one you **go on the swag**. If you have **a swag of** anything, you have a lot of it. If you are **looking for your swag straps** you are considering seeking another job. ANZ mid C19.

Swamp Foxes   Thames Valley rugby team.

swamp hen   A person with long, thin legs, as exemplified by the swamp hen or pukeko.

Swannie   Bush shirt, from the brandname Swanndri.

swatty-blouse   A wimp, from the alternative version of 'swaddy', a soldier.

sweet as   Strong teenage approval, 1990s. ANZ.

swell   Single woman earning lots of lolly, a female yuppie from late 1980s.

swept   Cleaned out of money. From 1930s.

swept up   Flash and upmarket, like the boutique shopping complexes put in the old customhouse in Auckland and the old BNZ in Wellington in recent years. The fashion originally applied to hair brushed up.

swerve, a Something you avoid. You might give a swerve to your former girlfriend's invitation to her party.

swiftie/swifty A trick, performed when you **pull/work a swiftie**. ANZ mid C20.

swill Drinking in a greedy fashion, as used to happen in the six o'clock swill.

swing one across To deceive somebody. Mid C20.

swipe Objectionable person, whom you might take a swipe at. ANZ 1920s.

swordie A swordfish.

TAB Totalisator Agency Board, state-run betting shop, beginning as off-course bookmaker on racehorses in 1949. ANZ.

tacker/wee tacker Child.

taddie tadpole. ANZ.

taiho! Wait! eg, 'We'll just taiho on this project till we get more funding.' A contraction of Maori word *taihoa*, 'by and by'. Late C19.

taiho the land court Advice to back off; local variant of the American phrase 'don't make a federal case out of it'.

taiho, touch your kick, your turn to cough up a quid It's your round of drinks; 'kick' was wallet, wherein was the required quid or pound note.

tailgunner Male homosexual.

tail-shredding Driving impatiently, tailing other cars. Adapted from fowlyard behaviour involving pecking out tail feathers. 1990s.

Takapuna surprise Steak stuffed with oysters.

take/take-down A swindle or swindler. ANZ late C19.

take a long walk off a short plank Go away. ANZ.

take a pull on yourself Admonition to improve your behaviour. ANZ mid C19.

take a swing at, To throw a punch. ANZ 1920s.

take out the back teeth Neutering the domestic tomcat.

take that and share it among you A pre-emptive remark from a belcher or farter.

take the bum off Change nappies.

take the burnt chops Work as a sheep musterer.

take the day off to carry bricks A working holiday. Latter C20.

take the dog for a walk To urinate. ANZ.

take the dog out for a run Clap on the effort, eg, 'If the guys decide to take the dog out for a run, we'll really make an effort.' Sarah Ulmer, New Zealand Commonwealth and Olympic cycling medallist on her women's team racing with the men's team, TVOne News, 4 February 2003.

take to 1. Attack. ANZ early C20.

2. Like someone. ANZ.

taki-a-wei Takeaway food, pronounced as if it were Maori.

talk a glass eye to sleep Boring.

talk braille To be drunk, eg, 'He's been drinking all day, he's talking braille.'

talk bullock Use bad language. Bullock drivers were known for it. From mid C19.

talk out the side of your mouth Surreptitious conversation, advisable in school assembly and among soldiers and prisoners on parade.

talk shit at the moon Talk rubbish.

talk the leg off an iron pot Talk too much, and/or persuasively. ANZ early C20.

talk through a hole in the back of your neck Talking nonsense. ANZ.

talk to a brick wall Complaint that audience not paying attention.

talk to your saddle Talking to yourself, eg, 'Poor Smithy, ever since that blow on the head he's been talkin' to his saddle.' From the condition of the lonely musterer. Mid C20.

Tall Blacks National men's basketball team from 1995.

tall poppy Outstanding person who has aroused the envy of lesser achievers. The phrase was popularised in 1931 by New South Wales premier J.T. Lang to describe those on government salaries above 10 pounds a week. The **tall poppy syndrome** is used of a high-flier attacked by those below.

tall timber   Lofty lineout forwards in rugby union. All Black lock Gary Whetton observed tall timber in the Queensland side on TVOne, 20 April 1991.

tangi   Dispute or wild party; the former meaning was used by Katherine Mansfield in 1919. Pakeha misrepresentation of a Maori *tangi*, wake, as a boozy party. **On the tangi** used for a celebration, **holding a tangi** for a setback or dispute.

tank   A safe, from c1932. Used in phrase **blow a tank** to open a safe with explosives. ANZ underworld extensions to the craft of **tankartist/tankblower/tankman**.

Tapanui flu   A debilitating longterm affliction with flu symptoms and chronic fatigue, named after the small Otago town where there was an early manifestation of this virus in 1980s.

Taranaki   Contemptuous adjective, mostly in the South Island, early C20, eg, 'Real Taranaki beast, that one, proper cow of a bull.' Taranaki has been singled out among Kiwi provinces to represent things excessively rural or hick, but some of the following entries would rate at the other end of the scale:

Taranaki bullshit   Boasting.

Taranaki cow   Any cow in poor condition.

Taranaki drive   A less-than-salubrious road.

Taranaki gate   Home-made gate of wire and battens.

Taranaki spanner   Bottle opener.

Taranaki sunshine   Rain.

Taranaki topdressing   Cowdung.

Taranaki violin   Cowbells.

Taranaki wind   Kapuni natural gas.

Tararua biscuit   A tramper's biscuit full of nuts, dried fruit, oats and other high-energy fodder. The Tararua region is favoured by trampers. It is where Sir Edmund Hillary learned his footcraft.

Tararua dishmop   The *Raoulia tenuicaulis* creeper favoured by trampers for cleaning utensils.

Tas/Tassie   The Tasman Sea, the latter also a Tasmanian.

ta-ta for now-now   Cheery farewell, as extension of babytalk for a walk 'going ta-tas'.

tat   Tattoo.

Tatts   Tattersall's Australian lottery ticket named after the Sydney hotel whose proprietor started it in 1881.

taz   Contracted form of 'sweet as', the favoured teen expression of approval.

Te Mama o Te Papa   Doughty Dame Cheryll Sotheran, inaugural and allegedly autocratic CEO of Te Papa, the Museum of New Zealand.

Te Ware Whare   The Warehouse stores.

teapot   Hands on hips. 'Angus Fraser gave it the old teapot,' Glenn Turner observed England vs New Zealand, Lancaster Park, 9 February 1991.

teararse   Treacle or golden syrup, with reference to its laxative qualities. ANZ c1920.

tear into   Attack, with fists, words or gusto, eg, 'He tore into his chores like there was no tomorrow.' ANZ C20.

tear up for arsepaper   Severe reprimand. WWI.

technicolour yawn   Vomit. ANZ 1960s.

teeth like a row of condemned houses   Decayed teeth. ANZ.

teeth on him/her like a donkey eating thistles   The big, strong variety.

Tegel pigeon   Kereru or native pigeon, employing jokey use of a popular frozen chicken brandname.

ten-pound pom   Assisted British immigrant mid C20, often proudly used by those who were. Alan Caddick observed in the *Dominion Post*, 22 January 2003, that he could never understand the term, as the ten pounds applied only to Australia and Canada; New Zealand offered free passage.

tenskin bowling   Term used to describe beating up skinheads.

Te Papa-ised   Dumbed down to the level of Kiwi kitsch, as it is perceived Te Papa, the National Museum of New Zealand, has reduced our heritage by promoting old refrigerators and corrugated iron craft at the expense of established Kiwi art. Late 1990s.

Terries, The   New Zealand Territorial Army. From c1930.

terror for   Enthusiastic about something, eg, 'I'm a terror for those new toffee pops.' Late C19.

TF   Tomato flavouring, if you are being polite; tucker fucker, if you are not.

TH Lowry   A Maori, rhyming slang from name of a Hawke's Bay farmer and racehorse breeder.

The Beach   Wellington's main thoroughfare of Lambton Quay from earliest settler times, brass footpath plaques marking where the water lapped, before reclamation.

that didn't touch the sides   The first or second beer on a hot day after hard yakker and the implied request for more of the same. Popularised by McPhail and Gadsby in the pub segment of their TVNZ comedy series.

that'll be the frozen fortnight   Indicative of doubt or rejection. Variation on Canadian 'frosty Friday'.

that'll steam your socks off   That will surprise.

that's a bit hot/much   Protest at something adjudged unreasonable. ANZ.

that's borer dust   Dismissing something as nonsense, probably a euphemism for 'bullshit'.

that's you pressed off and buttoned   Someone or something spruced up.

the fuck   Introductory intensive, often responding to a request or command, eg, 'The fuck I'll take the dog walkies, that's your job.' ANZ.

the way to a man's heart is through his belly and what hangs off it   How to keep a man content and not straying from the marital bed, yes? ANZ.

there goes the Ohakune nut   Spotting a redhead; Ohakune is carrot country.

there's an old boot for every sock   Longterm single people reassured they have a chance of intimacy, maybe marriage.

they're off, Mr Cutts   The race has begun. Possibly derives from the Cutts brush hurdle at Riccarton Racecourse. A variation of the British C19 phrase 'They're off, said the monkey' from early C20, to which New Zealand from mid C20 added: **when he got his balls/ tail caught in the chaffcutter/lawnmower.**

thick as pigshit   Very dim-witted, often with the addition **and twice as smelly**.

thick piss up the front bum   Male ejaculation into vagina.

thicker than maggots on an old ewe's bum   Plentiful.

thin as the back of a chair   Very thin, usually in reference to farm animals, mostly sheep in drought conditions or dogs the farmer half-starves.

things you see when you don't have your gun   Comment of resignation or regret, such as a randy man seeing a woman he cannot pursue.

Think Big   Ambitious and expensive state projects of the Muldoon era of late 1970s, early 1980s that were perceived as not delivering, making the phrase bywords for rash investment.

think your shit doesn't stink, but your farts give you away Your ego trip is not shared by us. ANZ.

think you're clever but your feet stink   You might well fancy yourself, but we don't. ANZ.

thinks only of his belly and what hangs off it   A man whose thoughts never stray from food, drink and sex; the implication is that there are other, perhaps worthier things in life. ANZ.

thinks with his dick   A man preoccupied with sex. ANZ.

third beer   A woman, usually a girlfriend, who is not attractive or very exciting; dull, ordinary.

thistle-peeper   The heading dog in a sheep muster.

Three Wise Men   The All Blacks selectors.

throw   The value of something, used in conjunctive phrases such as 'ten cents a throw', from the cost of a sideshow turn. From mid 1950s.

thugby   Rugby, to those who also regard it as a form of open-air wrestling or an excuse for a stoush.

thumb bird/thumbie   The rifleman, the smallest of our birds.

thunderplump   A downpour down south. *Otago Daily Times* 18 November 1977 sources back to Scottish dialect.

tickets on yourself   Conceited, as you would be if you purchased tickets on your own performance. ANZ C20.

tickle   To steal; **tickle the peter** is to rob the till. ANZ early 1930s.

tiffin   Midmorning smoko, possibly from the Anglo-Indian 'tiffin', a light lunch. Late C19.

Tigertigerumu   Paraparaumu, from when the World Number One golfer, the American Tiger Woods, played there in 2002.

tight as a bull's/duck's/fish's/gnat's/oyster's arse   Mean with money. The most popular 'duck's arse' carries the extension **. . . and that's watertight**, while the oyster has to endure being **tighter than an oyster's arsehole at low tide**. Other examples of tight include as **a nun's nasty** and **a Scotchman's purse**. ANZ.

tight five, the   1. The five forwards who bind the rugby union scrum, namely a hooker and two props in front, behind them two locks.

2. Late 1990s nickname for the new intake of New Zealand First Party Maori Members of Parliament Tau Henare, Rana Waitai, Tuariki John Delamere, Tu Wylie and Tukoroirangi Morgan.

tike/tyke   A Catholic. Orsman sources it to the popular Irish boy's name *Tadhg*, Partridge also to a pun on 'Mike', another popular Irish boys' name. It came here as abusive, probably from the Northern Irish Protestant usage.

tiki-tour   1. A quick trip around the tourist highlights of an area.

2. To look around.

3. Unlicensed driving, eg, 'When I was twelve I had an old BSA Bantam motorbike hidden on the farm, and used to tiki-tour all round the back of Cambridge.' *New Zealand Herald*, 22 February 1989. Derived from Contiki tourist operators.

tiku on a stick   The answer to 'What's for tea?'

tin arse/bum   Lucky person, from 'tin' meaning money. ANZ mid C20.

tin can   Old, noisy car. ANZ from mid 1950s.

tin of cocoa, tin of cocoa, tin of Coca-Cola   Cod-Maori greeting from 'Tena koutou, tena koutou, tena koutou katoa.' When invoked by Tom Scott in a satirical rendering of a speech by Governor-General Sir David Beattie, Sir David's response was to present Scott with a tin of cocoa.

tinpot   Insignificant and/or rundown. After the government reforms of the 1980s, many small towns looked tinpot. ANZ.

tin-teller   Money-dispensing machine.

tingle   Telephone call; eg 'Give me a tingle when you're ready.' ANZ mid C20.

tinnie/tinny   1. Lucky. ANZ from c1918.

2. A can of beer. Australian from mid 1960s.

3. Cheap and/or poorly made, as if made of tin instead of solid steel. ANZ c1925.

4. An aluminium boat or a raft made of a sheet of corrugated iron.

5. A measure of cannabis wrapped in tinfoil.

tinny house   Place where cannabis is sold.

tired and emotional   Drunk.

tired as a newt   Drunk; variant of 'pissed as a newt'.

titoki   Shandy that includes raspberry, which looks like juice of titoki berry. C20.

tit-puller   Dismissive term for dairy farmer.

tits and bums   Landscape painting.

tits and bums man   One who trumpets the attractiveness of women with prominent breasts and buttocks.

tits in a tangle   In difficulty, eg, 'Don't get your tits in a tangle.' Russell Tulloch on *Heartland*, TVOne, 11 July 1995. Refers to the problems associated with the clothes mangle attached to washing machines in the days before spin-drying. ANZ.

tits on toast   A serving on toast of bellypork, which usually has the nipples attached.

tizzy up   Dress up. Partridge suggests a combination of 'tidy and 'jazzy'. ANZ c1935.

to and from   A Pom, originally among prisoners of war under the Japanese, WWII. ANZ.

toa   Champion marble; from the Maori for a warrior.

toe   Power/speed ratio, which has been applied in a TV car ad 'more toe than an Aussie tank'.

toey   1. Excitable, anxious, touchy. ANZ.

2. Fast, usually of a car or sportsperson or animal. ANZ 1920s.

togs   Swimming or rugby costume. From early C20. In Northern Ireland togs are boots. ANZ.

toiler   Admirable worker, the Kiwi version of the 'little Aussie battler'. Often applied to hard-working, if unspectacular, rugby forward play. Early C20.

toity   The toilet. If something has **gone down the toity** it is lost or has failed, like the majority of Lotto tickets.

tom thumb   1. A tiny firecracker.

2. The bush wren, a tiny bird. Both mid C20.

tomato   1. A hundred dollar bill.

2. An attractive blonde, one with luscious curves. From American servicemen in WWII. However, at the same time a **tomato blonde** was a local lady of part-European blood to our servicemen in North Africa.

tomato sauce   An ANZ horse C20.

tommyaxe/tommyhawk   A small hand axe or tomahawk, ANZ from C19.

toney/tonky/tony   Fashionable, as in swanky and high-toned, usually used disapprovingly. From c1935.

Tongan steroids   Mashed taro. 'Taro gives Jonah his power,' said his mother Hepi Lomu in the *Evening Post*, 17 June 1995. 'We joke it's Tongan steroids.'

tonk 1. Effeminate male, possibly derived from above entry. ANZ from mid C20. Partridge suggests original English meaning was a fop, a perversion of an older word 'tony/toney', a fool.

2. In some secondary schools in Britain and Australasia 'tonk' was a term of abuse; in others, and in general, it meant to hit a cricket ball. Down Under from 1920s it meant to get the cane, which is closest to the original, mostly Midland, dialect *tank*, to strike.

too ducky to quack Too good to be true, as used by a member of a small North Island lodge of a solicitor who had conned the lodge of its assets.

too much hui and not enough do-ey More talk than action.

too much Weet-Bix Superior strength. The runners-up in the Ironman race could say the winner had too much Weet-Bix. It is not officially an ad for the breakfast cereal.

too right! Most certainly! Emphatic reassurance. ANZ early C20.

toot The bum. Multiple possibilities for its origin, as in the noise it can emit, the Maori name *tutae* for excrement, the Australian contraction of toilet, the dog-French *toute suite* — but not apparently related to the following entry. The popular phrase **a root up the toot** could be a kick in the bum or anal intromission of the penis.

tooted Grazing animal poisoned by the *tutu* plant.

top/top off/top on To inform on somebody, originally Australian police informer.

top shelf The best and/or most expensive, from where the best quality goods and liquor are kept. ANZ.

topdressing Deception, usually in surface presentation, from the fruiterer's habit of putting the best fruit on top. Mid C20.

toss Throw away, usually as useless. Australian from 1930s.

toss a reverse lunch/the tiger/your lollies To vomit. ANZ latter C20.

tote The TAB or Totalisator Agency Board which replaced private bookmakers on and off the racecourse precincts.

tote up To add up. ANZ 1920s.

touch Somebody's turn to buy a round of drinks.

touch your kick   Modest loan, adapted from mid C19 word for pocket.

touchy   Oversensitive, eg, 'Don't stare at the braces on her teeth, she's touchy about them.' ANZ.

towie   Tow-truck driver. ANZ.

town bike   A sexually available woman. ANZ mid C20.

town Maori   An urban Maori who has lost touch with tribal roots. 1970s.

townie   Dismissive rural term for an ignoramus from town. ANZ.

Toyota Corroda   Jokey reference to Japanese cars perceived as tending to rust, punning on the popular Toyota Corolla or Corona.

trace element Maori   Dubious claim to be Maori from a minuscule amount of Maori bloodline.

tramlines   The marked divisions down the sides of football fields, adapted from the doubles lines of a tennis court.

trammie   A tram driver or conductor. ANZ.

tramp   To go fast, from the 1930s.

trannie   1. Transistor radio from 1960s. ANZ.

   2. Transsexual. ANZ.

trap for young players, a   A danger to the young, inexperienced or naive, like taking out too many mortgages. ANZ from mid 1950s.

treacle-arse   Unlikeable or sycophantic, or both.

Treaty trout   Trout fished up by Maori under the broad umbrella of customary fishing rights enshrined in the Treaty of Waitangi; the phrase sometimes used resentfully by Pakeha.

trick   An amusing child. ANZ late C19.

trig   A trigonometrical station, a familiar wooden pyramid on summits as a survey reference point; used first here from at least 1849.

trim your language   Command to stop using swear words. ANZ C20.

tripe, don't bust a   Take it easy, you might pop a gut-string.

tripehound   Sheepdog. ANZ.

tripes out, I'll tear your   A threat unlikely to be executed. ANZ.

trog A rock cave, wherein a troglodyte or caveperson would have lived, combined with trampers' term 'trog', to tramp, and 'trog boots', the durable rubber boots trampers wear.

trol Female, less offensive than 'trollop'. ANZ mid C20.

trolley dollie Air hostess from 1960s, revived in TVOne documentary *Coffee, Tea or Me*, 1 March 2003.

trollied Wiped out on booze or drugs.

troppo Crazy. From WWII servicemen in the tropics, where they often **went troppo**. ANZ.

trot A person — usually affectionate, which is nice considering it was once an English word for a whore.

trots 1. Diarrhoea, ANZ early C20.

2. Horse harness racing. ANZ late C19.

truck and trailer Sycophant, down Otago way.

truckie Heavy-truck driver. ANZ mid C20.

true dinks Assurance of truth, a contraction of 'true dinkum', a variant of 'square dinkum' or 'fair dinkum', eg, 'True dinks, Mike, I never laid eyes on your bag of marbles.' ANZ early C20.

trunk-muncher Cunnilinguist.

try-hard Unwelcome, troublesome or unacceptable person.

tryondewondygong Thingummyjig.

tryontwentygobbler As you asked, that's what I'm cooking.

TTFN Ta ta for now, or goodbye.

tucker Food, originally goldminers' rations. Hence **tuckertime** for mealtime, unless one is unfortunately **tuckerless**. ANZ**.**

tucker fucker Army cook, or tomato sauce.

tugger Twit, or male masturbator.

tui A good singer, whistler or mimic, like the bird. Early C20.

tukus Male underpants. In the *Dominion* of 6 June 1997 Frank Haden wrote of hearing Lower Hutt schoolboys discussing birthday presents, one saying 'and I got some new tukus'. A reference to NZ First MP Tukoroirangi Morgan, who attracted much publicity by purchasing expensive underpants; any public extravagance is now referred to as **doing a tuku**, and the specific scandal was identified as **Tukugate**.

tulip muncher Dutch person.

tupperware Allegedly aerodynamic fins above the back boot or any other flash external addition to a car in 1990s.

turbo suckout A wave breaking hard and fast in shallow water.

turboburger Double hamburger with beetroot, mayonnaise, lettuce, cheese, pickle, onion, grated carrot, tomato sauce, mustard, all guaranteed to rev you up; speciality in downtown Whakatane hamburger joint.

turd bandit/puncher/tapper Active male homosexual. ANZ.

turd strangler Plumber. ANZ.

turkey off A sudden departure, ANZ 1930s.

turkey will roost on your lip, a Warning to a sulking or pouting child.

turn dog on To make trouble for someone by reporting them to authorities, or simply to attack or be unpleasant to someone. ANZ C19.

turn it in Give up a job or task. A less drastic adaptation of the Armed Forces meaning 'to die'.

turn it on Give a party or provide drinks. ANZ C20.

turn it up Make oneself sexually available. From 1970s.

turn on the Waipori Switch on the electricity; from an Otago river dammed for electricity.

turn to custard Anything which fails, eg, 'Halfway through the performance of *Hamlet* by the Upper Waikikamukau Players all turned to custard.' Later 1990s.

turnout Gathering, something politicians hope to see plenty of at election time. ANZ.

tussock jumper Stationhand.

tussocker Somebody arriving in time for tucker, but after work has ended.

tweeds Trousers. From early C20. Rarely an accurate indication of material. ANZ.

Twigs and Tweeters Conservationists, into protecting rare birds or little-known foliage, most notably the Royal Forest and Bird Protection Society of New Zealand from 1960s when the conservation movement got going.

twinset and pearls set Ladies of conservative upper middle class, from the way they dress. ANZ.

twist To con or cheat. ANZ early C20.

twist the tail Kid or tease. Possibly from 'tail', to drive or tend animals.

two bastards on bikes Reaction in game of two-up from those betting on two heads when two tails come up.

two bob each way Hedging your bets, acting indecisively. ANZ.

two, four, six, eight, bog in, don't wait Chant to urge tucking into a meal.

two kumara short of a hangi Simple-minded.

two ladies on bikes The two-up toss providing two tails or images of Britannia.

two pages stuck together Bit deficient mentally.

two-pot screamer Somebody with a low tolerance for booze. ANZ mid C20.

two-minute silence The *Hokitika Guardian*, or any other paper adjudged thin on content.

two shakes of a dog's hind leg A short interval of time, often used to assure somebody you will not take long. ANZ.

two thirds of five eighths of fuck all Very little, often used to indicate disgust.

two-up Illegal gambling game where two pennies are tossed and bet on coming down heads and tails or two of either. ANZ late C19.

tyrekicker Used-car salesman term for a car-yard browser who does not buy, now applied to a politician who is evasive.

u-ey A U-turn in a car from one side of the road to the other, eg, 'You guys want to do a few u-eys, burn some rubber, eh?' ANZ.

ugly enough to eat gorse Term of abuse that suggests a resemblance to those gorse-munchers, goats.

uglier than a cow facing south Rather ugly.

uma rapeti To escape or run away, from the Maori version of the song 'Run, rabbit'.

Uncle Tom Cobley and all Rubbish, in a roundabout fashion from the cobbler's last or awl being rhyming slang for balls.

under the affluence of inkahol, though some stinkle peep I am Self-condemned drunk. ANZ.

underdungas Underpants. 1980s.

underground mutton Rabbit. ANZ C20.

unemployed, the The penis, during period of sexual hibernation.

uni University. ANZ, later C20.

unit Wellington suburban electric train.

unreal Excellent, in teenage patois. ANZ.

Unsmiling Giants, the All Blacks up to the mid 1980s, when Auckland flair under coach John Hart spread upwards and outwards.

untold Adolescent add-on emphasiser to indicate huge number or quantities or condition, eg, 'The untold numbers at the Big Day Out music show included way too many untold drunk wannabe homies.'

up and down like a honeymoon cock/new bride's nightie Swinging to and fro between any extremes.

up and under A rugby ball punted high in the air to allow a team to descend on the unfortunate opposition at the same time as the ball.

up at Ross's having afternoon tea with a straw hat on   Facetious answer to the question, 'Where are you going?'

up burnt gully for the winter   Said of any person or animal of emaciated appearance.

up Cook's arse   Expression of disgust.

up in Lizzie's room behind the clock   The less-than-serious answer to a question where something might be found or, possibly, up to hanky-panky and having to hide.

up large   Heavy drinking, a contraction of 'piss up large'.

up Mully's gully shooting magpies with a goss knife   The reply to the question, 'Where are you going?'

up shit creek in leaky gumboots   In trouble.

up sticks   To pack your belongings and depart, or abandon your home and move on.

up the boohai for the rhubarb season/shooting peanuts with a sling/shooting pipis with a hayrake/shooting pipis with a long-handled shovel/shooting pukakas/shooting pukakas with a pitchfork/popgun/shotgun   Lost and maybe loony, but more usually some of the droll extensions of being 'up the boohai' as a dismissive answer to a pesky question about what you are doing or where you are going, which you do not want to answer.

up the chute   Wrong and maybe stupid or worthless, eg, 'Sorry, fella, you're up the chute if you think New Zealand's going to lose the next America's Cup.' ANZ c1920.

up the duff   Pregnant, perhaps by extension from being in the pudding club, which could also be a plum duff. ANZ C20.

up the Dutch shit   In deep trouble.

up the Mokau   Very lost, as you would be up this remote North Taranaki river.

up the river in a matchbox shooting pipis with a popgun Another of those evasively extended answers to where you are going.

up the scrub   In the bush.

up the wop 1. Pregnant. ANZ.

2. Broken or malfunctioning, as often happens to battery-driven toys. ANZ.

up to the mark Where people expect someone to be, such as a new test fastbowler in cricket. Also refers to health being in good shape. Late C19.

up you for the rhubarb season/for the winter Mildly abusive rejections, indicating you are talking rubbish, or you are rejected for a long time.

up your bum, chum/up your date, mate Abusive rejections. ANZ.

up your bum to the neck Said of somebody with high regard for self.

up your arse with broken glass/up your nose with a rubber hose/ up your vagina with an ocean liner Jokily abusive rejection, which can be topped with the responses, **higher and higher with barbed wire/twice as far with a chocolate bar**. ANZ.

useless as a fart in a bottle/a glass door on a dunny/a gumdigger's dog/a spare prick at a wedding/a submarine with screen doors/a tit on a hand/an arsehole on a broom/as ashtray on a pushbike/the bottom half of a mermaid Completely and utterly and totally useless or incompetent. ANZ.

user pays Bureaucratic euphemism for screwing money out of the public for traditionally free public services, one of the pettier examples of market-driven restructuring of the public service.

ute Utility truck or van. ANZ from mid C20.

vag   A vagrant. If you are **on the vag** you are on the road and maybe seeking work.

vaginamite   Sexually overactive heterosexual male.

Vandemonian   Literally somebody from Tasmania or Van Diemen's Land, but it can mean rough or aggressive, by association with the original meaning of a convict.

vees   Men's extremely brief bathing trunks with the V-shape of today's brief underwear. Mid C20.

veg/vegies   Vegetables. ANZ.

vegemite   Cute word for a child, perceived as a consumer of the yeast spread Vegemite. ANZ.

vegemite driller   Active male homosexual.

vegetable   Dazed. Used by streetkids to indicate a doped state brought on by substance abuse. ANZ.

vegetable sheep   A woolly, low-growing South Island plant.

verbal diarrhoea   Running off at the mouth.

vertical drinking   Stand-up drinking, the way it was.

very funny   Not funny at all, eg, 'You think letting down her tyres was a good joke? Very funny!' ANZ.

vid   A video.

Vinnie's Boutique   St Vincent de Paul op shop. ANZ.

violets growing out of your ears   Too good to be true, eg, 'The smarmy way that girl lisps and pouts makes me sick. She's got violets growing out of her ears.'

visual symphony, a   Ironic admiration of something way over the top, employed by Lyn of Tawa comic character of the extraordinarily kitsch set in her 1980s Mitre 10 TV ad.

Vitamin DB   Draught bitter from Dominion Breweries.

W   The toilet, short for WC, which is short for water closet. Katherine Mansfield wrote of one in 'Aloe', 1916. Recorded here before elsewhere.

wacker/whacker   1. Male masturbator. ANZ.

2. Stupid and/or nerdy person. ANZ.

Wadestown Wadical   Any mild, if not lapsed, socialist, after the cosy yuppies who inhabit the wealthy Wellington hill suburb of Wadestown without feeling the need to be any more radical than joining the local Labour Party branch.

wahine   Girlfriend or wife, from Maori for 'woman'.

Waiberia   Waiouru, bleak town and army training area in the desert surroundings of central North Island volcanic plateau.

Waikato dandruff   Sheep.

Waikikamukau   Imaginary archetype of Kiwi back-country town, a cod-Maori construction. 'Wakikamukau?' children ask, then answer: 'Because it kicked me.'

Waiouru blonde   A sheep handy to army training area.

Waiouru limp   An injury sustained in pursuit of Waiouru blonde.

waipiro   Alcohol, from Maori for 'stinking water'.

wait on   Hang on a minute, mate. Mid C20.

Waitangi   A fictional variety of potato.

waiwai   Beer or any booze, from the Maori for 'sodden', the end result of too much waiwai.

waka blonde   Maori woman. The reference derives from **Whakarewarewa wahines**, the Rotorua Maori women observed by tourists.

waka-jumping   Leaving the political party you came into Parliament with to join another. The *Evening Post*, 7 May 2001, reported 'waka jumper Tau Henare put in his first appearance at a National Party conference' and, on 27 August 2001, noted 'waka-jumping legislation'. The phrase is now popular in the general sense of changing allegiance.

waka soccer   Canoe polo, or waterpolo, basketball and a little bit of league thrown in, reported TV3 News, 26 August 2001.

wake-up call   Sharp reminder not to rest on your laurels, eg, 'The thrashing by the Blues was a wake-up call for the All Blacks in the Crusaders team ahead of the World Cup.'

wake up to   Aware of something, on your guard against being duped, eg, Sooner or later she'll wake up to his tricks. ANZ c1925.

walk off one's land   To abandon, from late C19 depression years, when many farmers walked off land they could not pay the mortgage on. ANZ.

walks as if he/she has grass seeds up his/her bum/is pinching sixpence   A mincer. ANZ.

walk-up/walk-up fuck   Promiscuous woman — you walk up and ask her. ANZ C20.

walloper   Male masturbator.

wally   Short back and sides haircut, named after Auckland barber Wally Buck.

wallyburger with cheese, fries and a large Coke   The ultimate 'wally' or idiot, an extension of the English 'wally' (not the barber above).

Wanganella weather   Good weather, from the several weeks following the *Wanganella* striking Barrett Reef off Wellington in January 1947, allowing the ship to be floated to safety a few hours before a savage southerly struck.

want to talk to the butcher, not the block   I want the boss, not you; or, I don't want your unsolicited advice. ANZ.

wants the penny and the bun too   Greedy; from the days when a bun cost a penny.

warmth in winter, shade in summer   A fat person.

warratah Fencepost.

waterburner Sheep shearers' cook.

waterfront solicitor Wharfie, because he is always working on a case.

watermelon Derisive name for a compromised Green politician, green on the outside and watery pink within.

wayback A remote rural district. ANZ late C19.

Way Down Under New Zealand, the way Kiwi soldiers sung it in WWII: 'For we are the boys from way down under, sons of the Anzacs are we.'

weak as cat's/gnat's/nun's/weasel's piss Feeble and unthreatening, eg, 'This local beer's weak as cat's piss.' ANZ.

wedding cake architecture Baroque Edwardian brick and plaster buildings, a much-used phrase when such structures were being tumbled in city centres in the 1980s demolition ball, notably the retail shops along Wellington's Lambton Quay. Remnants still attracting the phrase include the old Public Trust on the other side of Lambton Quay, the Dunedin Railway Station and the University of Auckland tower. The original was the Victoria Memorial outside Buckingham Palace.

wedgie The unpleasant result of **wedging,** twisting or lifting by the underpants until the bits between hurt, one of the less savoury playground tricks.

wee Little (though it can mean the opposite), often in celebration, such as **wee beaut/beaut wee**; eg 'That was a beaut wee bouncer.' British dialect word popular here from mid C19.

weekend root Casual sexual partner.

weekender Casual, as compared to permanent, resident.

wees Urine or urination. A euphemism of a euphemism of a euphemism, from English 'pee', to piss, evolving into 'weewee'.

weights up, put your Getting someone into trouble, perhaps from the weights carried in handicapped horseraces. ANZ mid C20.

weird and wonderful Anything unusual or interesting.

weka A Chatham Islander, where the weka bird is prominent.

well gone 1. Deeply in love. Early C20.

2. Severely wounded. WWI.

well, saw off me penis and call me Venus! Surprise, surprise! No sexual connotation. You might say it if you came home from work and saw a neighbour who'd neglected his house for 20 years busy scraping the paint and putting on primer.

well, what do you know? Indicative of maybe mock surprise, eg, 'Well, what do you know, Mehrts made the All Blacks.' From c1918.

well in Successful in an enterprise or project, eg, 'Cyrus is well in with the meat-processing plant.' From mid C20.

Wellingmonian Resident of the capital city.

Wellywood Wellington from later 1990s, when city council encouragement and Peter Jackson boosted the capital's filmmaking activity.

welter, make a Go to extremes. ANZ early C20.

were you born in a church/swing-door dunny/tent? Sarcastic encouragement to shut the door. ANZ.

West Coast sidestep Straight ahead, Greg Clark advised in the third rugby league test New Zealand vs Great Britain, 6 November 1993.

Westie Inhabitant of western suburbs of Auckland, perceived as rough beer drinker in tight black jeans driving a beaten up Holden ute. Those who adopt this image are said to be **Westicated**.

wet area An area that has voted to allow sales of liquor, which is now the vast majority of the country. ANZ.

wet bread and butter bowling Persisting in use of old cricket ball making the scoring of runs difficult. Commentators Parker and Galloway discussed such bowling during Radio New Zealand coverage on 26 February 1989.

wetboot man Bureaucrat, one who can't keep his boots dry in the bush.

whack into Enthusiastic approach to doing something, like whacking into the day's chores.

whack out   A good period of exercise, often in game of cricket.

whack up   Quick construction, like whacking up a kitset garage.

whackohthediddleoh!   Exclamation of pleased surprise. ANZ.

whale into   Attack vigorously. ANZ C20.

whare   1. A prison cell, from Maori word for a house.

   2. A palatial home, a humorous usage. It has been applied to the 'vice-regal whare'.

whare boy   A bachelor shepherd.

wharfie   Wharf labourer. ANZ early C20.

wharfies' sunshine   Wet weather, when wharfies do not have to work.

what are ya!   Chiding remark to somebody who has bungled or chickened out. ANZ.

what are you going to make out of it/do about it?   Belligerent challenges. ANZ.

what can you say to a pig that grunts?   Rhetorical question about somebody deemed hopeless.

what did your last slave die of?   Sarcastic suggestion you do the chore yourself.

whatever blows your dress up   Reassurance that you are entitled to your own choice, even if I maybe might question your taste.

what's the butcher's name?   Sarcastic response to an obvious question, such as 'Do you really like Cadbury's Roses chocolates?' The phrase spread from Feilding, where the butcher's sign read: 'Watts' the Butcher's Name'.

Wheel Blacks   National men's wheelchair team at the rugby world cup for wheelchair athletes in June 1998.

whanau, the   The immediate or extended family, from the Maori word for 'extended family' used informally by Maori and Pakeha.

where were you when they were handing out the brains?   You dolt.

where'd you get your licence, out of a Weet-Bix packet?   You are a bad driver.

whingeing Pom   The stereotypically complaining British immigrant.

whinger   Persistent complainer. From nothern English dialects, but applied extensively in Australasia from c1910.

whiny   Somebody who complains, or the complaining sound of a voice, like a hungry cat. Late C19.

whip behind   Hitching a ride on a horse-drawn vehicle, a children's game from early last century which could provoke advice to the driver to whip behind him. Extended later to trams and trains and lorries.

whip it up, whip it in, whip it out and wipe it   A sexual quickie for the man.

whip the cat   To moan or reproach yourself, make a fuss, particularly about something that has happened. ANZ mid C19.

whips of   Plenty of whatever. From British dialect 'whips' for a lot of anything. ANZ late C19.

white flight   Moving Pakeha children from schools with Polynesian majorities from mid 1980s, an adpatation of the United States movement of white families from black neighbourhoods.

white hairs, you must have   Said of somebody receiving an unexpected favour.

white homie   Teenage slang for middle class Pakeha kids wanting to live the life of streetkids.

white joker   The average Kiwi bloke mid C20.

white lady   Methylated spirits, which turns white in water and turns drinkers not white in the head. ANZ c1920.

whitebait   Skinny person. Glenn Johnston offers the example: 'He's built like a racing whitebait.'

whitebaiter   Maori activist, who baits whites, or Europeans.

white-haired boy   A favourite.

whiteman   A first-rate fellow, used here in 1880s earlier than most places.

who slapped Nelly in the belly with a wet flounder?   She's pregnant.

whojamaflung/whojamafiffle   Thingummyjig.

whoop along   To speed, diverting the 'whoop it up' idea of raucous fun to the Toad of Toad Hall notion of speed for its own sake. Late 1930s.

whopcacker/wopcacker   Outstanding person or thing, perhaps evolved from a 'whopper' or large lie. ANZ 1920s.

who's milking the cow?   Who is in charge here? I am. So get lost. ANZ.

whoshanwallah, ya little luggergate!   Go away, you little brat.

who's up who and who's paying?   Enquiry about what is happening, but originally a WWII sexual joke. ANZ.

why don't you go and raffle your doughnut?   Go away. Could be construed as a rude request, where your doughnut is the back or front bum.

why's a duck? The faster it swims. Quacker.   One way to confuse a child asking a question you don't want to answer. Could be an extension of the nonsensical Marx Brothers' question, 'Why a duck?'

wicked   Fashionable, to youngsters.

widgie   Female partner of a bodgie, dressed to outrage 1950s sensibilities with short blonde hair and short dress and heavy makeup. ANZ 1950s.

widow-maker   Loose limb of a tree, which can kill a forestry worker. From 1950s. Also applied to any dangerous machinery, notably on construction sites.

wigger/wigga   Teenage slang for someone trying too hard or attempting to join a group they do not fit, such as middleclass kids wanting to live with street kids.

wigwam for a goose's bridle   Jokey answer to a query about what you are making. Sometimes with the elaboration . . . **to wind up the sun on a wet day**. From 1930s, adapting British dialect 'whim-wham for a goose's bridle'. ANZ.

W

wild Irishman   Matagouri plant, its thorns making it difficult to handle. Late C19.

wild Spaniard   Speargrass, its leaves like a Spanish dagger.

Willie away   Rugby union tactic of peeling off the front of the line-out around the back of the other forwards and leading a surge upfield. Named after 1958-65 All Black captain Wilson Whineray and used as the title of his book.

willie-woofter   Male homosexual, an extension of 'woofter' to include the point of his exercise.

win against the head   Hooking a rugby ball the opposition has put into the scrum, converting their **loose head** into your **tight head**.

wind blows up your trouser leg and waggles your tongue   Windbag or boaster.

windie   A windsurfer from mid 1980s.

windler   Fun sailing of modern yachts, attributed to Aucklander Mark Steele, 1996.

Winebox Inquiry   The long-running investigation of alleged use of the Cook Islands as an illegal tax haven, from the cardboard carton containing Serious Fraud Office documents Winston Peters tabled in Parliament in March 1994.

Winterless North, the   Northland — but less so since 1988 Cyclone Bola.

wipe   To reject someone. ANZ from mid C20.

wobbly   A tantrum. Often used in the phrase **chuck /throw a wobbly**. From mid 1960s here, elsewhere later.

woo   A mild petting session. From c1930.

wood on, have the   Enjoy an advantage, from woodchopping competitions. ANZ c1926.

woodchook   Weka.

wooden   To hit. To **wooden out** somebody is to knock them to the floor. ANZ early C20.

wooden aspro   A truncheon or the result of its contact with your head, employed by protesters drawing attention to police treatment of them during the marching seasons of the early 1980s.

woody   1. A woodsman.

2. A wood-burning stove.

woofterish/woolly-woofterish   Unconvincing performance, as a macho man might rhyme 'poofter' or perceive the woolly-headed efforts of a woofter or effeminate male homosexual. Late 1980s. ANZ.

woolbug   Shearer. From c1890.

wool classer   The mustering dog that snaps at the heels of sheep.

wool king   A big sheep owner. ANZ c1920.

woolagoo   Instruction to huntaway or heading dog that it is finished, adapted only in New Zealand from a Gaelic word, reported in TVOne's *A Dog's Life*, 3 November 2001.

Woollies blackballs/Woolworth's blackballs   Sheep dags.

Woollies bladder/Woolworth's bladder   A weak bladder, as if it was a bargain purchase.

woopknacker   A rough diamond character. From 1920s.

wopwops   Remote place. Often said to be **in the/out in the wopwops**. Variation on Australian 'woop-woops'.

working for the Prime Minister   On the Welfare benefit, eg, 'Some surfers in the north jokingly say they are working for the Prime Minister, which means they are receiving the benefit.' Acting Director-General of Social Welfare Robin Wilson, the *Dominion*, 24 May 1991.

working the smorgs   Getting a smorgasbord of perks from your employer, from 1980s, when perks really kicked in as a way round Prime Minister Muldoon's ill advised wage and salary freeze.

worksburger   The entire range of whatever. In TVOne screening of *So You Think You're a Good Driver* on 18 December 2002 the ticketing officer observed an offender got 'what you call a worksburger — cops the lot. No warrant, no rego, towage and ticket. $500.'

worse than a man short   Useless worker.

would be if he/she could be   Talentless trier.

would fuck a blind man's dog/a hole in the ground if it smiled at him/the hairs off a barber's shop floor   Said of a man considered extremely randy. ANZ later C20.

would shit anywhere   Uncouth person.

would you rather walk a mile and climb a stile or eat a sunburned cake? Question addressed to somebody lagging behind, often a child.

wouldn't call the king me uncle Expression of high spirits, higher than being related to royalty.

wouldn't it! Expression of dissatisfaction, exasperation, disgust, often extended in such phrases as **wouldn't it make you spit/make you spit chips/rip your ration book/rock you/root you/rotate you/rotate your crops/rotate your socks**. ANZ mid C20.

wouldn't know her/him if she/he stood up in my porridge I have no idea who she/he is.

wouldn't know if his/her arse was on fire Exceptionally ignorant or vague person. ANZ.

wouldn't know if he/she wants a shit or a haircut Prize ditherer.

wouldn't know sheep dung from dried dates/beef from a bull's foot Dim, if not dense. The latter is a local variant form not knowing 'A/B from a bull's foot', traced back by Partridge to Shakespeare's not knowing 'a hawk from a handsaw'.

wouldn't know shit from clay — unless you tasted it Severely limited person.

wouldn't know someone from a bar of soap/if you fell over them Not known to the speaker. ANZ.

wouldn't know the postie was up her unless he blew his whistle A stupid woman.

wouldn't know your arse from a hole in the ground/from your elbow Ignorant or dim-witted.

wouldn't lend you the harness on his/her nightmare Mean person. ANZ.

wouldn't piss down someone's throat if their guts were on fire Held in contempt. ANZ.

wouldn't that rip the crutch/fork out of your nightie/undies? How annoying or disgusting. ANZ.

wouldn't touch it with a forty foot pole/red-hot poker Extreme distaste. ANZ C20.

wouldn't use him/her for shark bait   Contemptible whoever. ANZ.

wouldn't want him/her farting in my last pound of flour   Fat person who would be sure to spread flour explosively. ANZ.

wouldn't work in an iron lung   Lazy person. ANZ.

Wow   Area of Avondale suburb of Auckland near Whau Creek where the former psychiatric hospital, now Unitec, is known as **the Wow**.

wowser   Spoilsport or puritan, objecting to alcohol, cigarettes and any other joys that it is possible to kill. Originally a prohibitionist. Possibly from British dialect word *wow*, to whine, acronymically identified by John Norton as 'We Only Want Social Evils Remedied'. Promoting prohibition was **wowserdom**, the promoter **wowserish**, his or her behaviour **wowserism**. ANZ early C20.

wozzed   Very tired.

wozzle   Wireless.

wrap   Praise. Often used in sport in the phrase **to give someone a wrap**. ANZ.

wrinkled dick   Old man.

wrung out like a dishcloth   Exhausted. ANZ.

wuss   Weak or ineffectual person, often a comment indicating someone is so, ie **wussy**.

WWW   World Wide Wait. Computer-user frustration at the World Wide Web.

W

x-amount Unspecified amount. ANZ.

XXXX 1. Pimply young man in a white shirt who deals with foreign money exchanges, also known as a forex dealer, from 1980s.

2. Dark brown Waikato beer, challenged for the logo by Queensland tinnies.

yabber Chatter or talk unintelligibly. Partridge offers both Aboriginal *yabba* and English 'jabber', maybe in combination.

yachtie A person who sails yachts. ANZ.

yacker Chatter, from American 'yack'. ANZ.

yakker Work. From Aboriginal *yaga*, work. ANZ.

yammer To complain and/or talk hyperactively. ANZ.

Yank tank Any large American car. ANZ latter C20.

Yankee shout When nobody shouts and everybody pays a share. ANZ mid C20.

Yankee start A headstart or unfairly advantaged start, as Americans were seen to enjoy in making the rules that enabled them retain the America's Cup for over a century.

ya-yas German tourists, from their habitual deferential use of *ja*, German for 'yes'.

Yeah, right Derisively sceptical catchphrase popularised by Tui beer posters, eg, 'The bach sleeps four, max. Yeah, right.' Subjects veer from domestic, such as claiming to have spent the night on a mate's sofa, to provincial, such as Aucklanders are people too, to national, such as suggesting a politician gave all the money to education.

yodel To vomit, often with the addition **over the mahogany**, preferably involving the toilet seat rather than the hotel bar. ANZ latter C20.

you can beat an egg, but you can't beat a root Sexual boasting.

you can choose your friends, but you can't choose your rellies Relatives just have to be tolerated. ANZ.

you can put a ring around that   Something that you can be sure of. From putting a ring around a word or phrase to make it stand out on the page. From c1925.

you can take a Kiwi out of New Zealand, but you can't take New Zealand out of a Kiwi   You retain your national identity wherever you go, especially Australia.

you can't fatten thoroughbreds   Classy people are thin, okay?

you can't put a cow-cover over a horse and expect to get milk in the morning   You must be realistic.

you could eat your dinner off that floor   A clean house. ANZ.

you could knock me down with a feather   Expression of surprise. ANZ.

you could whip a cricket over it any time   Impoverished land.

you couldn't run a chook raffle in a country pub   You are worse than useless.

you get that   Indicating a resigned attitude; eg 'Floods most winters. You get that.'

you make a better door than a window   Indicating somebody is standing in your way.

you think you're a flowerpot because you've got a hole in your bum   You are vain.

you wouldn't make a bus arse's horsehole   You are hopeless.

you wouldn't read about it!   Exclamation of surprise or amazement. ANZ mid C20.

you're a you'rer   Exasperated assessment of a mischievous child by someone lost for the right expression.

you're as full of kid as a pregnant goat   You are a great teaser.

you're brave in the henhouse when the rooster's not there   Bully, coward.

Yuppie flu   Another name for Tapanui flu, probably because it was a wimp-inducing manifestation of the 1980s.

zack A sixpence. If something is **not worth a zack**, it is worthless. ANZ c1890.

zambuck Member of the Order of St John who gives first-aid and tends to injuries at sports events. From Zambuck, the all-purpose ointment. ANZ.

zeddy Z-class yacht.

Zimbo A Zimbabwean, specifically a member of the Zimbabwe national cricket team.

zipping Unzipping trousers, as a playful means of exposing what is beneath.

zonk 1. Dolt, eg, 'You zonk, you've spilled it everywhere.' ANZ.

2. To hit. ANZ.

zoo, feeding time at the When food is served at social functions and people pig in.

zoom University drinking game based on the Hokonui swindle, which can involve Italian words and eye contact. Roger Hall reports that at Otago University this 'game of skill' involves participants sitting in a circle going whizz/zoom/bounce, drinking each time they make a mistake.

zots Pimples, a variant of 'zit'.